Praise for Ruth Whitman

The Passion of Lizzie Borden

"With this book . . . she takes her place as a notable poet on the American scene."

—*The Boston Globe*

"She celebrates rich emotion yielding the most meaningful love—the verse itself has a deceptive simplicity, hiding allusiveness behind a straightforward style and unaffectedly uniting rhythm and subject matter."

—*The Saturday Review*

"Her control of craft, her fine wit and intuition create poems which are breathtaking."

—William Packard

Tamsen Donner: A Woman's Journey

"A work of beauty and force . . . a major achievement."

—*Booklist*

"It's simplicity and directness; its concrete evocation of time and place is just as vivid as can be. . . . It's a beauty."

—David Ignatow

"It has a sweeping and dramatic concision. I accept Tamsen fully and believe in her boggling trip to that pass in California. Maybe she has finally been made into American history."

—Edwin Honig

"Ruth has accomplished a kind of alchemy in distilling the inwardness of Tamsen's life. I think it's true to say that few people have been so remarkably lost and so remarkably found as Tamsen Donner."

—Ric Burns, director of *The Donner Party*, PBS

"Ruth Whitman has recreated the journal that Tamsen Donner lost on her nightmarish journey to California in 1846. . . . The journal, transforming historical fact into poetic insight, is a testimony to optimism, dogged survival, integrity, and courage of a woman pioneer."

—*The Boston Globe*

The Testing of Hanna Senesh

"For those who love Hanna Senesh, Ruth Whitman's biography, written in the form of a diary, will be a new source of inspiration."

—Isaac Bashevis Singer

"Whether she is probing the lyric mysteries of flesh and its bondings, or exploring her Jewish heritage, or celebrating—in an unprecedented series of long narrative poems—the witness-lives of heroic women, Ruth Whitman's work of almost thirty years exemplifies in all its phases her lively intelligence and the honesty and bravery of her spirit."

—Stanley Kunitz

Hatshepsut, Speak to Me

"Ruth Whitman joins the ranks of women writers exploring the deep past, where myth and history, sexuality and politics meet. This is a visionary book."

—Alicia Ostriker

"With wrenching power, Whitman revives Hatshepsut against the backdrop of her culture and time. Arias, recitatives, and interludes form the dialogue between Hatshepsut and the poet Ruth, mutually confiding their lives—the women and men they loved, their work, their children. Whatever else this richly layered book is about, it is also about time: the poet 'racing to leave behind / a few words arranged in a pattern / that will touch the living.' These Ruth/Hatshepsut poems do, and will."

—Carole Simmons Oles

"Ruth Whitman is one of America's best poets, and *Hatshepsut, Speak to Me* is one of her best books. The writing is both comely and powerful. What an inspired idea: to resurrect Queen Hatshepsut of Egypt as a woman for moderns. Cleopatra, move over; you've been trumped."

—Peter Viereck

"An altogether fascinating presentation of a fascinating major but little-known figure. By exploring Hatshepsut's life and her own, one reflecting on the other, Ms. Whitman brilliantly illuminates both."

—Theodore Weiss

Laughing Gas: New Poems

"The woman who shines out of these poems is large-hearted and full of feeling. The new poems are stunning. Her fourteen-part elegiac sequence, 'The Drowned Mountain,' swept me away."

—Maxine Kumin

Becoming a Poet

"*Becoming a Poet* is an exciting, instructive, readable guide to the poetic process, from its inception to the finished poem."

—*The Writer*

The Collected Works of Ruth Whitman

THE COLLECTED WORKS OF RUTH WHITMAN

Personas and Personhood

Edited by David Houghton

WAYNE STATE UNIVERSITY PRESS
DETROIT

ISBN 9780814352458 (paperback)
ISBN 9780814351246 (hardcover)
ISBN 9780814351253 (ebook)

Library of Congress Control Number: 2025932403

On cover: *Portrait of Ruth in Kimono* by Morton Sacks (1992). Courtesy of Schlesinger Library, Harvard Radcliffe Institute. Photography by Kevin Grady. Cover design by Will Brown.

Published with the assistance of a fund established by Thelma Gray James of Wayne State University for the publication of folklore and English studies.

Wayne State University Press rests on Waawiyaataanong, also referred to as Detroit, the ancestral and contemporary homeland of the Three Fires Confederacy. These sovereign lands were granted by the Ojibwe, Odawa, Potawatomi, and Wyandot Nations, in 1807, through the Treaty of Detroit. Wayne State University Press affirms Indigenous sovereignty and honors all tribes with a connection to Detroit. With our Native neighbors, the press works to advance educational equity and promote a better future for the earth and all people.

Wayne State University Press
Leonard N. Simons Building
4809 Woodward Avenue
Detroit, Michigan 48201-1309

Visit us online at wsupress.wayne.edu.

Contents

Acknowledgments vii
Editor's Note ix

An Introduction to the Work of Ruth Whitman 1
Jennifer Kronovet

The Poet Persona

The Passion of Lizzie Borden 17
Tamsen Donner: A Woman's Journey 23
The Testing of Hanna Senesh 59
Hatshepsut, Speak to Me 121
Isadora Duncan: To Dance Is to Live 175

The Poet Herself

Blood & Milk Poems 199
The Marriage Wig 227
The Passion of Lizzie Borden: New Poems 267
Permanent Address 291
Laughing Gas: New Poems 329
Atlantic Light 365

Becoming a Poet 397

Acknowledgments

The Passion of Lizzie Borden: Some of these poems first appeared in *The Antioch Review, Arion's Dolphin, The Atlantic Monthly, Boston Review of the Arts, The Carleton Miscellany, The Chicago Tribune, Commentary, The Editor, The Harvard Advocate, Hellcoal Anthology One, The Impressions Workshop, The Kenyon Review, The Literary Review, The Massachusetts Review, Midstream, The Nation, The New Republic, The New York Quarterly, The New York Times, Poetry Northwest, The Prairie Schooner, The Tuftonian, The United Church Herald*, and *Yankee*.

Hatshepsut, Speak to Me: Some of these poems first appeared in *Prairie Schooner, River Styx, Sojourner, The Women's Review of Books*, and *13th Moon*.

Blood & Milk Poems: Some of the poems in this book first appeared in *The Antioch Review, The Atlantic Monthly, Audience, The Carleton Miscellany, The Cambridge Review, Chrysalis, The Editor, Mademoiselle, Midstream, Midwest, Poetry, Poetry Northwest*, and *Prairie Schooner*.

The Marriage Wig: This book won the Alice Fay di Castagnola Award of the Poetry Society of America and the Kovner Award of the Jewish Book Council of America. Some of the poems in this book first appeared in *The Carleton Miscellany, The Chicago Tribune, The Harvard Advocate, The Impressions Workshop, The Kenyon Review, The Massachusetts Review, Midstream, Mimeo, The Nation, The New York Times, The New Yorker, Poetry Northwest, The Prairie Schooner, Premiere, The Tuftonian*, and *The United Church Herald*.

Permanent Address: Some of these poems first appeared in *The Agni Review*, *The American Poetry Review*, *Arion's Dolphin*, *The Bellevue Press*, *The Beloit Poetry Journal*, *The Bennington Review*, *The Boston University Journal*, *Counter/Measures*, *Green House*, *The Hudson River Anthology*, *The Massachusetts Review*, *Midstream*, *The New Republic*, *Ploughshares*, *Poetry Now*, *The Radcliffe Quarterly*, and *The Virginia Quarterly*.

Laughing Gas: Some of these poems first appeared in *American Poetry Review*, *The American Voice*, *The Boston Review*, *The Bridge*, *Choomia*, *Confrontation*, *Crosscurrents*, *Harvard Magazine*, *Helicon Nine*, *Hollow Spring Review*, *Images*, *Indiana Review*, *Kentucky Poetry Review*, *Manhattan Poetry Review*, *Ms. Magazine*, *Newport Review*, *Ontario Review*, *Ploughshares*, *Poetry Now*, *Prairie Schooner*, *Present Tense*, *Sandscript*, *Sojourner*, *Tendril*, *Virginia Quarterly*, and *West Branch Review*.

Atlantic Light: Some of these poems first appeared in *The American Voice*, *The Bridge*, *Free Lunch*, *Ms. Magazine*, *Negative Capability*, *The New Republic*, *Providence Journal Sunday Magazine*, *Sojourner*, and *The Yale Review*.

Editor's Note

> If my boundary stops here / I have daughters to draw new maps on the world / they will draw the lines of my face / they will draw with my gestures my voice / they will speak my words thinking they have invented them / they will invent them / they will invent me.
>
> —"Where is the West," *Tamsen Donner: A Woman's Journey*

Ruth Whitman, my mother, died on December 9, 1999, after a long battle with leukemia. As someone who still misses her, I can say with certainty that publication is not a path to immortality for an author. Yet, more than twenty-five years after her death, this volume will preserve her thoughts, creative ideas, and most powerful words, making them as widely available as they deserve to be.

The editorial process for this collection involved some reinvention: reducing the white space of the original poetry books for this more compact edition, updating her nonfiction volume, *Becoming a Poet*, and refining introductions, contextual notes, and acknowledgments. Even more important was deciding how best to present her work.

A chronological order of publications felt insufficient for illuminating the dual threads of the personal and historical in her poetry. As a lyric poet, Whitman boldly connected deeply personal themes to universal experiences, while her diverse interests led her to portray heroic women facing moments of historic struggle in the world. These two facets form a natural thematic map for the collection: *The Collected Works of Ruth Whitman: Personas and Personhood* captures the depth and breadth of her poetry, linking the visceral experience of human life to the broader historical currents that shape our existence.

This collection features Whitman's most famous and beloved poetry alongside previously unpublished works, including the volumes *Atlantic Light* and *Isadora Duncan: To Dance Is to Live*, which are as compelling as any of her other creations. As a single volume, *The Collected Works of Ruth Whitman* highlights patterns and themes that may not have been apparent in individual publications, and it celebrates Whitman's craft and contributions to American poetry, ensuring that her work remains accessible for both study and enjoyment.

AN INTRODUCTION TO THE WORK OF RUTH WHITMAN

Jennifer Kronovet

Ruth Whitman's admirers have typically stumbled upon her work in one of two ways. Some encountered Whitman as the author of *Tamsen Donner: A Woman's Journey* (1977), a book-length persona poem that reimagines the lost diary of the matriarch of the Donner party, whose failed journey from Illinois to California led to acts of cannibalism. When it was published *Tamsen Donner* was widely praised, and poems from within it were included in high school textbooks throughout the United States, giving, I imagine, nightmares to some American children, and to others a fiery interest in the way poetry can burst history open.

The second path to Whitman was, for many, including myself, *An Anthology of Modern Yiddish Poetry*, which she edited and translated. That book was the first bilingual anthology of twentieth-century Yiddish poetry, and before its publication it was difficult to find any modern Yiddish poetry in English translation. The anthology gave a voice in English to a literary immigrant culture and was the starting point of a flowering of further Yiddish translations.

The Donner Party and Yiddish poetry? It's hard to think how these two subjects are connected, yet through them, and other far-reaching voices—those of Lizzie Borden, Isadora Duncan, and the ancient Egyptian queen Hatshepsut—Whitman draws together the deepest threads of herself while exploring and expanding the boundaries of a self. Through this collected edition we see how Whitman's interest in and talent for inhabiting far-ranging lives and obsessions ultimately reshapes what identity means. The work is generous and exploratory, curious and risky, both rooted in history and ahead of its time.

Ruth Whitman was born to a Jewish family in 1922 in New York City and died in Rhode Island in 1999. She published eight books of poems, two books of translation, and one prose book on the practice of writing poetry. She was a classics scholar and an active participant in the life of poetry in the United States, supporting poetry organizations, attending residencies, and receiving fellowships from the Fulbright Scholar Program and the National Endowment for the Arts. She taught throughout her career at Harvard, Radcliffe, and MIT. She was married three times and had three children.

This summary, as impressive as it is, is an entirely inadequate description of Whitman when seen through the intensity of her work. Of course, all summaries of a life feel small compared to a whole person, but against Whitman's work, even the word *mother*, the word *wife*, the word *artist* or *scholar* or *Jewish*—any word that could define Whitman—is flat. Whitman's poetry takes concepts of gender and sexuality and uses them to plant a garden, which then blooms through seasons and generations. Whitman's excavation of motherhood lays bare its relationship to myriad kinds of losses. Whitman questions and embraces the ways her Jewish lineage does and does not define her. In Whitman's work "biography" is less what one does, and more the life of the mind and the act of imagination.

***

> It is innate in the female psyche to bring blood, conception, birth and death into close connection with one another.
>
> —Helene Deutsch, *The Psychology of Women*

This quote serves as an epigraph to Whitman's poem about the accused ax murderer Lizzie Borden. While some may see Deutsch's statement as prescriptive, reading Whitman you get the sense that she has taken it as a challenge. How can she connect the different parts of herself, her interest in female violence, her role as a mother, her devotion to her lineage, into one whole person? That drive to form connections results in Whitman using everything at hand throughout her career, from historical source material (trial testimony in the case of Borden) to experiences that were often ignored or dismissed in poetry when she wrote about them, such as miscarriages. Through "close connection," Whitman elevates and gives new meaning to living inside the body of a woman. In *The Passion of Lizzie Borden* (1973), Whitman moves seamlessly from inside the imagined Borden to a broader imagination of the self:

She'll hurl this pear against the door
until its ripe meat splatters,
like flesh torn in handfuls from the bone

She'll trap rage in her like a cage
trapping a bear. Not only where
her sex is, but where her veins
become its bars.

She'll think, as it draws her juice
to her nipples: that channel is why
I was made.
My roots curl under me
where they suck life
(I'll find the sun
I'll husband a flowering bough)

Through robust physicality Whitman draws a line between nurturing rage and nurturing domestic life, between one's anger and one's sex, one's freedom and one's gender. What I love here is the slippage from "she" to "I." Who is thinking that this is "why / I was made"? Whose roots suck life from the ground like a baby suckles from a mother? Whitman's or Borden's? And does the distinction matter? Is it scary if it doesn't? These questions are possible because of the obvious respect Whitman has for those she writes about. There's nothing salacious here to expose about Borden. What's salacious is domestic life itself, which Borden is a lens onto.

***

Must we devour ourselves
in order to survive?

—from *Tamsen Donner: A Woman's Journey*

Respect is everywhere in Whitman's work—respect for those of the past who are often dismissed and respect for what one often dismisses in oneself rather than face. Respect is where Whitman's insight comes from.

Without respect Whitman's book-length poem in the voice of Tamsen Donner would be satirical instead of epic. If Whitman had seen Donner as foolish or grotesque, her depiction of Donner's life would not have gone as deeply into the tangled tropes of marriage and land, of sacrifice and selfhood, of risk and motherhood. In the writing of *Tamsen Donner: A Woman's Journey* (1977), Whitman literally followed the path Tamsen and her fellow attempted settlers took from 1846 to 1847. In doing so Whitman gives the voice of Donner's despair a materiality that grounds this psychological work. "I forgot the anger of the land," Donner begins, and the doubleness of Whitman's voice behind Donner's gives every statement a stranded weight.

Links between Whitman and Donner ignite the work. Donner, like Whitman, was married more than once. She too traveled from home to recreate her life somewhere new. Donner's acts of devotion to her husband's plan are her downfall, and there is bravery in how Whitman inhabits that, how she admits to the pull of domesticity and its danger.

husbanded again have I finally learned
to let be let go? the need
to find oneself within a man
is not so great the second time

but we are like two voices of a strain
that come together and go apart
each echoing but singing independently
knowing the coming together in the end
will thread into a single theme

We know the theme that will draw this husband and wife together—the theme of death; knowing in advance where this story is heading could give it a leaden thump, but instead it reels the story into the unknown thrust of love, the unknown devastation of loss and loneliness.

. . . I see a woman:
long skirted in a bonnet
and beside her another woman
multiplied twenty times

who turns who stops
begins again even as I
turn stop begin
and then I understand

how the need for another being
is turned back on oneself
even as rays of heat
turn back and curve upward
against the reflected image

we discover we are traveling
beside no one
but ourselves

Donner, through Whitman, asks, "Must we devour ourselves / in order to survive?" Of course we know the answer for Donner, whose journey famously turned to cannibalism: Yes, you must devour yourselves, and you still might not survive. But for Whitman the answer isn't so clear. Must she devour parts of herself to survive domesticity? To survive as an artist? As an American Jew? Whitman's lifelong exploration of these questions keeps me riveted to her work.

***

> In 1947, when I was in my twenties, I suffered a crisis of gender identity. . . . When I read about King/Queen Hatshepsut, the woman pharaoh in ancient Egypt, I felt I had found a woman who could help me.
>
> —from *Hatshepsut, Speak to Me*

Whitman's strangest book, and the one I connect with most, is *Hatshepsut, Speak to Me* (1992). In it, Whitman's speaker converses with Hatshepsut—the ancient Egyptian who referred to herself with the pronouns he and she—and Hatshepsut speaks back. Through these conversations Whitman dives into her sensation of being both female and male, a feeling that I too contended with in a time before I had access to the beautiful terminology for these experiences now available to many of us. Whitman's poems are tactile explosions that remind us what poetry can do: give us a river of language for what is difficult to put into language and for what changes throughout a life and stays the same through centuries.

> Look: the sun is rolling out of the
> sky's vagina.

By making this book-length poem a conversation between "Ruth" and Hatshepsut, Whitman thematically binds the two figures while acrobatically showing their radical differences in life and in voice. "Ruth" asks, "Who were the women before you? / Where did you get your strength?" and then goes on to describe in a more confessional mode her grandmother who worked when most women stayed home. Hatshepsut replies by describing her influence, "Queen Menkara Metakerti, / the builder of the third pyramid," who invited her husband's murderers to a banquet and drowned them. The shift between confessional and epic traditions, between familial and political realms, is matched by lyric shifts that allow for differences to mirror each other in fascinating ways. These poems enact the variousness through which one navigates gender and the ways in which power is wielded through gender or subverted by it. They ask me to consider my own answers to the questions Ruth asks Hatshepsut.

> Ruth:
>
> boy-girl, boy-girl, boy-girl.
>
> What was I?
> I had no breasts.
> I was I, a lover of words,
> not yet male or female.
>
> Hatshepsut:
>
> If Hapi, the god of the Nile, can have breasts,
> I can have a beard.
> I live in the perfect justice of opposites

Both Ruth and Hatshepsut have been dismissed by those who are more powerful in different ways, and yet both are still here, speaking. Both reflect on how their power isn't lessened by their love of their children and state that they are attracted to both male and female lovers. Yet as much as we want it to be so, Hatshepsut and Ruth can never fully inhabit the same space. The longing to find a way, through writing, to Hatshepsut's presence and the knowledge she has can't be sated. It can only provide further fire.

Ruth:

For you death is a continuation of life:
you will eat the same bread, beer, wine, geese,
celebrate banquets and festivals,
your shawabtis will fish in the river, plow,
gather grapes in the vineyards for you.

For me, death is the end.
I'm racing to leave behind
a few words arranged in a pattern
that will touch the living.

***

Whitman carries the challenge of inhabiting difference (othering) and inhabiting what is familiar (coopting) into new territory, showing how far profound curiosity and empathy can take us imaginatively. Whitman's book *The Testing of Hanna Senesh* (1986) is an imagined diary based on the short life of Hanna Senesh, who, after fleeing anti-Jewish persecution in Hungary, fled to Palestine and then parachuted back into Nazi territory in an attempt to rescue her mother and others from the Nazi regime. It covers the period of Senesh's return to Europe and her capture, and ends with her execution at the age of twenty-three. Senesh, like so many of the women Whitman wrote about, was also a writer, and this project gives words to what Senesh never had the chance to record herself.

Whitman describes her interest in Senesh saying the "headstrong" resistance fighter, along with Donner and Borden, "have all been intense metaphors for my most basic concerns: refusing to be a victim, learning endurance, learning the skills of survival" (Preface, *Hatshepsut, Speak to Me*). Fascinating to me is that the women who taught Whitman about survival often did not survive, shifting the very definition of survival to that of living and creating on your own terms.

Braided together,
my mother and I
became strong through loss:
she watched my father die
in the bloom of their love,
and her mother, queen of the house,
sicken and slip away.
And then, skillful at parting,
she parted from me.

She let me go, knowing
I would carry her in me
even as she once held me safe
inside her own flesh.

Why then, with her center
in me, this tie
across time and distance,
across death itself,
do I have a longing
so sharp
it digs a hollow
beneath my heart?

What makes Whitman's imagining of Senesh so potent is not the depiction of outsized virtue or fearlessness but the focus on the familial bonds that Senesh's actions stem from. Whitman's Senesh poems portray the bravery of youth and link it to family as I have never seen done before. In this way Senesh's life is braided with the concerns of all the women Whitman wrote about, and what she addressed in poems that were presumably about herself: the bonds of family and also how the labors of family sometimes define us but not always. The boldness of Senesh's life heightens the stakes.

Writing a persona poem in the voice of another artist could blur the line between self and subject in a way that muddies both. This does not at all happen in *Isadora Duncan: To Dance Is to Live*, Whitman's collection of poems in the voice of Isadora Duncan, the choreographer and dancer who revolutionized modern dance. Instead, the similarities between Whitman and Duncan, their artistic ambition and their love of their children, lead Whitman to make daring leaps into language that is embodied and sexual. Instead of imagining Duncan's thoughts as Whitman would think them, Whitman writes like Duncan danced: with muscle.

> He has a pulse there
> under my hand   a sweet bird
> fluttering   my life
>
> I am starblossom burst
>
> out of stem's
> volcano
>
> I am leaf
> bud flower
>
> bearing the
> round secret
>
> full with its
> separate
>
> heartseed

Duncan's life was one of great romantic and artistic adventure and of great tragedy. Duncan's two children died in an accident, and Whitman does not shy away from imagining what most mothers do their best to avoid imagining.

two small black coffins
sit in the snow
black on white, black on white

a white room spins around me
three black ravens
beat against the walls

black on white, black on white
three black ravens
over two coffins

black birds flashing
on the blind white walls
white snow, black birds

As in all of Whitman's work, horror and devastation are not for their own sake. Instead, Whitman writes through devastation to understand survival.

***

Whitman did not only write persona poems. She also wrote work in "her own voice," but what I find most enthralling about reading Whitman's collected works together is how, as a body, it challenges the idea that one has a singular voice or should have one. Using the muscles developed by writing persona poems and reaching imaginatively into others and their imagined ways of talking, Whitman writes expansively about her own life without settling into a stagnant persona of the self.

   I am my grandmother
with her four sons, her outliving patience,
her patient hate.

I am my grandfather,
loved beyond usual lot,
stealing his delight.

I am my grandfather's mistress,
tending the alien land he left,
with no face for the face she loves . . .
—"The Old Man's Mistress," in *Blood & Milk Poems*

Like the other Whitman, Ruth contains multitudes. She grows bigger by erasing the borders between what is presentable and not, what is hidden and not, and brings it all into a bigger sense of what it means to be a person: containing contradictions, being inside a culture and critical of it, being of the past and at the same time rejecting the past.

I would steal light from any bush,
Rob any blaze from heaven for my vase,
Just as I danced once on your wooden floor,
Naked and sudden,
Whirling you in a waltz,
Or did you whirl me,
Shaking the yellow spring
From rafters winter-stained with penitence?

That's the way I'd always have my guilt,
Sudden, high, a theft of fire, a dance,
A secret flowering of forsythia.
—"Stealing Forsythia" in *Blood & Milk Poems*

Writing, for Whitman, is a potent act. It can unearth the desires of nuns and bring forgotten brides back into history. By writing about dismissed artifacts and moments, Whitman shines a curious and caring light on them, like the wig worn by married Orthodox women, which Whitman endows with nuance. Remembering and reconciling an abortion decades later gives that experience importance while rejecting it as self-defining. In one poem, seeing a chipmunk, of all things, becomes important enough to unite you with your own body:

WORD

A fur muscle ran across the road.

Only when I saw the pointed tip of it
waving, did I think chipmunk.

Sometimes we move inside our bodies
as inside a stranger. The sack
hangs loose, inviting us to think
I can be anyone, go anywhere, do anything.

But once your pen touches paper, all
choices become one, the word as single
as the chipmunk moving in one spasm
from green to green.

—"Word" in *The Passion of Lizzie Borden: New Poems*

All the women Whitman wrote through make her brave in the face of her often dire fascinations, such as her own mortality, her fear on behalf of her children, and her family's past. This bravery manifests formally in Whitman's later poems, where there is more white space and tighter lines. Whitman trusts that her writing, even condensed and elided, will carry the weight of meaning for her. To me, the following poem is the best description of the arc of Whitman's poetics, written out of decades of generous thinking and imagining:

she built a tower with her voice

she moved
breast first
across the curve of the globe

she arched over
the hidden geography
of the ocean floor

she sailed across
its peaks and resonant valleys

singing

—"Singing" in *Permanent Address*

***

You write because you want to celebrate being alive, even the grief and pain.

Everything human is significant. That is what poetry demonstrates.

Remember that self-definition is never final.

These sentences by Whitman are from the last book in this edition, *Becoming a Poet* (1982), a collection of essays on how to approach writing a poem. The book, full of boisterous and vulnerable advice, begins here: "I was sitting one morning on the porch of a cabin in the woods, where I had been given the gift of two weeks in which to do nothing but write poetry. I had left behind all my family responsibilities; there was nothing to bother me, except that no poem came." Ugh. What poet hasn't had a moment like that? Whitman lovingly shares all the ways she made it through this kind of moment. She does so by respecting her own process but also respecting her readers and what we might have to say. "Poets are in love with language," she says, including all of us in that love.

In *Becoming a Poet*, Whitman also connects her work to a larger canon. She imagines how poems by peers came to exist on the page, expressing how much she admires these writers, with her usual humility. Poets who provide models in *Becoming a Poet* include A. R. Ammons, HD, Zbigniew Herbert, Erica Jong, Denise Levertov, Adrienne Rich, Theodore Roethke, Muriel Rukeyser, Anne Sexton, Cesar Vallejo, and others. I hope that, with the publishing of this collection, Whitman is seen alongside these poets as an essential, expansive, and radical twentieth-century writer whose poetry continues to illuminate what is at the heart of so much verse: being alive, including the grief and pain.

Even beyond *Becoming a Poet*, I learn so much from Whitman's work about how to write. How the arc of a book-length poem can hold a reader in its sway. How to incorporate research into lyric so that it enlivens both. Reading Whitman makes me brave in my writing by showing me how robust language can strengthen you when you take personal risks. She gives me permission to explore the parts of myself and others, in writing and in life, that are terrifying, because language, when we use it to generously reach into what we don't yet know, can open up the beautiful complexity of being a person.

My favorite moment from *Becoming a Poet* is here: "One morning I pulled up my shade and saw nothing. A summer fog had rolled in from the Atlantic and covered the entire view. There was nothing but a large gray blanket hiding what I knew was out there. I looked at the fog and thought, 'It reminds me of something. What is it like?'" This moment is quintessential Whitman and why I will always be drawn to her work: Whitman found likeness when she saw nothing at all and sought connection in the nothing to arrive at a poem.

THE POET PERSONA

THE PASSION OF LIZZIE BORDEN

On the morning of August 4, 1892, during an intense heat wave, Lizzie Borden's father and stepmother were found brutally murdered in their house in Fall River, Massachusetts. Their daughter Lizzie, a thirty-three-year-old spinster, secretary of the Young People's Society for Christian Endeavor and active in the Fruit and Flower Mission, was arrested for the murder, tried, and acquitted.

> It is innate in the female psyche to bring blood, conception, birth and death into close connection with one another.
>
> —Helene Deutsch, *The Psychology of Women*

> Q. I ask you again to explain to me why you took those pears from the pear tree.
> A. I did not take them from the pear tree.
> Q. From the ground. Wherever you took them from. I thank you for correcting me; going into the barn, going upstairs into the hottest place in the barn, in the rear of the barn, the hottest place, and there standing and eating those pears that morning?
>
> —Inquest testimony of Miss Lizzie Borden, Fall River, August 9–11, 1892

> We were talking in the afternoon, me and Lizzie Borden, and I says, "I can tell you one thing you can't do," and she says, "Tell me what it is, Mrs. Reagan." I says, "Break an egg, Miss Borden," and she says, "Break an egg?" I says, "Yes." "Well," she says, "I can break an egg." I says, "Not the way I would tell you to break it. . . ." And she did get the egg, and she got it in her hands, and she couldn't break it, and she says, "There," she says, "that is the first thing that I undertook to do that I never could."
>
> —Testimony of Mrs. Hannah Reagan, matron at the Fall River police station, on the ninth day of the trial, New Bedford, June 14, 1893

THE PASSION OF LIZZIE BORDEN

1.
Heat cracks the skin of Fall River.
Soot hangs flat
over the moist city.

Pears
sweat in the backyard.
Sitting alone in the kitchen

Lizzie feels
chunks of leftover mutton
heavy in her

belly. Her father
has left for the bank. The ring
he gave her long ago

pinches her finger.

2.
Openeyed last night she felt
her blood pounding
the back of her neck,

tidal waves from the sea
that poured up the Taunton river,
tore open the breakwater,
ripped apart her corsets
and pumped breath, air,
sealife into her,

sunstorms, volcanoes, astral debris,
until she was pregnant with a pregnancy
that puts an end to wishing.

3.
She woke, thicker around the shoulders, heavier
under the jaw. The birds
had left the burning pear tree.

This house has killed the girl she was
Narrow, gray, grudging in windows,
bare of guests or laughing,

the parlor's only pleasure is to lay out
corpses or tell tales of each new
disease, step by fatal step.

What holds her here, eating pears?

4.
In the August heat
she irons handkerchiefs for her stepmother,
heating the iron on the kitchen fire
in the black stove.

The center of the earth is always boiling,
and she must have the trick of eye to see
how she can liquefy
stones, trees,
slash air so she can breathe,
take life to make life, break
the blind wall open with her fist.

5.
She'll hurl this pear against the door
until its ripe meat splatters,
like flesh torn in handfuls from the bone

She'll trap rage in her like a cage
trapping a bear. Not only where

her sex is, but where her veins
become its bars.

She'll think, as it draws her juice
to her nipples: that channel is why
I was made.
My roots curl under me
where they suck life
(I'll find the sun
I'll husband a flowering bough)

6.
this sprung and spiralled wrath
won't uncoil till she's invented death

Her father is napping in the parlor,
her stepmother is sitting
at the vanity upstairs.

7.
Shake the murderous mountains and dance
a step or two before you turn to rain.

Then in the sky that gives you lightning,
in that same sky
your meteor will hurl;
will singe the tops of trees and bring
spring to the dry hedges of the moon
and set a clanging in the world
and break
by twos
the timbrels of the stars.
Who's to judge me? When I sleep I sleep
curled on the shoulder of God

8.
At last
I feel hallelujah in my hips
my son the day comes out of me the morning

She raises the ax.

TAMSEN DONNER

A Woman's Journey

When I began writing Tamsen Donner's lost journal, I did not know who I was writing about; only that I was writing in the person of a pioneer woman in the mid-nineteenth century, who was approaching a last range of mountains in the western part of the continent. When I finally identified her by name, I recognized her immediately, as though she were someone I had known.

Tamsen Donner was born in 1801 in Newburyport, Massachusetts. She was a teacher, wrote poetry, and had been married and widowed before she moved to Springfield, Illinois, where she met and married her second husband, George Donner.

Ten years later, in 1846, Tamsen and George decided to travel to California, where they could buy cheap land and where Tamsen planned to start a ladies' seminary. They traveled in style with their own three little girls and George Donner's two older daughters by a former marriage.

They planned the journey as a summer holiday, but it took months longer than they had anticipated. They followed an untraveled route across the Wasatch mountains. They miscalculated the time it would take to cross the Salt Desert. They lost animals, wagons, food. When they reached the Sierra, only a hundred miles from the Sacramento Valley, they were caught in a series of blizzards in one of the earliest and worst winters in western history. Snowed in for six months in the mountains, without provisions, many of the party resorted to cannibalism. Some of the children and the adults who could still walk were brought out by rescue parties. Tamsen refused to leave her husband, who was dying of an infected wound.

Tamsen had published poetry in the *Sangamon Journal* in Springfield and wrote a letter about the journey to her friend, Allen Francis, editor of the newspaper. But most of what she wrote—her diary, her poems, and all but three letters—has been lost.

In 1974 I followed her path along the Oregon and Mormon trails and along the Hastings cutoff across the Salt Desert to the Sierra mountains. During the trip I kept a journal, as I knew she had done. I discovered again—what I already knew—that in a poet's journal, prose passages become interlinked with lyrics, like recitative and aria, and these together help to weave back and forth between immediate and symbolic levels of reality.

Ruth Whitman
January, 1977

Where is the West?
Who shall fix its limits?
He who attempts it will soon learn
that it is not a fixed but a floating line
—Eleutheros Cooke, 1858

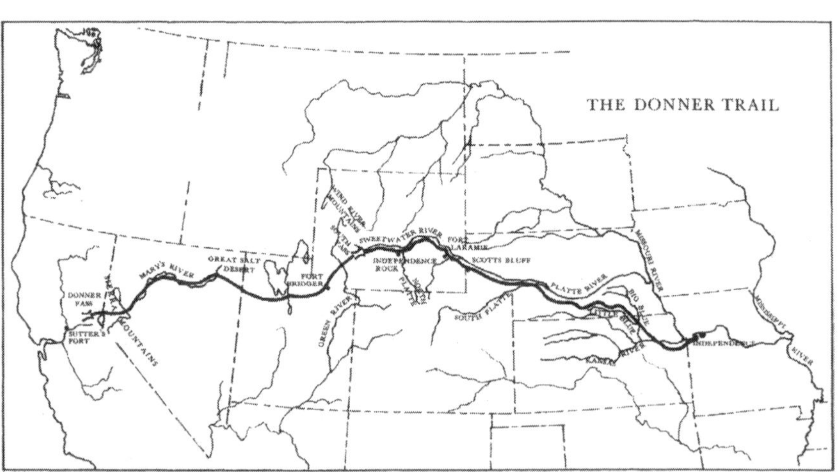

how could I foresee my end
in that soft Illinois spring?
I began my journey certain
that what was unknown
would be made smooth and easy

I forgot the anger of the land

now in the white silence I remember
wind blowing back the hair of the ocean
sunlight slicing through clouds
spring birds circling south

under the cities of snow
under the whirlpool of leaves
my beginning stirs again:
out of the white spring of my unbelief
a far blue country parts the sky

I. PRAIRIE

Westward Ho! For Oregon and California. Who wants to go to California without costing them anything? As many as eight young men, of good character, who can drive an ox team, will be accommodated by gentlemen who will leave this vicinity about the first of April. Come on Boys. You can have as much land as you want without costing you anything. The Government of California gives large tracts of land to persons who move there. The first suitable persons who apply will be engaged.

—George Donner and Others, *The Sangamo Journal*, March 26, 1846

Some are leaving this fall, for Texas, and more are going in the spring to California and Oregon. For my part I have no desire to go anywhere. I am far enough west now and do believe some people might go west until they have been around the world and never find a place to stop.

—Elvira Powers Hynes, in a letter to her sister, Illinois, March 1852

APRIL 15, 1846, LEAVING SPRINGFIELD, ILLINOIS.

The wagons move first,
one directly behind the other,
but then straggling—
friends want to ride beside friends,
and we pass back and forth.
It is like a large summer party
    except for rumors that the Mormons
    who are also moving west this spring
    will massacre as many of us as they can;
    that the Indians will steal from anyone who
    separates from the train; that there may be
    war in California.
But we are surrounded by our friends
and at night outside the hollow square of wagons
we drown out the howling of the wolves
by singing hymns and old ballads around the campfires

Just sometimes, when we are fairly on our way
one behind the other
undulating over the prairies
we have much the appearance
of a large funeral procession.

APRIL 20, 1846, ON THE MISSOURI PRAIRIE.

The land flattens out most suddenly, long stretches of fertile land, stands young corn. The horizon is everywhere. We picknicked by a huge flat field with a sky broader and lower than ever in the East I could imagine. Broad, low and blue, with herds of clouds. The stretches themselves are punctuated here and there with little isolated exclamation points—a house, a barn, a shield of trees planted by an emigrant. Trees show either that water is present or someone brought a sapling to shade his house. Otherwise there are none. Only immensity and loneliness. We change in relation to the land. We become smaller.

MAY 11, 1846, INDEPENDENCE, MISSOURI.

My dear sister,

I commenced writing to you some months ago but the letter was laid aside to be finished the next day and was never touched. A nice piece of pink letter paper was taken out & now has got so much soiled that it cannot be written upon & now in the midst of preparation for starting across the mountains I am seated on the grass in the midst of the tent to say a few words to my dearest only sister. One would suppose that I loved her but little or I should not have neglected her so long.

My three daughters are around me, one at my side trying to sew, Georgeanna fixing herself in an old India rubber cap & Eliza Poor knocking on my paper asking ever so many questions. They often talk to me of Aunty Poor.

I can give you no idea of the hurry of this place. It is supposed there be 7000 waggons start from this place this season. We go to California to the bay of San Francisco. It is a four months trip. We have three waggons furnished with food & clothing drawn by three yoke of oxen each. We take cows along and milk them & have some butter though not as much as we would like. I am willing to go and have no doubt it will be an advantage to our children and to us. I came here last evening and start tomorrow morning on the long journey.

Farewell my sister, you shall hear from me as soon as I have an opportunity

Love to Mr. Poor the children & all friends

Farewell
T. E. Donner

MAY 26, 1846, ON THE KANSAS PRAIRIE.

Where are the seagulls?
                                                                        crossing
the prairie, I keep mistaking hawks
for gulls: a thick wind
blows inside my head full of salt
and seafog

                    now in my dreams I find
wild rosehips on the beach
at Newburyport: I'm a child
chasing waves across the sand
sails sting white against the blue

in these feathery seas of grass
traveling towards the steep
heart of America, why do I
keep watching for seagulls?

MAY 30, 1846, ALONG THE BIG BLUE RIVER.

Talking to my friend, Mrs. Reed, who is fearful of the journey and has a constant headache from the jolting of the wagon, I see it is not with me as it is with the other women. It is easier for me to change my life, to think of a new kind of living.

As a girl I traveled from Newburyport in Massachusetts to North Carolina to teach in the seminary in Elizabeth City, and there at the age of twenty-eight I married Tully Dozier and bore him two children, thinking this would be my life forever. All three were taken from me by fever in the space of two months.

My brother in Springfield asked me to come and take care of his motherless children. So I began a new second life. I journeyed for weeks in my grief, crossing Massachusetts, going by waterway through New York, by railway and coach through Pennsylvania and Ohio. I found I had a taste for travel.

In Springfield, teaching my little scholars simple botany in a farmer's field, I met George Donner, twice Widowed, who gave me my second family. He is a big man, in soul as well as in body, and gives himself freely to new things. So to sell our farm and pack up our household for this journey seems to me not so frightening. I carry my roots with me into a third life. I am willing to make a home wherever we choose to sleep.

JUNE 2, 1846, ALONG THE BIG BLUE.

I find it awkward at first to bake out of doors but now that I am becoming accustomed to it I do it quite easily

Our table is the ground,
our tablecloth an old India rubber spread,
our dishes of tin:

tin basins for tea cups,
iron spoons and plates
and several pans for milk

I find the wagon's jolting
can churn a pail of cream to butter
in a day's journey

JUNE 8, 1846, ON THE PLATTE RIVER.

Eliza follows a rabbit into some woods and brings me back two enormous purple thistles and a cluster of daisies. The fields along the river incredibly rich and rolling. The immense sky full of gray clouds, mist, and small rain.

In the tangle beside a stream at noon
we find large patches of strawberries
wild and sweet and small wild roses

slowly the clear sky of morning
begins to breed thick clouds
                                        until at sunset
we are bathed in black and orange light

we start down a road
where the air hardly parts to let us through
we are suddenly blinded by a rain
that drenches our clothes, our wagon tops,
our bedding

but it is a small sparse rain after all
not enough to fill the shallow river
or moisten the ground

JUNE 12, 1846, ON PRAIRIE CREEK.

We dress in our night dresses for washing clothes, build a fire almost in the center of the creek on some stones, warm some water, and commence washing in the kettles as we have nothing else to supply the place of washtubs. We could get on well were the water soft but that being hard, it takes all our strength and a great portion of our soap. Besides, our clothes will not look well, which spoils our anticipated merriment, but we find that we can heat water, wash, boil, and rinse in the same kettle.

One of the company brings us a little wild honey; we have a little sport with the fire running in the dead grass.

JUNE 17, 1846, ON THE NORTH PLATTE.

The morning is fierce with fresh smells:
prairie grass   clover   and the familiar
lupin paler than the sky bluer
than the periwinkle starring the ground
around the stream under willows and alders

I pick the wild blossom and mark the joining
of leaf to stem the design of
petal to petal
                                        and I remember
the kiss of fingers
the joining   the holiday of eyes
in an Illinois meadow

    I had brought my class
    to study the wildflowers
    not knowing the tall farmer watching us
    owned the field and would be my future
    refuge

    a widow of thirty-five I had thought
    my body would not stir again
    my lifelong fires were banked
    but in his rich earth
    winter buds unclenched their tightness
    under his sun his unaccustomed rain

I shed my widowhood
and let a new self burgeon

husbanded again have I finally learned
to let be let go? the need
to find oneself within a man
is not so great the second time

but we are like two voices of a strain
that come together and go apart
each echoing but singing independently
knowing the coming together in the end
will thread into a single theme

JUNE 18, 1846, ALONG THE PLATTE.

We watch the land dry out. Trees grow smaller and disappear. Patches of light sand, and then, on the plains, long low hills. We keep crossing and recrossing the Platte,—ugly, shallow, and as the mountain men say, a mile wide and a foot deep.

We pass a dead ox and two graves of children.

We sometimes see
the shattered wrecks
of ancient clawfooted
tables, well waxed and rubbed
or massive bureaus of carved oak
sitting along the track:
once loved relics
flung out
to scorch and crack
on the hot prairie

JUNE 21, 1846, NEAR ASH HOLLOW.

Strange moundlike formations begin to appear out of the dry flat bottoms. At Ash Hollow we are obliged to pull our wagons and oxen over the high ledge with ropes and pulleys. George and the men work well together and we are able to pass through without damage.

There are strange alkali smells from the surrounding earth. The land is powdered with traces of white sour salt. The sparse water poisons the cattle. Many of the families are constantly sick with dysentery. So far our little ones have been spared that misery.

JUNE 25, 1846, ON THE LARAMIE PLAINS.

We creep along the Platte
in shifting sands and quicksands

the dusty earth is covered with a salt
so poisonous it spoils the springs

my woolen skirt is stained
my shawl is torn from catching

sharp corners in our crowded wagon
my bonnet is limp from sudden rains

rising ahead in the flat valley
a monstrous chimney

towers like an obelisk:
ruins and castles

turrets knobs violent peaks
like shapes our children see

when they awaken frightened in the night
and here I find among these monuments

a cactus shape
            low to the ground

with ears and spines and a sudden flower
like a giant buttercup above

the green:
            a smile of yellow in a twisted land

JULY 4, 1846, AT FORT LARAMIE.

Dressed in our best clothes, which we have saved for this occasion, we come together in a grove and open the bottle of wine our old friends in Springfield gave us. They promised they would toast us today, facing towards the west, as we drink to them, lifting our glasses to the east.

So do we make a link
between what we were
and what we have become:

we are inventing
the body of a land
binding together

two halves of a whole
as we touch each other
across a thousand miles

and I who started
a thousand miles before
feel in my flesh

the stretch of the land
as we give it birth
the long spill of it
unrolling before us

JULY 12, 1846, NEAR INDEPENDENCE ROCK.

At night when the fires have died I think of my New England, which now seems tiny and cramped compared to the enormous spaces we are living in. We are watching Laramie peak ahead, sprinkled with snow like confectioner's sugar. The ground is cracked, baked, covered with colonies of small sage brush. We stop at the Rock and read the travelers' names scratched there, despite the brutal mosquitoes that aim for scalp and ears. But that is no worse than the hot wind that blows perpetually, covering us with bitter dust.

Sage brush:
a two-foot tree
with rough bark spiny foliage twisted boughs
a delicate graygreen spreading its tint
over hill and desert:

smells like our herb
but sharp as turpentine
pungent in campfires
hardy:

in deep sand among barren rocks
everywhere peopling the peopleless spaces
like us
where nothing else in the world would grow

JULY 15, 1846, NEAR THE END OF THE NORTH PLATTE RIVER.

Moving down-sun
I learn to read water
by willows and alders:

a line of cottonwoods,
a green stripe across a desert,
scrubby cedars on a hillside

signal a spring in a gully:
pines on a mountain
announce a running stream:

moving down-sun
our water has been rank
men and oxen are sick with it

but now in the unexpectable land
we come to an untainted stream
cold and fresh Sweet Water

most beautiful of names
the last stream
on the eastern side of the mountains

as we start to climb
there leaps out of the distance
north of west

a city
of stony mountains
under a roof of perpetual snow

the first snow I have ever seen in summer

JULY 18, 1846, CROSSING THE GREAT DIVIDE.

An end or a beginning:
is this the place where being separates
from itself the precise moment
the space between pulse and pulse

at one instant we are moving towards:
transporting the furniture of our lives
bringing the particularities of one existence
to an imagined point where we are taken in
formalized justified like an embrace
without an end

but no love is so final merely
having traced ourselves back to our
Atlantic beginnings
we change from source to source
leap to a new love plunging westward
where once we looked backward all the way

now hesitant among the mountains
we pass across the invisible boundary
that divides self from self
and move forward heartlong towards the other sea
a twin
a mirror of ourselves

II. DESERT

The most direct route, for the California emigrants, would be to leave the Oregon route, about two hundred miles east from Fort Hall; thence bearing west southwest, to the Salt Lake; and thence continuing down to the bay of San Francisco.

—Lansford Hastings, *The Emigrants' Guide to Oregon and California*, 1845

The Californians were generally much elated and in fine spirits, with the prospect of a better and nearer road to the country of their destination. Mrs. George Donner was, however, an exception. She was gloomy, sad, and dispirited, in view of the fact that her husband and others could think for a moment of leaving the old road and confide in the statements of a man about whom they knew nothing but who was probably some selfish adventurer. Mercury at sunrise 46°; sunset 52°.

—Jesse Quinn Thornton, Oregon and California, 1849

JULY 21, 1846, ON LITTLE SANDY CREEK.

As we come down the western side of the Divide we
find patches of purple flowers and orange daisies. But
the country is still windy dry, uninhabited, and the
children are beginning to tire. The wagons too are
aging more rapidly than we expected and must be
tarred constantly. But George remains his cheerful self
and talks continually of that wonderful California land
where it is always spring. I wonder what flowers would
bloom perpetually.

Tumbleweed:
a densely branched spherical
Amaranthus plant

withered broken off
and rolling wildly across the plains
in the wind
or huddled together
against the wagons
clasped in each other's spiny arms

the children chase the bristly creatures
as though they were chasing
hoops or balls

the rootless chasing the rootless

JULY 25, 1846, ALONG THE BIG SANDY.

Thus we scatter as we go along
the arid stretches are so dry
the hills are so steep
that we must constantly tar
and mend the wheels

it would have been better
not to bring
any baggage whatever
only what is necessary
to use on the way

if I were to make this journey again
I would make quite different preparations
to pack and unpack so many times
and cross so many streams

the custom of the mountain men
is to possess nothing
and then you will lose nothing

JULY 27, 1846, ON THE WAY TO GREEN RIVER.

A white blindness of salts:
it makes us squint
it glares like snowfields under the sun
it glimmers and quivers in snaky heat waves
our hair clothing wagons
covered with white dust
we cannot stop to wash away

the children complain
of grit in their mouths
as we pass plains filled with shimmering lakes
that quench no thirst

JULY 23, 1846, AT FORT BRIDGER.

After miles of brown-gray hills and buff-colored deserts, Fort Bridger appears wonderfully green, with rushing brooks and groves of trembling aspen. It eases our thirst just to look at the trees.

There has been a change of plan. A Mr. Lansford Hastings has sent us a letter from Sweetwater promising to meet us here and guide us across a shorter route to California. But he is not here.

It is a two-hundred-mile cutoff around the Great Salt Lake and across a small salt desert. George and Jim Reed are eager to try it, and Mr. Bridger encourages them, but Joe Walker, the mountain man, cautions us against it since there is no clear trail.

My heart misgives me. We are all weary, many of us are sick. In a month summer will be over. Our supplies diminish. How can we trust an absent guide?

AUGUST 14, 1846, CROSSING THE WASATCH MOUNTAINS.

We are traveling blind.

The trail thins and disappears
                    diminished
like a river to a stream the stream snakes down
to a trickle in the ground

we age in the youngest canyon and still we climb
carving out on the steepest ridge
an inch-long place

chaos of brush and boulders
tangles of cottonwood and willow
                    we fumble through

the same unpassable passage
our days become
like cliffs   around   around

we are playing blindman's buff, hands outstretched:
we are children in the dark who cannot find
one mapped familiar face

AUGUST 27, 1846, NEAR THE SALT LAKE.

It has taken us twenty-one days to go thirty-six miles, wandering through blind canyons, long ascents, narrow defiles choked with brush. We finally come down the ten-mile descent into this lovely valley circled by snowy mountains. If I were leading the emigrants, I would be tempted to settle and build a new city here.

AUGUST 28, 1846, IN THE SALT LAKE VALLEY.

Here in the cracked earth
twenty deep pools:
pure eyes from another world
without salt or alkali
each spring so bewitched
that when you dip water
out of the smallest or the greatest
it comes filling back to the brim
not flowing over
not an inch below the lip
but inexhaustible

is it a sign
as in the fairy tale
that charity
            that love
will not go dry?

SEPTEMBER 1, 1846, AT THE EDGE OF THE SALT DESERT.

We find scraps of paper with bits of handwriting scattered on the ground at the foot of a post. Perhaps it is a message for us.

   Spread on my lap where I
   have gathered blossoms, held
   my babies, I hold this
   future:
      random shreds of paper
   have a scheme the listening
   hand the patient hand must
   find.
      I ask the angles
   where they want to go. The

pattern is all in the
being.
    And I am the
instrument to find their
form, as the hazel wand
finds water:

            hard drive   two
days and nights
                no water

SEPTEMBER 5, 1846, IN THE SALT DESERT.

After three days and nights in this desert of salt I am obliged to give the children little cubes of sugar to suck on, to ease their thirst, and flattened bullets to chew on, to keep their juices flowing. Finally, in the cold night, we sleep. Towards dawn with a mouth dry as paper, I dream of a morning rain storm:

That gray satin quilt the ocean
is ruffled by first rain

sterling arrows fall on it
iron muscles underneath the quilt

loll and flinch, unwilling to combine:
pour sky and become ocean

let the steel drumbeats celebrate
the yielding beast the mixing elements

let gray behemoths of rain
enter and flood my valleys

SEPTEMBER 6, 1846, IN THE DESERT.

Go light go light I must walk lightly

as I moved from one life to another
more and more followed me:
gowns books furniture
paints notebooks

now the seven of us—even the little girls—
must have substance
to carry into the new country

we are transporting a houseful:
barrels of flour stuffed with porcelain
pots tin plates silver service quilts
salt meat rice sugar dried fruit
coffee tea
        the wagon sags
and the oxen falter
                one wagon founders

what shall I let go? books:
                    the least
needed for survival: in the cold
desert night
            George lifts my heavy
crate of Shakespeare, Emerson, Gray's
Botany, spellers and readers for my school
and hides it in a hill of salt
while the children sleep parched
and the cows and oxen stand mourning:
I put aside my desk with the inlaid pearl
our great fourposter with the pineapple posts
my love my study

what else can I part with?

I will keep one sketchbook one journal
to see me to the end of the journey

go light
go light
I must walk lightly

SEPTEMBER 7, 1846, IN THE DESERT.

Across the white plain of salt
I see an army of wagons
teams dogs children
passing near the horizon
and rejoice to think
another company
is breaking way for us
heading towards the water

and I see a woman:
long skirted in a bonnet
and beside her another woman
multiplied twenty times
who turns who stops
begins again even as I
turn stop begin
and then I understand

how the need for another being
is turned back on oneself
even as rays of heat
turn back and curve upward
against the reflected image

we discover we are traveling
beside no one
but ourselves

SEPTEMBER 25, 1846, NEAR MARYS RIVER.

We are facing
the last mountains:
sometimes we walk
with the children
beside the wagon
to rest the lame oxen

the mountains rise
unscalable
the road is
a fiction
I am not inside this story
I am sitting
beside my husband
a frame
to the picture

there is surf I know
on the other side of the pass
somewhere beyond this wall
the end of land
and a summer sea

III. MOUNTAIN

. . . here I met Mrs. Reed and two children two still in the mountains, I cannot describe the death like look they all had Bread Bread Bread Bread was the beging of every child and grown person except my wife I give to all what I dared and left for the scene of desolation and now I am camped within 25 miles which I hope to mak this night and tomorrow we had to camp soon on account of the softness of the snow, the men falling in to their middles.

—James Reed's diary, Feb. 26, 1847

... O Mary I have not rote you half of the truble we have had but I have rote you anuf to let you now that you dont now what truble is but thank god we have all got throw and the onely family that did not eat human flesh we have left everything but i dont cair for that we have got throw with our lives but Dont let this letter dishaten anybody never take no cutofs and hury along as fast as you can.

—Twelve-year-old Patty Reed's letter to her cousin,
May 16, 1847

OCTOBER 12, 1846, NEAR TRUCKEE MEADOWS.

There was a film of ice on the bucket of water this morning.

We followed Marys river until it disappeared into the ground. But we are no longer surprised at distortions of nature.

Now after traveling across another miserable alkali desert, through dusty hills and dry miles, we come to these green meadows. We will stay to replenish ourselves and our oxen. We are tired and disorganized almost beyond repair.

OCTOBER 28, 1846, ON THE TRUCKEE RIVER.

Straining downhill
our axle breaks
the wagon falls
to one side but
George scoops out the
sleeping children

he starts to cut
a piece of wood
to mend the break
the chisel carves
an angry gash
across his hand

It is starting to snow.

NOVEMBER 3, 1846, BY ALDER CREEK.

Stopped.
    We can go no further.
Here steep in the mountains
the flakes thicken down
heavier and heavier
the white veils swirl between us
and the pass

George with his injured hand
starts to fell the trees
to build a shelter
but the snow falls and falls
fat flakes
sent to wind us in a
thick sheet
we have no time to pitch a tent
we make a shed of brush
roughed over with pine boughs
rubber coats blankets and skins
the two little ones sit on a log
snug in a buffalo robe
cheerfully watching us work
thinking it fun to catch the snow
on their tongues

inside this strange
dwelling place
I must build a fire
and make another nest

NOVEMBER 8, 1846, BY ALDER CREEK.

Storms hammer us:
snow covers our shelter,
our wagons, oxen alive and dead

we cut steps upward
to get to the light
watch westward over the crest

for help: no one comes

looking for food
George has shot
a Coyote, an owl,

a wounded bear:
not food enough
to cure our hunger

NOVEMBER 12, 1846, BY ALDER CREEK.

The wound on George's hand does not heal. He feels ill and cannot stand up, although he protests it is nothing and will pass. The poison seems to be traveling up his arm to his shoulder. I bathe it in melted snow, salve it, bind it up, assuring him with all my love that it will improve. But it worsens. I think it begins to smell of decay, although it is hard to distinguish smells, we have lived so long in this close wet space.

The children were glad at first to stop in one place and play in the snow, but now they prefer to lie quietly in bed, keeping each other warm.

So it falls to me to fetch twigs for the fire, prepare our little food, and make the time pass until help comes. I have told all the stories I can remember and sung all the songs.

NOVEMBER 25, 1846, BY ALDER CREEK.

When I look at this strong man
lying injured on his bed of boughs
or watch him sleeping vulnerable

I remember him
as a motherless boy:
what makes the ordinary features

of an ordinary man
suddenly uncommon
or the events of a usual life

mythical and rare:
I think of him as a boy of eight
sent out into the fields to play

in clean new overalls:
and the skunk he met
braver than he   who baptised him

with its generous stink
and the farmer's wife
who buried his shoes

and his spoiled brandnew overalls:
how ashamed he was
the frightened boy

now my tidy husband elegant
and courteous
even in his pain

lying here with his festering wound

DECEMBER 5, 1846, BY ALDER CREEK.

All the oxen and cows that were alive are dead and lost beyond recovery under the snow. Fires are unsafe, all water frozen, and the light shut out. I still have some tea and sugar left, and a few hides from the cattle The thousand dollars sewn up in the quilt that Covers the children is nothing but dead paper to us.

We hear that a party from the other camp at the Lake is attempting to walk out on snowshoes made of split oxbows and strips of hide to get help from Sutter's Fort in Sacramento.

DECEMBER 26, 1846, BY ALDER CREEK.

I have come up out of our black hole beneath the snow
(where the children sleep all day in damp clothing
and George lies without stirring)
to breathe the sharp white air

these mountains
comfort me

a blazing army
straddling the sky
with their long pyramidal pines
dark green black green
trees trees a profusion of trees at last
against the emerald lake

these shapes these colors cleanse my eyes
and I turn back to our evil-smelling cave
a little stronger to confront
the next meal and the next day and the next

JANUARY 7, 1847, BY ALDER CREEK.

I thought of mother's bread, as a child would, but did not find it on the table.

The field mice
that creep into the camp
we catch and use
to ease the pangs of hunger
pieces of hide
we cut in strips
singe scrape and boil
to glue: hard-to-swallow
marrowless bones
boiled and scraped
we burn and eat
we chew the bark
and twigs of pine
to keep from crying
for meat and bread

FEBRUARY 19, 1847, BY ALDER CREEK.

There is no choice. We have somehow survived these months in our dark hole under twenty feet of snow with nothing to fill us but gristle and dried buffalo hide, but now I must send George's two older girls with the kind men who have come to lead them over the pass to Sutter's Fort and California.

Many have died of hunger, of cold, of despair. And I am not sure, with only a few skins left, how long we can keep from eating the bodies of our dead as others are doing.

George begs me to go with the children, but I can not, I will not leave him to die without my comfort.

MARCH 1, 1847, BY ALDER CREEK.

Must we devour ourselves
in order to survive?

    is this new continent
    a place where we can live

only by thrusting down
that fragile barrier

    the ancient loathing
    to eat each other's flesh?

for my children I find it
not so hard:

    I must give them
    nourishment

from whatever source
they will not question where

 but for me
 I cannot see

how I could bear to live
by eating my friend's death

MARCH 15, 1847, BY ALDER CREEK.

I send my three little ones away with the second rescue party. I dress them in layers of their best clothes and tell them to be sure to say to everyone they meet that they are the children of George Donner. I take them to the other camp, kiss them each, and beg them not to cry. I walk back alone to our empty nest.

My children move in my mind
like miniatures
painted on ivory:
one light and willowy
one rosy dark
and the littlest
a frisky animal
that refuses to be tamed:
she reaches through the frame
and pulls at my skin
a baby sloth
clutching its mother's fur

I etch them in my brain
like diamond scratches on a windowpane:
arrest their images as though I were
a limner passing through, a peddler
of portraits

APRIL 10, 1847, BY ALDER CREEK.

How can I store against coming loss?
what faculties of the heart
can I bring against this parting?

we traveled across the land
towards winter not towards spring
I watched the children become solemn and thin
our wagons and housewares
brittle
        depleted

when I buried my boxes
my watercolors and oils my writing desk

I felt I had given all I could part with:
that was what the desert demanded of me:
then the canyons and boulders

ate at the wheels of our wagons
squeezed the life from our oxen

and we learned to part from our
livestock our friends
our comfort

how can I part with
my sustaining love
who was father

to the whole camp, orphans and families
who whistled us up at dawn

who nooned me in the shade
and fed me at sunset
the darks and lights of his eyes

playing over me like sun and clouds
on a highhearted summer afternoon:

how can I learn to sleep
without his shoulder
to bed down my griefs?

the sun stays hidden
for months the sky has wept its snow

APRIL 12, 1847, ALDER CREEK.

Hunger. The lightness of it. I feel my legs will not hold me up any longer. Sounds enter the senses sharply, colors are very bright, I am filled with light, a music that the saints sought and called God. I am not quite in touch with the ground, I am outside my own body. It would be easy to join the air and float into nothingness.

APRIL 15, 1847, IN THE MOUNTAINS.

Cobblestones of light
have poured my path
east to west:
the gull swoops
in the low tide
leaving little crab claws
washed out pink
where the atlantic sun
sucked out the quick

From notes by Thomas Fallon, leader of the final salvage expedition to Donner Lake:

books calicoes tea
coffee shoes percussion caps
household and kitchen furniture
are scattered about

the body of George Donner
is carefully wrapped
in a large clean white sheet
in the midst of filth

Mrs. Donner's body
is nowhere to be found

WHERE IS THE WEST

If my boundary stops here
I have daughters to draw new maps on the world
they will draw the lines of my face
they will draw with my gestures my voice
they will speak my words thinking they have invented
them

they will invent them
they will invent me
I will be planted again and again
I will wake in the eyes of their children's children
they will speak my words

THE TESTING OF HANNA SENESH

Yet even in death you will have your fame,
to have gone like a god to your fate,
in both your living and dying.
—Sophocles, *Antigone*, ll. 834–836

And let us remember the parachutists, emissaries from Israel, who were the first to come to the aid of the nations besieged in Europe, and who did not return.
—Abba Kovner, *Scrolls of Fire*

CONTENTS

Preface

The Historical Background, Livia Rothkirchen

I. Budapest
June 1944

II. Yugoslavia
March 1944 to June 1944. Three Months Earlier

III. Budapest
July 1944 to November 1944

PREFACE

I want to express my thanks for the personal testimony and assistance of Reuven Dafni, who allowed me to interview him for many pleasant hours, and the late Joel Palgi, both of whom were in the parachute rescue mission with Hanna Senesh in 1944; to Hanna's mother and brother, Catherine and Giora (George) Senesh of Haifa, who filled in many details of Hanna's life; and to Miriam Neeman, curator of the Hanna Senesh Archives at Kibbutz Sdot Yam.

I am also grateful to Mishkenot Sha'ananim, the center for artists and writers in Jerusalem, where I began this book in 1977; to the Martin Tananbaum Foundation for two grants that allowed me to visit Israel in 1979 and 1981 to continue my research; and to the Rhode Island State Council on the Arts and the MacDowell Colony of Peterborough, New Hampshire, for supporting me while I did the writing.

Hanna Senesh's most famous poem, "Blessed Is the Match," appears here in my translation from the Hebrew. The farewell letter she actually wrote to her mother before her execution, in my translation, is also reproduced here. (This may not have been the last letter to her mother, since the Hungarian officer who ordered her execution refused to surrender that letter, as well as one written to her comrades in her last hour of life.) All the other poems, as well as the prose passages, are my re-creation of what she might have written during the last nine months of her life.

THE HISTORICAL BACKGROUND

Livia Rothkirchen

Hanna Senesh's life—from 1921 to 1944—spans the most crucial period in recent history, a period that includes the rise of Nazism in Europe and the Second World War. She was twenty-three years old when a firing squad executed her in her native city, Budapest, on November 7, 1944. In sensitive prose and poetry Ruth Whitman explores the last nine months of Hanna's dramatic mission as a British emissary behind enemy lines in Nazi Europe. *The Testing of Hanna Senesh* is a moving imaginative postscript to the diary of the legendary young poet, pioneer, and hero of World War II.

Hanna Senesh was born on July 17, 1921, in Budapest. Her father died when she was still a child, and her mother, Catherine, nee Salzberger, became the central figure in Hanna's life. Surrounded by a closely knit family, Hanna was brought up in an elegant and assimilated Jewish milieu which fully identified itself with Hungarian society and was rooted in its cultural heritage. This essay will attempt to trace Hanna's spiritual growth and transformation against the background of the major historical events both in her chosen land of Israel and in her native country, Hungary.

The record of Jewish life in this enclave of East Central Europe reaches back to Hungary's early history. For centuries the Jews of Hungary prided themselves on the knowledge that as far back as the Magyars' national territorial conquest in the tenth century, Jews had resided in this area. Grave inscriptions from Pannonia and Dacia in the Roman period, as well as epitaphs and relics of Jewish settlement in the Middle Ages and during the Turkish occupation of Hungary, also provided evidence of Jewish presence in this region.

During the seventeenth century the first Jewish families immigrated to Hungary from neighboring Austria, Bohemia, Moravia, Silesia, and Germany. Later, there was a massive influx of immigrants from Galicia and Poland. By the beginning of the eighteenth century, when most of Hungary came under Hapsburg rule, only a few remnants of the ancient Jewish settlements remained. A century later, with the onset of the liberal era, the Jewish population of Hungary experienced a spectacular transformation. As a result of the Emancipation Law of 1867 and a policy of equality and tolerance, Jews came to be respected citizens, sharing fully in the economic and cultural development of the country.

After the First World War and the dissolution of the Austro-Hungarian monarchy, however, the public attitude toward the Jews underwent a radical change. The Treaty of Trianon on June 4, 1920, defined new frontiers: two-thirds of Hungary's territory, with about three million Hungarian nationals, was annexed to Czechoslovakia, Yugoslavia, and Romania, an event regarded as a national humiliation. By the early twenties there was a strong right-wing anti-Semitic force in the country. The *numerus clausus* law was enacted by parliament, which set limits on the number of Jewish students allowed to attend institutions of higher learning. Fifty years after the emancipation of the Jews, Hungary became the pioneer in anti-Jewish legislation in Europe.

Nevertheless, many Jewish writers and musicians continued to enjoy popularity within Hungary. In Budapest, ridiculed as "Judapest,"

Jews comprised 30 percent of the population. The works of talented Jews were translated into several languages and were performed in leading theaters abroad. One of the most popular playwrights was Bela Senesh, known under the pen name of "Coal Man," father of Hanna Senesh.

It was from her father that Hanna inherited her literary talent. With her Grandmother Fini's help, Hanna produced her first literary efforts. Six years old, uncertain about the rules of spelling, she dictated her first poems to her grandmother. Later, she and her brother, George, a year older, issued "The Little Senesh Papers," dealing with current affairs and including a special feature on humor. Occasionally, well-known writers, friends of her father, contributed to this journal, among them Zsolt Harsanyi.

Life was filled with amusements: excursions to Lake Balaton and the Tatra Mountains, holidays in Italy and France, and concerts, performances, and parties. Hanna's teacher observed at the end of the school year in 1929 that "her imagination is colorful, rich, abounding in ideas. She never fails to fulfil her duty, anxious to accomplish the tasks entrusted to her." A recommendation for entrance to secondary school issued two years later commented, "Her style and her poems are reminiscent of her father's gift for expression." Her teachers at the exclusive Protestant school recognized her talents by awarding her various literary prizes. In what was considered a special favor, Hanna's mother paid only double tuition for her daughter and not the triple tuition that most Jews had to pay.

Hanna's teens were marked by a growing desire for artistic expression. At the age of thirteen she started a diary, which she kept for ten years. She wrote about her experiences at school and in her family circle and also commented on political events in Hungary and the world. In 1936 she made her first attempt at playwriting with a historical one-act parody, *Bella gerunt alii, tu, felix Austria, nube*, a school performance in which she was both actor and director. She wrote four humorous sketches in which suitors from four different historical ages proposed marriage to their loved ones: a B.C.E. suitor; a medieval knight; a petit bourgeois in 1836; and an astronaut in the year 2036 who proposes to a woman astronaut after a flight to Mars. She mentions food tablets and television, apparently influenced by the writings of Huxley. She also wrote thoughtful papers on history and literature, exploring for the first time a Jewish theme in an essay entitled "Jewish References in Hungarian Literature," a prelude to her more mature writings on "Our Nation" and "Zionist Foundations."

The incorporation of Austria into the Reich on March 13, 1938, brought the boundaries of Germany to the gates of Hungary, creating a highly tense political climate in the whole region. Wanting Hitler's favor, the Hungarian government acted quickly to show its sympathy for the "New Order" in Europe by further restricting the rights of the Jews. In April 1938, the "First Jewish Law" was introduced. It was intended to "ensure with greater effectiveness the balance in social and economic life."

The deteriorating status of Jews throughout Europe and the increase in anti-Semitism in her immediate environment stimulated Hanna's interest in Palestine. In the same high school where she had been praised and rewarded, she was now not allowed to keep her elected position as president of the literary society. In late 1938, as Hanna stood on the threshold of her matriculation, she began to find her way toward Jewish consciousness and Zionism. Everything she wrote from this time onward was colored by her passion for Eretz Israel. On October 26, 1938, she wrote in her diary: "I am a Zionist. That word conveys a lot. I am more aware now of my Jewishness and sense it with all my heart. I am proud of being Jewish and I hope to go to Eretz Israel to help in building up the country. Of course, this idea did not come to me overnight. When three years ago I first heard of Zionism I was definitely opposed to it. Now I have land under my feet and a purpose for which it is worthwhile working." Hanna started to learn Hebrew and made up her mind to immigrate to Palestine when she graduated from high school. Before leaving Budapest, she collected photographs and information on the lineage of her family. She compiled this into a booklet, which she intended as a farewell to her past.

The "Second Jewish Law" was put into effect on May 8, 1939. Its main innovations were the reduction of the proportion of Jews in economic and cultural occupations to 6 percent and forbidding Jews to occupy any controlling managerial or influential positions in newspaper offices, theaters, cinemas, film studios, or in the armed forces. A special instruction provided that in war "Jews were to be engaged only in the line of fire." The term "Jew" was redefined as a person whose "parents belonged to the Mosaic faith to the extent of 50 percent," that is, if one or two grandparents were Jews. At this stage, exemptions from the law were still granted to Jewish war veterans who had medals, to invalids, and to Olympic champions.

This new definition of "Jew" on racial grounds resulted in a wave of conversions to Christianity in all the Jewish communities. It is estimated that at the turn of 1938, approximately fourteen thousand Jews converted, in the hope of becoming exempt from the anti-Semitic laws. Many of the outstanding writers, artists, and leading figures of the Hungarian economy became Christian, but in late 1939 it became clear that conversion was no protection against racial persecution.

The outbreak of war on September 1, 1939, the strengthening of the extreme right-wing parties, especially of the Arrow-Cross Party, and the increase of the Jewish population from Hungary's newly acquired areas placed a heavy burden on Jewish community leadership. The leaders of the community in Budapest, reacting to the anti-Jewish laws, issued this declaration: "Hundreds of thousands of Hungarian citizens of Mosaic faith who had always labored for their fatherland and were ready to sacrifice their lives for it, are now being excluded from the national partnership which has been maintained for generations."

In this atmosphere of disappointment and frustration, Hanna decided to leave Hungary. She set out for Palestine on September 19, 1939, on board the *Bessarabia*. Her mother remained behind in Budapest; her brother had already gone to France to study engineering. As soon as she arrived in Haifa, Hanna began study at the Nahalal Agricultural School, eager to learn how to work on the land. In 1940, while she was still a student, she wrote her first poem in Hebrew, on Yom Kippur Eve. At the same time she started to write her diary entries in Hebrew, determined to make it her own language. She consoled herself for her errors: "It is better to write a little in Hebrew than a lot in Hungarian."

In 1941 Hanna joined the young pioneering kibbutz, Sdot Yam, near the ruins of ancient Caesarea. As a member of the settlement, she performed various duties: working in the kitchen, the garden, and the laundry, scrubbing floors, tending chickens, and performing guard duty. In her free time she swam in the sea, climbed the rocks, and meditated about the past and future. In Sdot Yam she wrote her most moving poetry.

Much of Hanna's diary is valuable as a chronicle of Palestine during the war. She reported the fate of the refugee ships, news from the European war zone, and the activities of the Yishuv [the Jewish community residing in Palestine before the establishment of the State of Israel in 1948]. There is no problem or idea that did not attract her analytic mind. She discussed the future of the kibbutz, the role of the working class in a socialist society. Her one-act play, *The Violin*, reflects her own conflict between her artistic aspirations and her commitment to the kibbutz. The heroine, Judith, a talented violinist, faces the choice between collective society and art and decides to devote herself to the collective, since service to the community is a higher and more significant goal than the success of an individual. Obviously, Hanna's commitment was nurtured both by the precarious situation of the Jews in Europe and the thriving, hopeful atmosphere she encountered in Palestine.

During the thirties Jewish colonization in British Mandatory Palestine had made great progress. In the famous words of British minister Malcolm MacDonald: "They have made the desert bloom. They have started a score of thriving industries. . . . They have founded a great city (Tel Aviv) on the barren shore. They have harnessed the Jordan and spread its electricity throughout the land." Ironically, the same MacDonald signed the infamous Statement of Policy known as the White Paper of May 17, 1939, in which the British government limited the number of Jewish immigrants to seventy-five thousand for five years, making the Yishuv dependent in subsequent years on Arab acquiescence. This curtailing of Jewish immigration—a breach of British pledges—was meant to appease the Arabs, but dealt a serious blow to the Yishuv because it sealed off Palestine as a refuge at the moment when the survival of European Jewry was threatened.

With mounting persecution in Germany, the late thirties saw an increase in the stream of refugees, which began with Hitler's advent to power in 1933. The refugees were chiefly Central European Jews—German, Austrian, Czechoslovak, and some Romanian and Hungarian. They set out from eastern Mediterranean ports on discarded Greek or Turkish cattle boats, leaking tankers, or old freighters, paying exorbitant sums to private entrepreneurs or boat owners for their passage. Some of these "little death ships," as Arthur Koestler described them, sailed clandestinely to Palestine, landing their human cargo by night; others were intercepted by the British navy. In accordance with the White Paper, those caught were brought to Haifa and to the island of Mauritius, or sent back to their ports of embarkation in Europe. The odysseys of the sunken ships *Patria*, *Pacific*, *Milos*, *Struma*, among others, were reported by the survivors of these vessels. Despite British interception, however, the influx of illegal Jewish immigrants grew considerably in the summer of 1939, fostered occasionally by the Irgun Zvi Leumi (the National Military Organization). The British admitted fifty thousand refugees into Great Britain, but feared that a massive exodus to Palestine would provoke the Arabs and thus unbalance the mandate's policy.

The fall of Mussolini and the turning of the tide on the fronts had, of course, positive repercussions in Mandatory Palestine. Since the fall of 1939, the leadership of the Hagana in Palestine had proposed various plans to the British authorities for the active engagement of a Jewish force. One of the proposals was to provide a Jewish unit of volunteers to operate behind enemy lines in Nazi-occupied Europe. But it was only in late 1943 that the reluctance of the British was overcome and a handful of Palestinian Jews were allowed to participate in this enterprise. The proviso was that "they be used as individuals under SOE [Special Operation Executive]." Most of the young men and women were in their early twenties, each selected for outstanding physical and intellectual qualifications, from the elite stock of the pioneer settlements. The women were recruited into the Women's Auxiliary Air Force and the men into the Buffs or Pioneer Corps.

As the news of the plight of European Jews under Nazi occupation began to leak out to Palestine, Hanna became increasingly worried about the fate of her mother and the Jewish people. Hanna learned about the political developments in Hungary and the fate of the Jews there not only through the media but also through her exchange of letters with her mother. Still living in Buda in the family's villa on Bimbo Street, Hanna's mother described the changes that were affecting the everyday life of the Jews. Then Hanna made a decision. On January 8, 1943, she wrote in her diary: "This week has been most agitating. Suddenly the idea occurred to me: 'I must go to Hungary, be there at this time, help in organizing Youth Aliyah and bring my mother out.'" She had heard that the British were organizing volunteers to act behind the enemy lines in Nazi-occupied Europe and was eager to join them: "This is just what I dreamt of . . . I feel herein the hand of destiny, just as before when I left for Palestine. Then, too, I was not the master of my own will. I was caught by an idea that gave me no peace. I knew I would go to Palestine, no matter what obstacles were in my way. This time again I feel the same drive toward an important and necessary task and its inevitability."

She enlisted in the Hagana and prepared herself for her departure for Cairo, where she would receive training with British Intelligence. Before leaving, Hanna copied her Hebrew poems in a notebook, signed them "Hagar"—the code name she was given for her mission—and entrusted the book to Miriam Yitzhaki, her closest friend in the kibbutz.

At that time the Allied forces were in great need of volunteers in the Balkans to help with the rescue of military personnel stranded or imprisoned in enemy-occupied territories. The mission of the Palestinian volunteers was twofold: first, they were to relay to British Intelligence firsthand information regarding enemy strength, location of factories and bridges, and troop movements; second, they were to organize Jewish resistance, establish rescue centers, and devise means for the evacuation of Jews into liberated partisan territories.

Despite the obvious risks the Jewish emissaries were likely to face in Nazi Europe, the volunteers of the Yishuv were eager to embark on their mission. The situation in early 1944 still seemed favorable for such enterprises. There existed in southeastern Europe a sizeable Jewish population—about one and a half million Jews—the largest diaspora in Hungary and the remnants of Jewry in Slovakia, Romania, and Bulgaria. Swift actions by guerrilla fighters might have been of great value in these areas. But because of delays and technical obstacles, many precious months had been lost.

Tragically, Hanna and her fellow emissaries arrived in Europe too late. The general turmoil prevailing in southeastern Europe, the drastic security measures employed by the Nazis, and their ferocity in dealing with captured Allied personnel thwarted rescue activities from the outset. The first group of volunteers had landed in Romania in the fall of 1943. In March 1944, Hanna flew with the other paratroopers, Sergeant Nussbacher (later known as Joel Palgi) and Peretz Goldstein, together with Reuven Dafni, to Bari, Italy; they were assigned to "Operation Chicken I" in Hungary, as it is named in British Intelligence records.

Two days later they parachuted into Slovenia. They stayed in Yugoslavia for about three months with Tito's partisans, waiting to cross into Hungary. They witnessed battles waged by Yugoslav partisans, the destruction of towns and villages by enemy troops, and the plight of the local population. In Srdice Hanna wrote her poem, "Blessed Is the Match," an apotheosis of self-sacrifice, which she gave to Reuven Dafni, who stayed behind in Yugoslavia when she crossed the border.

Meanwhile, in Hungary, events had reached a climax. By March 1944 the German High Command had its plans ready for "Operation Margarethe," the code name for the military occupation of Hungary. On March 12, Adolf Eichmann brought his *Sondereinsatzkommando* (Special Task Force, which would eliminate Hungary's Jews) to Mauthausen, Austria, in order to prepare its activities. On March 17 Hungary's regent, Nicholas Horthy, was secretly summoned and persuaded to give his consent to the occupation. The Anglo-American invasion of Normandy on June 6, 1944, and the advance of the Red Army toward the Carpathian Mountains and the borders of Hungary spurred Eichmann to work feverishly to achieve his final goal—the total removal of all Jews from Hungary. After clearing out the provincial areas, his principal target remained: the capital city, Budapest, with its 220,000 Jews. Their deportation was planned for July. Between June 17 and June 24, more than 20,000 Jews of the city were crammed into buildings marked by the Star of David. On June 9, 1944, at the height of the deportation of the Jews from the provinces, Hanna Senesh managed to cross the border from Slovenia into Hungary. The next day she was denounced to the Hungarian police by an informer and taken to a Gestapo prison in Budapest. The other two parachutists—Nussbacher and Goldstein—were arrested a short time after their slightly later arrival in Hungary. British Intelligence sources reveal that at one point the comrades were placed in adjacent prison cells. Hanna was able to tap out to Nussbacher a good deal of information before she was taken away for further interrogation and torture. Meanwhile, two young Jewish escapees from Auschwitz revealed authentic data and figures about the extermination of millions of Jews in the death camps. Members of the Jewish Council brought these so-called Auschwitz Protocols to the attention of Regent Horthy. The information eventually reached Switzerland, where it was given wide publicity in July 1944. Both the Catholic and Protestant churches continued to demand an easing of the plight of the persecuted, though their main concern was for the fate of their converts. The reading of a joint pastoral letter that they prepared in protest was delayed for two months, but was finally read as a formal declaration from the pulpits on July 16. By that time, however, five hundred thousand Jews of the provincial areas had already been deported.

At noon on October 15, the very day the Germans kidnapped his son by a ruse, Regent Horthy, in an effort to get Hungary out of the war, announced over Budapest radio that Hungary was proclaiming its armistice with the Allies. Representatives of Hungary and Russia had already signed an agreement in Moscow on October 11. In his address Horthy referred to the Jewish question, "the solution of which the Gestapo had dealt with in its well-known way, against the principles of humanity." But Horthy's attempt to save Hungary failed.

Budapest's Jews were doomed to further suffering. By late in the day on October 15, Ferenc Szálasi, the nation's new leader, announced on the radio his takeover of power, promising to continue the war on the side of the Reich. On October 17 Eichmann appeared in Budapest to begin the final removal of the Jews. Since rolling stock was not available, the remaining Jews had to travel by foot to the German border. In the rain and cold on November 8, the day after Hanna was executed, the first group of Budapest Jews started on this death march, among them Catherine Senesh, Hanna's mother. It is estimated that about sixty thousand Jews were removed from the capital in this way. Budapest was filled with confusion and terror. Jews who did not possess protective passports were locked up in a ghetto in Buda. The streets were controlled by the mob, everyone competing for the booty of Jewish property. At every hour of the day, Jews could be seen being dragged by men of the Arrow-Cross Party to some unknown destination, usually a dark cellar or the banks of the Danube, where thousands of people were shot. The Russians had begun their systematic bombing of Budapest; the city was under siege, and the terror increased. At the end of December Otto Komoly, president of the Zionist Federation in Hungary, was kidnapped by the Arrow-Cross and vanished. Jews in hiding places were constantly in danger; children were hidden in orphanages and monasteries. The Swedish rescue team headed by Raoul Wallenberg, and including Professor Valdemar Langlet and his wife, Nina, Asta Nilson, and other Righteous Gentiles, among them individual priests and nuns, risked their lives to save the remnant of Budapest's Jewry. One part of the city, Pest, fell to the Soviet army on January 18, 1945. Buda became free on February 13. The gardens in the ghetto, the courtyards of the Jewish Council offices, and the ritual baths were covered with heaps of cadavers, victims of the Nazis' last vengeance.

The liberation of Budapest came too late for many and too late for Hanna Senesh. On October 28, after four months in the Budapest prison, she was tried by a Hungarian military court. American bombers were pounding the city, and Soviet guns could be heard on the outskirts of Budapest. Although she had not received an official sentence, Hanna was executed by a firing squad on November 7. Her execution was ordered by a Hungarian officer, Captain Simon, who acted on his own initiative. Peretz Goldstein, her fellow parachutist, perished in one of the concentration camps. Only Nussbacher, Joel Palgi, survived, managing to escape from a locked deportation train. He made his way back to Budapest, dug up the transmitter he had buried when he arrived, and was able to communicate for a few weeks with headquarters in Britain.

Hanna's last days were recalled by some of her fellow prisoners and parachutists who survived and by the Hungarian guards who came into contact with her during her imprisonment. Her mother, who was jailed for a time in the same prison and, through the goodwill of some of the guards, was occasionally permitted to meet with Hanna, has written her reminiscences of that harrowing period. Eyewitnesses related that during one point in Hanna's trial, everyone was asked to leave the courtroom, and Hanna was left alone with the judges. It was reported that she presented her own defense boldly, analyzing the moral decline of Hungary in siding with Nazi Germany and warning that those participating in the crime would pay for it. She refused to ask for clemency from "hangmen and murderers."

Since the Jewish burial society was no longer functioning in Budapest, Hanna's body was buried by merciful gentiles in the martyr's section of the Jewish cemetery. After the establishment of the State of Israel, Hanna Senesh's remains were transferred to Jerusalem and buried on Mount Herzl in the military cemetery, beside fellow parachutists who were also executed in Europe. A mourning nation paid its tribute to the young woman who would become a legend. Since then, monuments have been erected in her memory throughout the country. Farming settlements, a ship, a forest, several streets, and a species of flower now bear her name.

On November 2, five days before Hanna was executed, Bill Tone, a British officer serving with the partisans in Yugoslavia, wrote to a friend in Jerusalem: "I had the pleasure of meeting a young woman from Palestine, who parachuted to my headquarters in Slovenia and proceeded overland to another part of Europe. She was a grand girl and as plucky as anyone could be. Should you hear of her when she returns, please put yourself out to meet her. She was accompanied by two other men from Palestine. They were all excellent and will be regarded as great heroes as time goes on."

Hanna's literary legacy became public domain after the war. Her diary and poems have been translated into many languages, and some of her poems have been set to music; several have been recorded and are often performed. They are now part of the folk heritage of Israel. On January 11, 1944, before embarking on her mission, Hanna Senesh wrote the last entry in her diary: "I want to believe that what I have done, and will do, are right. Time will tell the rest." She could never have imagined that forty years later an American poet would pick up the thread of her life and would spend several years in the effort to relive and re-create her last days with so much empathy and insight.

Historian **Livia Rothkirchen** (1922–2013), editor of *Yad Vashem Studies* from 1968 to 1983, was the author of many monographs on the Jews of Slovakia, Hungary, and Bohemia-Moravia and the author of *The Destruction of Slovak Jewry: A Documentary History*.

BLESSED IS THE MATCH

As a little child
I heard a voice

calling me, commanding me
it was dim at first,

but knew I was chosen:
it called me, called

until I followed:
now I hear it clearly:

I must be the match
to strike the flame:

I must be the flame

—Hanna Senesh

I. BUDAPEST
June 1944

1

They've been beating me for three days.

My ribs ache.
I think my wrist is broken.
And my jaw is throbbing where the police
knocked out a tooth.

The Gestapo agent was furious
when I threw the book of French poems out of the train
and tried to jump after.
He didn't know the transmitter code was in the book,
he was just angry that I tried to escape.

Now I can't tell anyone the code, even if I wanted to.

2

After the first shock
it's like letting a wave of flame singe your hand:

first a sharp sensation, then no feeling.
I watch myself like a person in a dream
while they invent devices to break me down.

But I never scream.
Screaming means it's happening to me.
I step back and watch it happen around me.

Anger helps. Anger makes a barrier between the whip and me
They tie me up
and beat my soles, my palms, my back:
                                    I say

no no to myself
don't let them have a sign that I feel it:

think of the blue-green sea that I saw every night
from my tent under the old stars,
the cool Winds of evening:

think of that hill in Jerusalem,
the little lights shining in the villages,
breathe the aromatic Judaean air,
watch the sun set over the Old City,
the shadows creeping up the towers,
pulling the bruised light behind them:

you see: I feel nothing.

It is only my body flopping like a fish.

It is only my body that bleeds.

3

the self
becomes small and thin
a single taper
burning
        in immense darkness

4

In this small cell on the top floor of the prison
I count:
        chair,
            bed,
                table.
The window is high and horizontal, out of reach.
I push the bed beneath it,
lift the table with my aching arms,
and place the chair on top.

I climb up and stand on the peak of my shaky mountain
Now I can see sky, trees,
even the street where I once lived—
Bimbo Street.
But that was long ago and another me.

5

Four Gestapo policemen are taking me to Military Headquarters
on Horthy Miklos Boulevard.
They won't tell me why.
I'm sitting with my eyes closed,
trying not to feel the throbbing of my bruises,
the pain in my head.

I imagine I hear my mother's voice.
The door of the room opens,
a large man steps out and says.
"Bring the girl in."

The police push me roughly through the door.
My mother is standing there.
I break out of their hands and fly into her arms.
For the first time, I let my tears come.

"Mother! Forgive me!"

My mother, my beautiful mother has aged, her hair is gray.

"Aniko, what has happened to you?
What have they done to your poor face?
Why?"

"Yes," says Mr. Rozsa, the civilian interrogator,
"tell your mother why you're here.
We'll leave you two alone."

"Aniko, did you come back because of me?
I could never forgive myself for that."

"No, I hoped you were already in Palestine with George."

"Then why, why?
Didn't you know the Germans were in Hungary?
Look at your bruises, your skin, your hurt wrists.
They've even knocked out a tooth!"

She begins to embrace me, weeping, and the men rush in

"No secrets!" they shout.

Rosza says, "Now tell us what you were doing
with the transmitter, or watch us
torture your mother."

I look at my mother and see
although she doesn't understand what I'm doing here,
she trusts me. She doesn't flinch.

"I have nothing to say."

They take me away.

6

Trapped in this gray square
I know the earth
is moving across the dawn
from meridian to meridian

all night I keep watching,
searching the walls, the floor
for an opening
into the light:

dreams stream down my face,
my breath stops in my throat,
my bones crush against each other

as I beat at my own absence

7

A round reflection of sunlight flickers on my ceiling
At first I think it's accidental, but it moves around.

Then I realize it is being done on purpose,
with a mirror.

Someone is talking to me.

This afternoon, when the sun is on my side,
I'll try to answer.

8

Behind my closed lids I see
the late afternoon sun
shining through the petals
of a red flower:
a transparent red light
as though the petals
were of glass
except for the shadow
that falls across them
and the secret black center

II. YUGOSLAVIA
March 1944 to June 1944
Three Months Earlier

1

Sitting in the dark inside the plane,
I hear the dispatcher dumping the bales,
each attached to its own parachute.

It's bright moonlight.
we're over Slovenia, which has just been liberated
from the Germans.
The partisans
are expecting us. Below I can see
the fires marking the letter E
to show us their position.

It's time to jump.

Every fiber in my body is against it.
But I know that when I let go,
when I let myself fall into open space,
I burst open my limits and feel I can do anything.

The hatch opens.

I jump against the moon.

2

Stepping out,
I'm delivered to air:
I'm swept into turbulence,
tumbling down
past twenty-five feet
of nowhere:

the laws and patterns of space
unfold my arms and legs:

my parachute blossoms,
a spray of the milkweed,
as my pendulum body
swings beneath it:

now I'm falling slowly,
alive:
I see the trees below me:
I come to the end of sky,
stem first,
ballooning then collapsing
flower string wind:

I cut the cord
and the world is mine

3

I land on six feet of snow in the moonlight.
It's like falling into a featherbed.

The wind has blown me off course
and I've floated away from the others, out of sight.
As I jumped behind Reuven I heard him curse the pilot
for dropping us on the wrong side of the wind,
away from the flaming E.

I blow the whistle they gave me.
The sound cuts across the silence.
Tall Yugoslav mountains are all around me,
nothing but snow and rock.

Reuven and Abba come out of a patch of trees, shouting,
"There she is!"
We hug each other, laughing with relief.

A band of strange men appear and come towards us,
holding rifles.
Reuven puts his hand on his grenade,
in case we've been betrayed to the Nazis.
But then we see the men are wearing red stars on their caps

They're Tito's partisans.

Standing in the snow, they are barefoot

4

The Germans have marched into Budapest.

What will become of the million Jews in Hungary?
They'll be killed by the Nazis while we sit here in the snow.

"Reuven," I say, trying not to cry with disappointment,
"What about the plans we made
to help the refugees escape to Palestine?
Let's cross the border now, quickly,
before the Germans bring the storm troopers."

"No," he says, "it's hopeless.
We tried to reach Budapest before the Germans,
but they were too fast for us."

"You mean we were too slow," I say bitterly.
"Why didn't the British arrange to drop us sooner?
The longer we wait, the more impossible it will be.
Let's cross the border now."

"No, Hanna," he says, "it's too late.
You'll only be endangering all of us
and then there'll be no one left
to contact the underground."

"I don't care. It's better to take the risk now
than never to try at all. How can you
sit back and do nothing?"

"That's enough," he says, getting angry.
"You'll get us all wiped out if you keep on like this."

"But we must cross the border. And find a new escape route
Yugoslavia, Hungary, Rumania, are all being shut off.
How can we reach the ships
that will carry the refugees to Palestine
unless we go now?"

5

I remember the battered ship
that waited for months in the Turkish harbor
and was never allowed to land:

6

The death ships. The Struma.
It lay in the harbor at Istanbul
Without food or coal.

Don't let it land,
said the Ambassador.

Jews are enemy aliens,
said the British.
Tow them out to the Black Sea,
send them to Crete, Mauritius,
to Rumania, Germany, Jamaica,
but don't let them come to Palestine.

That was December 1941.

Safe in my kibbutz at Sdot Yam
(meadows of the sea),
                    I looked
at the peacock-blue Mediterranean
and cried, let them come,
we have room.

No, said Lord Moyne,
if one ship comes
they'll all want to come.
Let the children come.

Children?
What will we do with children?

The hold was airless.
Sickness, filth,
layers of excrement, vomit.

The ship could not sail.
The ship could not stay.
No land would take them.

In February the ship exploded
outside the harbor at Istanbul.
Eight hundred lives flew up,
their rags, arms, legs, hopes
falling like rain.

One was saved.
He was allowed to enter
Palestine.

7

We're hiding in the forest near Semič.
The Germans keep pushing us south
through woods and mountains.

I've had my hand on my pistol several times,
but haven't fired it yet.
                I try not to think of
soft human flesh.
When we trained in Cairo, we shot wooden dummies,
But a man, even an enemy, is real, with blood,
thoughts, hopes.
            How can I destroy that?

We haven't changed our clothes or had a bath
since we joined the partisans.
                I never expected
to live like this, playing hide and seek
with Nazi murderers in the mountains of Yugoslavia.

Reuven and I have hardly spoken since our quarrel.
He knows I'm determined to find a way
to cross the border,
even if I have to do it alone.

8

Every day we walk farther away from the Slovenian border
Now we're moving into Croatia.

One part of my mind watches for an enemy patrol.
The other part notices the white birches around us,
the long trunks of pines, the poplars by the streams.

Even now, part of me observes with a cool eye.

9

I think of the pine tree
beside my tent
on the dune
at kibbutz Sdot Yam:
I watched the sea,
I walked on the fragrant shore
and my blood lifted
with the salty lift of the tide:
now under the pine trees
in a foreign land
I live day and night
with strangers:
I'm a drop of oil on water,
sometimes floating,
sometimes sinking,
but always apart

10

Everywhere I go the partisans are startled to see me.
Perhaps it's my British Air Force uniform.

Last night there was a party in a village
of lavender-painted houses.
                                        The men and women
Came into the meeting house, laid down their rifles,
and began to dance and sing.
someone had a gusla, a kind of Yugoslavian guitar,
and we clapped to the music as the dancers danced.
I danced most of the night.
The table was heaped with cheese, bread, pancakes,
cherries, peaches, wine, slivovitz,
but I was too excited to eat.

They asked me to say a few words to our comrades.
I stood on a table and shouted,
"Death to Fascism! Freedom to the people!"
holding my fingers in a V.

They clapped and cheered.
I could see that Reuven was pleased with me for once
He smiled and touched my shoulder.

11

Surrounded by Nazi patrols hunting for us,
we crouch in the forest for ten hours,
not daring to speak or breathe,
afraid the flutter of a leaf will betray us.

When we huddle in the bushes like this,
when we can't even whisper among ourselves,
I've learned to let my mind wander out of my body
to other times and places.
                    Hiding here in the mud and twigs
I remember how I used to take care of the cows
when I first arrived in Palestine.

12

Shoveling manure in the barn
I breathe the heavy lurid smell
of cows' excrement:
it is not so unpleasant,
it is full of sharp hay and grass
and fields of sweet clover

But the pile is a mountain,
soft and endlessly yielding:

I reach across with my shovel
and my foot gives way
as I slide into it
up to my waist

At that moment
my whole life changes

The dainty schoolgirl,
the airy pioneer
who used to play Chopin
with delicate white fingers
begins to laugh
and curse the cows
in salty Hungarian

13

Thinking of my arms and legs covered with manure,
I begin to laugh, and Reuven shushes me sternly.

The forest is finally clear,
and we can crawl out of the underbrush.
My legs are so cramped it takes a while to unbend them
I can hardly walk.

14

An uneasy wind
blows through the trees
bending the tall pines;
one small bird
flies over my head,
chirps a warning,
then hides in the leaves

15

We're resting in a cave with the partisans.
It's a radio station, a hideout with food and medicine.
Marking time again.

Here in Croatia the partisan general
has asked us not to tell the fighters
that we are Palestinian Jews.
Our British uniforms would convince them—
what they've already been told—
that the Jews rule Britain. So when we speak
Hebrew among ourselves,
we tell them we're speaking Welsh and they believe us.

With nothing to do,
I start to think about September 1939,
when I left Hungary for Palestine.
The Germans had invaded Poland. The war had started.
I took the train from Budapest to the mouth of the Danube
in Rumania, where I caught the *Bessarabia*, bound for Haifa

16

Haifa. Overhead the crown of Mount Carmel
above the Mediterranean;
the port, gold in the sun, was crowded with ships,
the streets full of excited men and women,
loud voices, extravagant gestures.

I went south from Haifa to Tel Aviv—
a new city built on sand dunes—
and up through orange groves leaning fragrant
in the arms of cypresses
along the narrow road to the Judaean hills,
up and around until I saw

Jerusalem, the Old City and the new,
a halo of diamonds above the desert.

Then across the desert to the Dead Sea
and the fortress of Masada
where the last remnant of free Jews
was trapped by the Romans
two thousand years ago.

In the end,
when the Romans were climbing up the walls,
the men killed their wives and their children:
then they killed themselves.

17

I sit here in the mountains of Yugoslavia,
breathing the hot dry air of Masada.

18

In the midst of the Judaean desert
Masada rises, rock fortress
streaked with tan, brown,
the colors of thirst.

A hot wind blows.

Crows cut across the air below me,
their corrugated cries
the only sound
in the ancient stillness.

King Herod's bath, once a mikva
for the Jews who hid here,

bakes in the heat.
Tails of field mice

flick between a jumble of rocks:
the paint in the throne room dims,
victors and victims
shrivel to dust

19

The Germans are moving Jews from the towns outside Budapest
into ghettos, to round them up and deport them.
An eighty-four-year-old woman was dragged from the operating
table where her foot was being amputated. She was thrown
bleeding into a wagon. Her son tried to shoot himself, blew off half
his face, and was hurled in the wagon with his mother.
Where is my mother, my brave mother,
who let me leave her behind in Budapest?
It is the end of April,
we've been wandering for more than a month,
and I'm farther from her than ever.

20

We're taking our first bath, here in Čazma,
in a house with running water.

Reuven has found two Allied pilots who were shot down.
He draws maps for them, showing them how
to get to the Adriatic coast
where British boats will come over from Brindisi
and take them to southern Italy.

"Reuven," I say, "don't spend your time
looking for British or American flyers.

Let's cross the border now. Let's save
the Jews who are being hunted in Hungary."

"Hanna, Hanna," he says sadly, "you must be patient.
We can't take foolish risks. We must wait
Until we have some chance of success.
And we must keep our promise to the British
to help Allied pilots get back safely."

He makes me angry.
                    Doesn't he realize
we're the ones who must make way,
who must keep the escape routes open?

21

Root cells.
At the farm at Nahalal
I learned how those pioneer cells
go first into the earth:

they make a way
for the root that follows
so the plant may bloom:
and then the root cells die.

22

Joel, my special friend,
has been dropped into Yugoslavia to join us.
We played together in Cairo while we trained with the British. Joel taught me how to shoot a pistol. We learned how to take apart and repair the transmitter, to translate the code, to repel an attacker. After class we'd go sightseeing: to the pyramids, the zoo, the theater. We wandered around the city, holding hands.

I love his pixie smile, his arched brows, his intense blue eyes, He looks
like a hero.

I know he has a sweetheart somewhere—perhaps many
sweethearts.

But now there's not time for that.
I feel a different love. I'm burning with it,
this terrible need to give myself to this mission,
to justify my being here.

23

I remember the two Polish women
who came to Palestine
escaped from a death camp
and the news they brought:

some did not believe,
but I knew:

now I follow a path
back to the fiery center

to rescue a live ember

24

We watch a fight between an American plane
and 3 German Messerschmitt.
Both are shot down.
The American plane falls near us.
We rush over and find the pilot unconscious
but alive.

Some German tanks
have seen him fall and start coming towards us.

We run through the underbrush, carrying the wounded pilot,
and come to a large underground hospital. The pilot
sips some brandy and says some words in English to Reuven.

In a corner I see the partisans are gathered
around a young girl with a shattered leg. The woman doctor
works with a saw because she has no instruments.
And no anesthetic, only brandy.

I can't bear to look. The girl makes no sound.
I think, if she is brave enough to bear it,
I must be brave enough to comfort her.
I take her hand and watch the tears
run silently down her cheeks.

25

We're sick with diarrhea, we're covered with lice.
The British promise to send us new uniforms
from Brindisi by parachute.

The orchards are now blossoming and the May woods
are alive with young oak trees and mauve crocuses.
The sun is so warm we take off our heavy uniforms
and spread them out to catch the fleas and lice.
Heat makes the insects sleepy.

I stretch out on the ground behind some bushes.
My skin feels the sun.

I know I'm not pretty, my face is too round,
but I have large blue-green eyes and thick curly hair.

And Joel says my long legs are well-shaped.
Will I ever feel a lover's hand on me?
I know, I feel sure there is someone
somewhere in the world as clever as my father,
as cheerful as my brother, as generous as my mother,
waiting for me.
Will I live long enough?

26

I remember swimming at Lake Balaton
when I was fourteen:

the sand felt warm and smooth
as I waded in:
I lay on my back
and floated on top of the world.
I closed my eyes,
felt the sun on my face.

I picked a cluster
of dark blue ripening grapes
from a vine on the hillside:
bit into a plump warm grape
and the sharp juice
gushed into my mouth:

and I thought of the lake,
how it held me up,
touching me gently everywhere,
how the sun kissed my face.

27

We've now managed to keep out of reach of the Germans
for almost two months, but Reuven says we still
can't cross the border.

The partisans share their food and shelter with us
but won't give us papers from their huge document factory
and won't let us deal with their chief operators.
They still don't trust us.

I worry, "What will become of our people in Hungary?
We have no right to sit here doing nothing.
No right not to go."

Joel says, "There's no logic in going now."

"This is no time for logic. I'd rather try and fail
than go back home, safe and selfish. Even if we fail,
word will get to them that they're not abandoned,
their suffering is known. That someone at least
risked her life to help them."

"Yes," said Joel, "but if you are captured
it will be a terrible waste. Don't be so obsessive.
You're sometimes very stubborn. That makes life hard
for the rest of us. Please, Hanna,
try to be patient."

"I have been patient," I shout, "I've been patient
for two years, since I first asked the Hagana
to let me join the parachutists.
            I'm tired of waiting.
Now it's time to act."

He is silent.

28

As I was waking up this morning I heard an explosion in my
head as though a light bulb flew apart inside my brain.
Behind my eyes white slivers of glass burst through the
black air. Was I dying?

I woke, my heart pounding, terrified.

I keep hearing tree branches snapping inside my head.
It's hard to breathe. My heart beats like a hammer, even
when I lie still.

Perhaps I'm not equal to this task. I feel breakable, as
though my heart, my breath, may stop at any moment.
The trees, my hands, the faces of my comrades look unreal.
The whole world distant and transparent.

I lie on the ground all day, not wanting to eat, not wanting
to talk.

29

The middle of May.
The partisans say the way is now clear
and we can move north toward Hungary.
I still feel weak and sick, but I know I must go
I will cross alone. Joel will cross later.

It's a rainy night.
We're sitting together, waiting near the airfield.

The partisans are singing around the fire.
Joel and I whisper together, remembering
Jewish partisans singing songs of Eretz Israel.

I want to share my heart with him.
I ask him to come and walk with me in the darkness.

We're going to part and I want to remember this moment.

I say to him, "I know I'm headstrong and stubborn
and I sometimes make Reuven angry,
but I want you to understand me."

He puts his arm around me and says,
"Hanna, don't worry. I know how soft and sweet
you really are."

His arm is warm on my shoulder.
I kiss him, a kiss that perhaps is sweeter
to me than to him.

We agree to meet in two weeks
at the Great Synagogue in Budapest.

30

I'll cross the border into Hungary
and find my mother
and lead her to safety.

31

Braided together,
my mother and I
became strong through loss:
she watched my father die
in the bloom of their love,
and her mother, queen of the house,
sicken and slip away.

And then, skillful at parting,
she parted from me.

She let me go, knowing
I would carry her in me
even as she once held me safe
inside her own flesh.

Why then, with her center
in me, this tie
across time and distance,
across death itself,
do I have a longing
so sharp
it digs a hollow
beneath my heart?

32

I'm dining with a partisan general
who has invited me to come to his cave.
He wants to see the girl who insists
on crossing the border into Hungary.

He serves me beef roasted on a spit,
arranged on a platter of branches and leaves.
It's the first meat I've seen for weeks.
I stuff myself shamelessly.

He warns me my mission will end in disaster.

33

The partisans are using wagons and oxen
to cart our guns and provisions.

We have to keep moving.
I'm learning to sleep while walking behind the wagon,
I rest my arms on the back of the cart, put down my head,
and my legs move behind automatically.

The roads are muddy from the late spring thaw,
Some roads are flooded.
I trudge along, my legs caked with mud
up to my knees.

34

We meet two young Jews escaped from the Budapest roundup
They have just managed to come across the border.
They're on their way to Palestine
with a French prisoner of war named Ivan.

We beg the boys to guide me back.
But they hesitate.
              They're lucky to escape
this far, and they want to go on to Palestine.
We finally persuade them
just to take me across the Hungarian border.

Reuven is worried. He says, "Your documents
are obviously counterfeit. Why not wait
until we persuade the partisans
to give us better documents?"

I say, "I know it's dangerous.
But I have to go."

I can see he is upset and irritated.

"Then go," he sighs, "I know I can't stop you."

35

There's a fire in me:
it must not go to waste.

Sitting in the snow,
I fan it with my breath

I cup it in my hands:
it must not be lost.

I am the fire.
I am the moth.

36

We're in Apatovač, on the border
between Yugoslavia and Hungary.
It's seven in the evening, the ninth of June.
The three men and I are setting out
from this frontier village. We'll hide until morning
then make a dash for Nagykaniza
and the eight o'clock train for Budapest.

I hand Reuven a scrap of paper,
a poem I've written, saying, "If I don't come back,
bring this to my comrades at Sdot Yam."

"I'll wait for you," he says.

The four of us—the two boys, the Frenchman
and I—have a map and a compass.
We cross over to a little village.
Ivan and I hide in a cornfield
while the two boys go to look around.

A Hungarian policeman sees them wandering about
and arrests them for vagrancy. He says
he wants to examine their documents.

One of the boys panics and shoots himself.

The police send word to the Gestapo,
who have been watching every move we make.
A peasant points out where we two are hiding.

A detective pulls me off the ground.
He slaps my face and knocks out my tooth.
He wants me to tell him the radio code
I'm carrying in my book of French poems.

But I am iron.

37

Perhaps I'm not iron.

At first I felt nothing could bend me,
but now I'm not so sure.
They laughed at me when I said I was shot down

They know I've been with the partisans.
They keep beating the palms of my hands,
the soles of my feet.
They keep asking for the transmitter code.

I'm not sure I can stand more beatings.
The detective twists my arm,
telling me I am now state property,
I say I am no one's property.

38

Blessed is the match that burns and kindles fire,
blessed is the fire that burns in the secret heart.
Blessed are the hearts that know how to stop with honor . . .
blessed is the match that burns and kindles fire.

III. BUDAPEST
July 1944 to November 1944

1

A Gestapo prison guard named Hilda,
a friendly Hungarian who was born in Germany,
whispers to me when she brings my food
that Joel is here.

So Joel was caught too.
Perhaps it is he who sends me those little circles
of sunlight across the courtyard every morning.
If only I could talk to him!
I ask Hilda to bring me a mirror.

I will signal to him somehow.
I will light up the black center.

2

Mother is in the prison.
Hilda tells me to stand on the chair tower
in front of my window and look across the courtyard.
And there is my mother, waving to me sadly.

I want so much to give her something,
some encouragement, some love.

I look at the dust on the window and slowly, with my forefinger,
I draw four Hebrew letters, as big as I can:
shin, lamed, vav, mem—shalom.

She smiles, not understanding.
And then I decide, I will teach her Hebrew.
But how? Something will come to me.

3

Four letters of the alphabet
sit on my windowsill
like birds in migration:

four sparrows who spiraled
out of the south
on luminous air:

they rest briefly here
before they travel
their half-arc north:

the letters are white
fragments that gather together:
the word is a blessing,

a connecting ribbon
I fling like confetti
across the void

It is to me the Word is speaking

4

In the evening Hilda comes and whispers
mother is waiting in the bathroom near my cell.
I rush into the room
while Hilda keeps watch in the corridor.

Mother's thin face is full of joy
at seeing me. We hold each other close,
then look at each other. I take her hands and see
her wrist is bandaged.

"What have they done to you?"

"No, no, it's not what you think. It's nothing."
"You're hurt!"
                "No," she says, "I did it myself.
I was full of despair, the night they brought me here
Some women in the cell woke and found me
and stopped the blood. It's nothing. I've forgotten
that moment of weakness.
                    But what about you,
darling girl? What happened to your tooth?
What are they doing to you? Why are you here?"

"I'm a parachutist for the British.
They sent me here on an intelligence mission
to get in touch with the underground for them,
but I wanted to come mostly to help our people
escape to Palestine.
If all I lose is a single tooth, it's worth it."

Hilda knocks on the door
and we must go back to our cells.

5

July seventeenth. My twenty-third birthday.
Sometimes I thought I would never live this long.

What have I accomplished? Nothing.
All my plans, my mission, all have come to nothing.
If only the Russians would enter the city,
we would gather up the survivors,
set the old escape routes in motion,
and start the exodus to Palestine.
But will there be anyone left to save?

Hilda brings birthday gifts from mother:
a jar of marmalade made from Haifa oranges,
a handkerchief, a sliver of soap, a sponge.

I am rich.

I climb up on my bed-table-chair tower
and draw a Star of David on the window
to thank her.

The sunny taste of these Haifa oranges
reminds me of my last night in Haifa
before I left for Cairo.
George had just arrived in port
the night I was supposed to leave.
He looked at my British uniform, puzzled and worried

"Don't worry," I said, "I'll be back soon
and then I'll tell you everything.
You must go to the kibbutz and wait for mother."

We sat above the bay and watched the lights
of Haifa over the water.

6

the city
is a crescent of light
curved around the bay

the evening sea and sky
merge into
one dusky surface

only the reflection
of a single small boat—
a night fisherman

alone on the water—
define: the difference
between sky and sea

7

We walk for ten minutes every day in a circle in the prison courtyard. Because I'm still in solitary, I'm not allowed to walk with the other prisoners, but must walk behind them.

I see that there are children among us and I wave and smile to them across the circle. Poor things, there is nothing for them to do all day in this terrible place.

If only I had paper and string, something to write with, I would make them some toys.

8

Hilda brings me a few pieces of paper,
a pair of scissors and some colored crayons.
I can't imagine how she got them.

Now I can make paper dolls, little doll pioneers
for the Polish children I see in the courtyard.

9

Out of thin tissue, hand in hand,
small shapes of boys and girls stand in a row.

I poke my finger through the skin of their world:
it is all made of paper. A puff of breath

could blow it away, could blow away these walls.
Walking up to death, I know I'd find

a hole in the shallow dark, a tear in the veil.
Now my eyes can see the truth of stones:

they are brittle and flat. Transparent. Paper thin

10

Today in the courtyard, by stopping every few feet
to fix an imaginary shoelace,
                    I lose my place
at the end of the line and manage to come beside mother

She squeezes my hand and whispers, "How are you?"

"I'm fine, mother."

"Aniko, tell me really why you're here.
What have you done?"

"Mother, I have done nothing wrong.
If the Nazis consider me a criminal,
that's their law, not mine.
When the war is over, what I've done will be
praised and celebrated, I promise you."

I can see she's not convinced.

"Be careful," she says. "You're dearer to me
than my own life."

11

Marietta, the cruelest of the matrons,
stands in the yard and cracks her whip,
making us run around in a circle,
faster and faster.

Later, I'm in my cell, standing on my tower,
spelling out the Hebrew words to mother,
when Marietta bursts in, shouting
that she has caught me signaling, which proves
I'm a spy, and when she tells the guards,
I'll certainly be shot.

"I'm not a spy," I shout back at her,
"I'm teaching my mother the Hebrew alphabet."

She's astonished, stops for a moment, then stalks out

12

I never see Joel. They keep
the men and women apart. But we two talk
every day with mirror language.

13

My circle of fire—
a kiss—
                moves on your ceiling,
                its borrowed light
speaking to you
and your circle comes
                yellow as a yolk
                a buttercup moving
across my wall,
speech of the sun
                I try to translate:
                I want to grasp it
with my fingers,
press it against
                my breasts until
                each syllable of light
enters me
                our sun-shadows
                our two worlds
of reflected fire
no longer separate

14

They've put me in a cell with the children.
I dreamed once of teaching children in a classroom,

or having children of my own.
But now I know this will never happen.

I'm teaching the little ones to read and write.
I teach them songs and their eyes shine
as they lift their thin voices. They'd forgotten
they could sing.

The grownups come and want to learn the words.
There is a place, I promise, waiting for them.

15

Today is my mother's twenty-fifth wedding anniversary
I remember the picture she used to show us
after father died: the two of them
sitting on a bench in our garden
on Bimbo Street, my mother like a young girl,
reading a book, perhaps a book my father
had written—and he beside her, elegantly
dressed in a jacket and white trousers.
Now that world is completely destroyed.

I cover an empty can with silver foil
and insert twenty-five straws from my mattress.
On each straw I paste a paper flower
so it looks like a bouquet of white roses.
I make a little bride to hold
the tissue paper bouquet.

There's no bridegroom. Not for her, not for me.

16

I am already
the widow of my life!

I chose a way separate
but paved with light,

a promise that I would be
a gift accepted,

that the world and I
would join rejoicing:

but now I am
married to solitude,

sister of death,
a gift that went astray

17

Joel and I are being transferred to a Hungarian prison,
As I come down the stairs I see him waiting in the hall

"Joel!" I cry and reach out to touch him.
The Gestapo officer roars, "Silence!"
and pulls out his pistol.

We're pushed into the same van, which takes us
to Margit Boulevard Prison.
There the guards are cordial, even fawning.
Joel and I ask if we can talk together,
and they agree to give us half an hour.

I want to hug him, I'm so happy to see him.
He tells me when he reached Budapest,
he was shadowed constantly by the police.
They arrested him and took him to the Hill
for questioning. They tortured him until
he felt he couldn't stand it any more.
He found an aluminum disk left behind
in the cell of an American flyer
and cut his wrists.
            But the jailers found him,
revived him, and went on with their questioning.

"They know they're in trouble now," Joel says.
"When the Germans surrender the Allies will hold them
responsible for the Jewish massacres.
Now they want to protect themselves,
and that should be to our advantage."

But now our time is up.

"You're still lovely," he says, holding my hands.
"You look thinner, more experienced. It becomes you."

18

The Hungarian police have set mother free.

She brings me warm clothes and some cheese and bread
And my little sewing set I used to play with
when I was a child, sitting on a low stool
beside her chair.
            We cry and kiss each other,
thinking of those lost times.

I ask her to find me a Bible in Hebrew.
I need those words to remind me
there is a language, a white lightning
to pierce this blackness.

19

They tell me my trial is set for October twenty-eighth
Mother has found a lawyer who will defend me.
He says he feels sure I'll be released
when the war is over. There's no question
of a death sentence.

20

My cell is getting colder and colder.
The soup is now nothing but thin gruel
I'm always hungry.

I lie on my bed and let visions
of the Haifa market rise behind my eyes.

21

a fist of life
thrusts up through sand
and opens its palm:

a rainbow of vegetables:
black olives, seas of oranges,
eggplants, shiny purple,
artichokes, small
scarlet tomatoes, parsley

curled in bushes
raisins   garlic   cumin

seeds fall through the air:
the sun is a cauldron
of hot oil

22

Not to despair, not to be diminished.

23

I'm driving with Joel along the Dead Sea:
shining turquoise on one side of us;
on the other, dusty mountains, muscle and sinew:

we come to the oasis where ibexes run
at Ein Gedi among the palm trees,
we climb up through a green cavern,

up stone steps carved out of the mountain
and come to the first waterfall, the lowest,
pouring out of a cave:
                    thirsty, hot,

we run through the drops, laughing, chasing each other.
we climb through underbrush, along a winding
uphill slope to the second waterfall,

a heavier pouring: we let the cool
fingers comb us:
                above, the spring begins
at the top of the mountain:
                        we push each other up

to the pool of David, where we swim and loll
as the third waterfall gushes diamonds
over our eyes, our backs.

we stop at noon in the airless shade
of a thorn tree and break open the watermelon
we bought in the Bedouin market:

we break the melon open
and the pink meat fills our mouths with juice,
the sweet liquid gives us back

our strength under the gray beaten thorn tree.

24

They're bringing me into the court. The judge says:

"Hanna Senesh, do you plead guilty to the charge of being a spy,
a traitor to Hungary?"

"I'm guilty only of returning to Hungary to save it from the crime
of destroying its own people."

"Didn't you come in the uniform of a British officer,
wearing the disguise of a secret agent?"

"I am a British officer from Palestine."

"You're lying. You are a Hungarian traitor. You could
save your life, even this late, if you would tell us the code you used
for sending military secrets to the Allies."

"What would you do with the code, even if I had it?
The Germans are running away, the Russians are in the suburbs
of Budapest. You Hungarian Nazis are the real traitors.

Would you use the code to tell the Allies to stop
bombing Budapest? No one would believe you."

"The prisoner is insubordinate, incorrigible, and guilty.
Take her back to her cell.
We will announce the verdict in a few days."

25

As they lead me out of the courtroom I see a crowd waiting
I had no idea my trial would be important.

And there is my mother,
who is risking her life to see me.
She's hiding the yellow star
by holding her purse against her chest.
I throw my arms around her, crying,
but the guard drags me away.
He says we'll be allowed to talk
after sentence has been passed.

"But the sentence has been postponed," I protest.

"Then she can visit you in prison," he says.

Mother follows us down the stairs
and when the guard goes to get the prison car
to take me back to Conti Street prison,
we embrace, tearful and wordless.

26

Driving back to prison in the car,
I stare out of the window hungrily,
wanting to see ordinary people doing ordinary things.

It hurts me to watch the real world outside my window,
but I cling to everything I see
as though it could prolong my life.

27

Why doesn't my mother come to see me?
The prison is almost empty.
My only visitor is a lizard on the wall.
I spend hours waiting for him to come
and keep me company.

28

A transparent twig
stands on the wall
sleepy as a century

he and the wall
are brothers:
colorless
patient

a flick of membrane

a motion of mind

29

Because I'll be leaving soon,
I feel my senses closing down.

I know the sun is shining, the sky is blue,
the stones are shimmering in the noon glare,
but I'm shut behind a black door.

30

A messenger from the Hungarian court is here:
"I have come to tell you a verdict has been reached."
"Don't I have to be taken back to court?
Shouldn't the verdict be made in public?"

"There's no time."

"No, there's no time. The verdict has been reached
for the Arrow-Cross too. Your punishment will come
when the Russians take over the city."

"Don't be insolent. I'll read the verdict:
The military tribunal has found Hanna Senesh
guilty of treason
and has demanded the supreme penalty."

"Does that mean I'm sentenced to die?"

"You have one hour. You can write a farewell message
if you wish."

"I want to see my mother."

"There isn't time."

"At least let me see my mother."

"We must evacuate the prison. No one
must be left behind."

31

Mother dearest
I can only say this to you: a million thanks.
And forgive me if possible. You alone will understand
why there is no longer any need for words.

With endless love—your daughter

Truly, there is no need for words, and there are none.

32

I see my mother marching in the cold November rain
with a long bedraggled line of friends, neighbors, strangers,
all carrying their pitiful bundles of blankets, keepsakes,
things they've snatched up in the last moments
before beginning the forced march to Auschwitz.

I know she has slept on the cold ground under the sky
for several days. She is ill.

I see her slip away from the crowd, tear off her yellow star,
step into a shop beside the road.

The shopkeeper, a kind woman, hides her.

Now she is riding back to Budapest,
concealed in a wagon of hay and vegetables.

And now—she is lying in a hospital bed in a convent,
protected by the nuns, who know who she is.

She scarcely wants to live.

Will she die?

A man is coming through the doorway.
It is Joel, my Joel, escaped from the death train,
dressed in rags, but shining.
He holds her visa in his hand.
He takes her tenderly away, across the Danube.

I see water—she is on a ship, coming into port.
It is Haifa, golden Haifa sparkling in the sunlight.

George is waiting for her.

She is home at last.

33

Janos runs in, wringing his hands.

"Everyone is running away. One truck after another is pulling out."

We hear a shot.

"Are they shooting the prisoners?"

"Yes, miss," he says.

HATSHEPSUT, SPEAK TO ME

Then, my friend, no practice or calling in the life of the city belongs to woman as woman, or to man as man, but the various natures are dispersed among both sexes alike; by nature the woman has a share in all practices.

—Plato, *The Republic*, Book V

For here again, we come to a dilemma. Different though the sexes are, they intermix. In every human being a vacillation from one sex to the other takes place, and often it is only the clothes that keep the male or female likeness, while underneath the sex is the very opposite of what is above . . . for it was this mixture in her of man and woman, one being uppermost and then the other, that often gave her conduct an unexpected turn.

—Virginia Woolf, *Orlando*

This is the place.
And I am here, the mermaid whose dark hair
streams black, the merman in his armored body
We circle silently
about the wreck
we dive into the hold.
I am she: I am he

—Adrienne Rich, "Diving into the Wreck"

CONTENTS

Preface

Historical Note

Looking for Hatshepsut

Beginnings
Hatshepsut, speak to me
When I was six
Birth
Beginnings
Before my father came to the throne
Nile Dawn
Hatshepsut, who were the women before you?
When I think of the women before me
At nineteen, I fell in love
I remember my grandmother
I was married to my brother
Politics

The Two in One
Hatshepsut, how did you convince the people
If Hapi, the god of the Nile
Hapi
I came to my little brother-bridegroom's body
Senmut, my steward
Still a child
A bride at nineteen
In the birthing room
Lullaby
When my daughter was born
Do you know the story of Isis
Funeral Song
Hatshepsut, I grieve for your pain
I said to Senmut
The mouth of my girl
My god, my lover
I embrace you
The Two in One
After two marriages
Marriage

Monuments

Hatshepsut, in the fullness
Across the river from my palace
On the right side of the temple
On the south side
My father Amon-Re spoke to me
In the fifteenth year
Tamsen Donner
Sahara Wind

Divisions

I began to hear jealous rumors
My nephew Thutmose has outgrown his priesthood
Festival
Spell
Thutmose looked at my temple
King-Queen, who has seen my face?
A young student, I brought my poems
Desert

Endings

Hatshepsut, my friend
In year sixteen of my kingship
In the Great Place among the cliffs
I came into a room
After Senmut's body
The Boat of the Sky
Senmut never lay in his tomb
Crossing the River
I passed through the sky
Epitaph
I watched Hatshepsut
Hatshepsut Osiris
Sister Pharaoh
I followed Hatshepsut
Egypt

PREFACE

In 1947, when I was in my twenties, I suffered a crisis of gender identity. It was the period after the Second World War, in the forties and fifties, when women were generally regarded as second-class citizens. I felt guilty about my ambition to be a writer and at the same time anxious about my femininity. When I read about King/Queen Hatshepsut, the woman pharaoh in ancient Egypt, I felt I had found a woman who could help me. I began to write about her. But then other events intervened. I married, had children, began to publish.

Thirty-five years later, when the Metropolitan Museum in New York opened its new Egyptian galleries, I walked into a room devoted exclusively to Hatshepsut. Here were her enormous statues, some depicting her as a sphinx, some as a male pharaoh, some as a tender young woman. I felt a powerful connection to my old friend. I knew I had to write about her.

I spent several years reading everything I could about Hatshepsut and her reign in the Eighteenth Dynasty, a period of exceptional achievement in painting, sculpture, and poetry. In 1985, when I was in Jerusalem on a Senior Fulbright Writer-in-Residence fellowship, I traveled by bus to Egypt, where I had my first glimpse of Hatshepsut's landscape and architecture. On the walls of her magnificent temple at Deir el Bahri she tells, in words and pictures, the story of her life. In 1988 I went back for a longer period to steep myself in the haunting atmosphere of ancient Egypt. I found that south of Cairo, Egypt reverts in many ways to the landscape and customs of four thousand years ago.

Hatshepsut is the fourth woman I have been drawn to write about. The others—the oppressed nineteenth-century rebel, Lizzie Borden; the brave pioneer of 1846, Tamsen Donner; the headstrong Israeli parachutist, Hanna Senesh—have all been intense metaphors for my most basic concerns: refusing to be a victim, learning endurance, learning the skills of survival. In each of these books I have spoken in their voices only. But I wanted to have a dialogue with Hatshepsut. I wanted to juxtapose our two lives across the twenty-five centuries between us and see what parallels might emerge. I wanted to examine her life and tell her about mine.

Ruth Whitman

HISTORICAL NOTE

Hatshepsut reigned in Egypt during the Eighteenth Dynasty, more than three thousand years ago. Daughter of a pharaoh, Thutmose I, and a royal mother, Ahmose, Hatshepsut I felt a special entitlement to the throne, a position traditionally handed down through a royal mother, but usually to a male. At first, according to convention, Hatshepsut married her young brother, Thutmose II, and reigned with him until his early death. He left behind a small son, Thutmose III, born of a slave girl named Isis. Because the child was too young to reign, and also because his mother was not royal, it was possible for Hatshepsut to take on the pharaoh's power. She had two daughters, one by Thutmose II, her brother and first husband, and the other possibly by her beloved architect, Senmut. She was experienced, in her thirties, a gifted and imaginative woman who had advocates and followers among the priests of the temple of Amon.

To reinforce her claim to the throne, she declared that the god Amon, king of all the gods, had impregnated her mother, making her claim to the kingship both royal and religious. In her wall paintings and statues she depicted herself as male, wearing a beard and the kingly double crown of Upper and Lower Egypt, the stiff kingly kilt, and holding the crook and flail. At other times she showed herself as a slender young woman, innately feminine. She refers to herself in the hieroglyphic account of her life as both "he" and "she."

In subsequent centuries, and in fact immediately after her mysterious death, many of her works were destroyed by her nephew, Thutmose III, who succeeded her. Her buildings were defaced, her sculptured face gouged out, and her name erased.

She has suffered neglect by many historians and Egyptologists who think of history as predominantly male. Some leave her entirely out of the registry of pharaohs, or barely mention her name; some describe her as a usurper who was "unable" to wage war or lead men in battle. No one knows exactly what political conflict brought an end to her unprecedented reign of over twenty years.

Ruth Whitman

LOOKING FOR HATSHEPSUT

I climb down a limestone staircase
that ends in a false chamber.
I slide the roof aside,
start to go down a blind passage.

The real passage leads
to another false chamber,
a sliding trap door
There is a false door

to the true chamber.
An immense stone roof
weighing forty-five tons
is lying on the ground.

It once sealed up her tomb.

Thieves have torn her secrets
out of its belly,
leaving charred bits
of diorite and lapis lazuli
scattered on the stone floor.

But here in a room
carved from a single block
of yellow quartzite, I find
a plaited girdle made of palm leaves,
an alabaster dish
in the shape of a duck,
a small headless sphinx
of black granite

and an empty stone sarcophagus
inscribed with her name:
Hatshepsut.

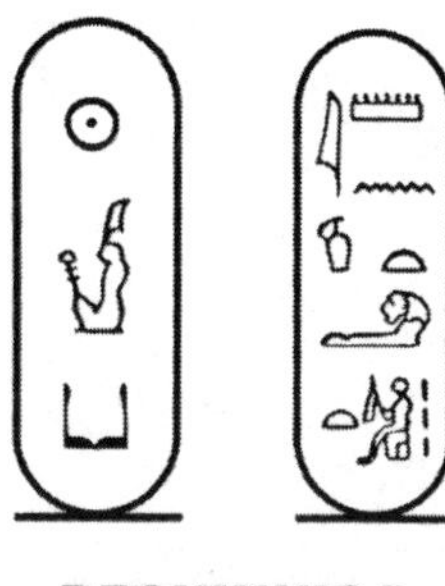

BEGINNINGS

RUTH:

Hatshepsut, speak to me.

I'm a woman like you,
ambitious, passionate like you.

I often dream of speeding
alone, downhill, without brakes.

When I was six
I drove with my father
in his new gray Buick.

I sat on his lap,
pretending to be driving,
feeling like a queen.

At nine
I wrote my first poem.
I stood in front of my fourth grade,
loving the awe of my classmates,
the praise of my teacher.

At eleven I sold my poem
and bought Untermeyer's book

of American poets.
I read every word, thinking
I want, I want, I want
to be one of them.

HATSHEPSUT:

When I was six
my father Thutmose the First
lifted me up to sit beside him
on his throne of Amon.
He said, Flower of Egypt,
you will be a ruler.

He took me with him on his royal barge
down the Nile to Memphis, to Sakkara,
to Giza, to see my kingdom.

He said to the farmers and nobles
crowding the water steps
This is my goddess daughter Hatshepsut
who will be crowned with the crown
of Upper and Lower Egypt
when she becomes a woman.

I knew that Amon-Re, Lord of Thebes,
King of Karnak, took my father's form
and came down to my mother, Ahmose,
as she slept in the beauty of her palace.
She woke at the fragrance of the god
and rejoiced at the sight of his beauty,
and he went into her and his love
came into her body. And my mother said
How wonderful to see you face to face,
your dew is in all my limbs.

And Amon, Lord of the Two Lands, said to her
Khnumit-Amon-Hatshepsut is the name of the daughter
I have planted in your body. She shall be king
in this whole land. My soul is hers,
my crown is hers.

BIRTH

Khnum the Potter
father of fathers
mother of mothers
molded my body
out of clay
out of spirit he
made another me
my ka to stay
on earth when I die:
she'll slip away,
unhindered, free,
while ba the bird
wing of my soul
will fly from my tomb
back to the sky

BEGINNINGS

Atum, the great He-She,
the breath of chaos
before the world began,
in the brooding emptiness
of waiting space
stirred his hand in Nun,
the primeval waters,
rubbed himself with his fingers

until his seed spurted into his mouth
and out of his body came
air and moisture, Shu and Tefnut,
and out of these came
earth and sky, Geb and Nut.

Atum, the Two in One.

HATSHEPSUT:

Before my father came to the throne
there was chaos in our double kingdom—
from the Great Green Sea on the north
to the land of Nubia on our south.

Men without breasts love war.
They measure their height
by the mountains of severed hands
piled up, cut from their enemies.

But I saw our land laid out in peace:
Thebes, the southern city, the horizon of earth
stretching east to west
and the fecund river cleaving the land
south to north.
Sun and moon
sail from east to west
across the Nile,
from life to death
and back again.

Symmetry. Order.
The Nile
floods, recedes, floods.

And over us stretches Nut,
the goddess who is the sky.
The sun travels by night
through her body,
the moon and stars by day.
Her toes touch the east,
her fingers reach to the west,
she arches over us,
rainbow mother of night and day.

NILE DAWN

A line of palmtrees
against a pink sky
echoes the trees
standing upside down
in the still river

An egret skims its surface,
flies smoothly against
the north-running current:

Tomb paintings
of headless men,
of amputated legs
walk against the current
of Maat, of justice:

Violence and stillness
as the vulture of protection
fans out her lovely wings:

Look: the sun is rolling out of the
sky's vagina. Lady Nut has swallowed
all the stars

RUTH:

Hatshepsut,
who were the women before you?
Where did you get your strength?

My grandmother, strong and black-haired,
went out into the world
when most women stayed at home.
She bought and sold land,
made money, educated her three daughters
and sent her son to medical school.

She fell in love with a young tenor
while her husband sat in his wheelchair
designing silver with his delicate hands,
murmuring poetry.

She wore a string of bright red beads
over her breast, she was large and fragrant,
a fullfleshed presence.

I often think of her, feel like her,
feel her power in me,
her round-bosomed sensuality.

HATSHEPSUT:

When I think of the women before me
I think of Queen Menkara Metakerti,
the builder of the third pyramid.
When her husband was killed,
she invited his enemies to a banquet
in a subterranean chamber.

There were seven kinds of wine,
baskets of fruit, roast goose,
dancing girls with their flutes
and little naked slave girls
who held lotus flowers
before the guests.

The killers were laughing,
winking at each other,
until at a signal from the queen,
a hidden gate was lifted
and the Nile waters rushed in,
drowning the murderers.

RUTH:

At nineteen, I fell in love with my
first mother-in-law,
a New England woman
frustrated in her ambition,
nearer to my nature than my own mother.

I now live in her house by the sea.

Whenever the furnace goes on,
I hear her heart beating,
warming me.

She sat in the sun on the porch,
her quick fingers sewing costumes
for daughters and granddaughters.

Her rage to nourish the world
fed every stray.

I see her, a low brown figure
with a cane and a dog,
walking the beach,
inventing schemes for fame, politics, war.
Then she'd go home and bake bread, rolls, pies,
cook turkey, turnips, squash, potatoes
until we could hardly rise from the table.

But now I have lost her:

how she was once young and passionate
and hid her passion under a long brown dress.
How she boasted of sleeping with a moral sword
between herself and her bridegroom.

She kept school in this tiny house, teaching
Shakespeare and manners to each truant and orphan

She was one of my mothers.

HATSHEPSUT:

I remember my grandmother
Queen Ahmose Nefertari, called God's Wife
and Female Chieftain of Upper and Lower Egypt
who reigned in place of her young son,
Amenhotep I, and founded Deir el Medina,
the village for artists and sculptors
in the Valley of the Kings.

She told me about Queen Sebek Neferura,
called the Horus, Beloved of Re,
the living beloved of Sebek, the crocodile,
Royal Daughter, Lady of the Two Lands.

She built the temple that contained
the labyrinth: twelve courts
with doors opposite each other,
fifteen hundred rooms above ground
and fifteen hundred below,
the tombs of kings and crocodiles.

I even remember my greatgrandmother Aah-hotep
who outlived husband, sons, grandsons
When she died during the reign
of Thutmose the First, my father,
she was almost one hundred years old.

I remember her coffin, bright blue
with a huge gold cover
painted with a replica of her face.

Her body was covered from neck to feet
by the great folded wings of Isis,
goddess of love, protector.

I was married to my brother Thutmose the Second,
seven years younger than me.
I was twenty-four, he was seventeen.
A sweet boy, but fat and dull.
Not interested in politics,
only in eating and playing checkers.

My father said, This daughter Khnumit—Am on-Hatshepsut,
the loving one, I put in my place.
Listen to her words,
obey her commands.
Whoever adores her, he will live,
but he who speaks evil against her majesty,
he will die.

And so I was named with my names:
The Horus, mighty by his Kas,
the Lord of East and West,
the Good Goddess, the Pious Lady,
the Golden Falcon, divine in her risings,
King of Upper and Lower Egypt,
Ka-Ma-Re, daughter of Re the Sun
Khnumit-Amon-Hatshepsut.

When my father died and joined the gods
my brother sat on the throne by law,
but I, his sister, his divine wife Hatshepsut,
was master of the country.

POLITICS

the labyrinth
beneath the throne
protects the beard
protects the crown
confuses those
who seek my tomb
who want to steal
each precious stone
and chisel out
my secret name

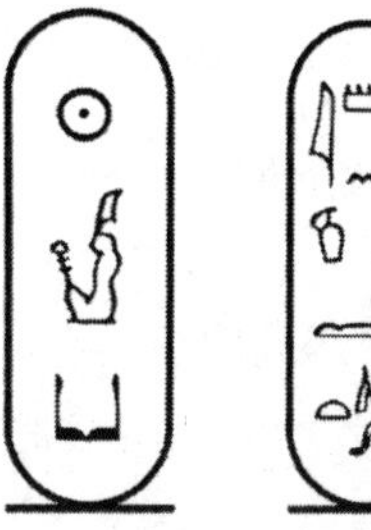

THE TWO IN ONE

RUTH:

Hatshepsut, how did you convince the people
that you were king? Couldn't they see
that you were a woman?

When I was seven
my mother cut my hair
in a short boyish bob:
my hair felt slick,
close to my head.

On the street
in front of the butcher shop
boys and girls surrounded me
pointing and chanting
boy-girl, boy-girl, boy-girl.

What was I?
I had no breasts.
I was I, a lover of words,
not yet male or female.

HATSHEPSUT:

If Hapi, the god of the Nile, can have breasts,
I can have a beard.
I live in the perfect justice of opposites:

He bisects the earth north to south:
on each shore lies a strip of fertile green,
beyond each strip yellow desert,
beyond each desert red mountain:

red yellow green blue green yellow red
mountain desert field river field desert mountain
rock sand leaf water leaf sand rock:
power and compassion lie side by side in me,
breast and phallus, milk and seed.

At feasts with my friends, nobles and priests,
and my dear companion Senmut the architect—
in the great cedar and brick palace at Thebes
I wear a transparent clinging skirt
and my jewelled collar of gold and lapus lazuli.

But for the sacred feasts
and the yearly procession of golden Amon
in his cedar boat
from Luxor to Karnak

I wear the stiff kingly skirt,
the elaborate wig with the serpent
on my forehead,
the double crown of Upper and Lower Egypt
and a small straight beard
tied on with linen thread,
as did all the kings before me.

HAPI

In the midst of the waters
there's an island
called Elephantine
from which man-woman Hapi rises

It is the beginning of the beginning,
the joining of the land,
the primeval hillock of earth,
the throne of the sun.

Two caverns
is the name of the water:
the two breasts of the Nile.
Hapi lies on his bed,
she impregnates the soil
mounting the land as a bull,
spreading her waters every autumn
and bringing forth
from the milk of his breasts
from the seed of her phallus
everything that grows.

Black silt covers the earth
until the crops come,
shimmering green,
sunyellow, yellowgreen
crowned with Nile blue:
sun earth river
reborn in each grass blade
each frond of palm.

HATSHEPSUT:

I came to my little brother-bridegroom's body
and savored its girlishness:
plump, white, with delicate fingers and knees.
I didn't care who he was, who I was,
girl-boy, boy-girl,
I loved him as though he were
my mother or sister—
and he—did he see in me
the men he longed for
as he took me from behind?

Senmut, my steward and architect,
born of a humble family,
grew to be my close companion.

He became my twin soul, my hands.

I wrote on the stele at Aswan:
Senmut, the companion greatly beloved
keeper of the palace
keeper of the heart of the queen
making the Lady of Both Lands content
making all things come to pass
for the spirit of her majesty

Still a child
concerned with childish things,
my nephew Thutmose
played war games in the palace
garden,
tore branches from the sycamore and acacia trees
for his swords.

Son of Isis the slave
by my dead husband, Thutmose the Second,
how could this child be king in my place?

I said: I will not be a king's ornament.

Thutmose said: I will shoot seven lions
in the space of a minute
and bag twelve wild bulls
in one hour.

I said: I will trade kindly with the Nubians.
I will open the mines of Sinai.

Thutmose said: The foreigners will abandon
their land in fear.
I will hack up their towns and villages
and set them on fire.
I will take their food away,
burn their corn, cut down their fruit trees.

I said: I will make Thebes the horizon on earth,
beautiful with temples and palaces,
the eye of the sun, his heart's throne.

Thutmose said: I will turn their land
into red dust where no foliage
will ever grow again.
I will make mountains of their severed hands.

RUTH:

A bride at nineteen,
I spent the years of my first marriage
in conflict and fury.

I said:
I want to study ancient Greek poetry,
I want to read all the books in Widener Library

My student husband said:
You must be docile and obedient.
You must earn money so we can eat.
You must type my thesis.

I became pregnant. He cursed,
"That's another nail in my coffin."

But now I knew I wanted books and babies.

In Greece, I let him persuade me
to have an abortion.
Lying on the table,
I suddenly realized
I did not want to part with this child.

I saw myself in the lava mold of a girl
caught in the rain of stone under Pompeii,
stripped of house, breast, throat, eyes,
floating burned and tattered
face down in the eyeless sea.

HATSHEPSUT:

In the birthing room
I kneeled on the warm mudbricks
like any other woman, giving birth
to Meryt-Re. A daughter.

Senmut was beside me
when my second daughter Neferura was born

He helped me see how I could be
mother, ruler, wife, king.

He was nurse and tutor
to little Neferura who sat,
nestled in his robe,
her head beneath his chin,
while we discussed
how I would build my temple
in the Valley of the Kings,
how raise my obelisks at Karnak,
how prepare for my voyages of discovery.

LULLABY

Senmut, man of peace,
sang to Neferura:

Sleep little daughter
Hathor will bring you
fragrance of clover
garlands of onions
combs of honey

clover to give you
dreams of abundance
onions to guard you
from jackals and deserts
honey to sweeten your tongue
and to soothe you

sleep little daughter
in fragrance of clover
in garlands of onions
in sweetness of honey
sleep safe on my breast

RUTH:

When my daughter was born,
I finally understood why my mother
spent her life pouring love
into her children:

Daughter, turning on the breast of the world,
turning slowly in your vernal equinox,

what can I give you?
War and peace, the condition of your birth?

Feet like seashells, hands like maple leaves,
a white birthday dress strewn with roses?

A seedpod of words? Bach, kisses,
the pleasures of silence? The muscular back of the sea

with its sweet and terrible secrets? You have,
you are all these.

I send you—from the very cave
and core of your beginning—the strength to bear

your peace and war, your music,
your flourishing in the century's despair.

HATSHEPSUT:

Do you know the story of Isis, who was
traveling with her small son Horus in the desert?
A mysterious fire broke out all around the baby
sitting alone on the sand.

There was no water anywhere.

Isis, out of the power of her love,
stood over him, legs outspread,
and urinated such a flood
that she quenched the tire and saved her child.

I was not able to save my little princess,
who suddenly sickened with a lever
Senmut too was helpless and heartbroken.

In the tomb of Princess Neferura
carved out high in the face of a cliff
we placed, along with her necklaces, her tiny cat,
little toy animals carved out of alabaster,
wreaths of sacred persea leaves,
mimosa, and the blue flowers of water lilies.

FUNERAL SONG

Lotus bud,
small and dainty,
I remember your slim arms
as you swayed with the dancing girls,

your eyes laughing
beneath your heavy wig
your child body graceful
under the gauze of your dress:

you danced
with solemn gestures
to the tune of the flute
the lute the oboe the lyre.

Live, my lotus,
open your petals,

let your fragrance fill the air,
dance with garlands in your hair—

do not die,
unopened bud,
do not enter the boat of the sun,
do not cross the horizon.

RUTH:

Hatshepsut, I grieve for your pain
and for Senmut's.

It was hard for me
to part with my three children:
the separation at birth,
the flight of each
into the world:

Where once below my navel
I carried a universe, the promise
of an end to grief,
a reason, a surfeit—
now I was hollow,
the beds were empty,
my son and daughters scattered

and I must become myself

HATSHEPSUT:

I said to Senmut:

My heart is balanced
by your heart

take my breast
its gift overflows for you

I'd rather spend
one day in your arms

than a hundred thousand
anywhere else

my love for you
swims through my veins
like salt dissolved in water
like milk mixed with cream

so come quickly to your love
like a stallion on the track

like a falcon swooping
towards its papyrus marsh

HE ANSWERED:

The mouth of my girl is a lotus bud
her breasts are mandrake apples

her arms are vines
her eyes set like berries

her brow a snare of willow
and I am the wild goose

HATSHEPSUT:

My god, my lover,
it is pleasant to go to the river

and bathe in your presence
I shall let you see my perfection

in a garment of royal linen
wet and clinging

When you ask me
I'll enter the water

and come out holding
a red fish

who will be happy
in my fingers

AND HE:

I embrace you
and your arms open wide

I'm like a man in Punt
overcome with incense

I kiss you
your lips open

and I'm drunk
without beer

As Amon lives
I come to you

my loin cloth
slung over my shoulder

THE TWO IN ONE

I long have known
the tender tip between my legs
is a twin of the phallus

an organ of pleasure
when the spasms of love
run from there
to the mouth of the womb
and back again.

My love inside me
touches both my source
and my twin part,
womb and clitoris,
complete.

RUTH:

After two marriages
I found a man, an artist,
who has given me more than twenty-five years
of tenderness, space to grow,
delight:

I said to him:

When your skin is strapped
to my bones, when I breathe
with your breath, wear your small
of the back, smile, eyelashes,
I'll be home again:

but I might cry for your marrow,
parching for your tongue,

and you might still turn away,
so slowly grows our grafting—

until your sex takes mine,
finally, as it was
before the beginning, before
the pregods envied us
and split in two our one

MARRIAGE

Goddess Hathor says to Horus at Edfu.

Here alone in my temple at Dendera
I long for my husband, the living hawk.
It is two weeks since he came downriver
in his cedar boat
to visit me, to make me
once again the house
of his royal temple.
Husband, you need not come this far
if you are busy.
I'll tell my priests
to prepare my gilded boat
and I'll come halfway to meet you

Horus answers Hathor at Dendera:

Wait my love,
until the Nile is higher.
Here at Edfu we measure it
as it rises every day.

I am busy, as you are,
accepting the king's offerings, receiving

the four corners of the universe
to keep against her death.

When the flood crests I will sail downriver
to celebrate our wedding again. I need
to hear your sistrum, your singing.
Horus the sun needs Hathor the sky.

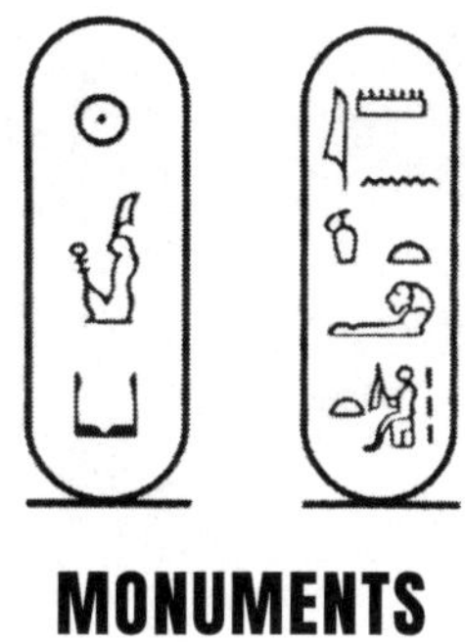

MONUMENTS

RUTH:

Hatshepsut, in the fullness of your strength
you began to create your monuments:

I too create my own kind of monument.

I want to find my own woman's voice, reveal
women's voices in other eras,
women who have transcended the cruelty,
the wars of men.

So I come finally to writing in your voice,
exploring your strength,

your brave assumption of power,
your monuments
marked with tenderness and strength—
your signature.

Hatshepsut, teach me to use my strength without fear
Teach me to overcome those centuries of docility.

HATSHEPSUT:

Across the river from my palace
in the valley where my ancestors lay
in the shadowy life of the soul,
Senmut and I found the place to set my temple

The cliffs of rock rose high in a semicircle,
forming a perfect resting place, as though
the mountain held my temple in its arms:

cradled in the belly of the cliff,
my three terraces rose one above the other,
terrace on terrace of white limestone columns,
ivory white courts, the chapels and colonnades
shining like alabaster.

Two rows of sphinxes,
each wearing my likeness;
and on each side
oases of flowerbeds
and hundreds of myrrh trees
filling the courts with their incense.

Here we raised two rows of eleven columns,
some square, some round,
and on the second terrace,
again two rows.

In the north colonnade
my mother gives birth to me
while Khnum the Potter
shapes me and my ka on his wheel
and Bes the dwarf dances his delight.

On the right side of the temple
I built my chapel to Anubis,
Opener of the Way,
who will guide me
through the underworld
to the fields of Amenti.

Black Anubis,
with the body of a greyhound,
the tail of a jackal,
creature of darkness.

On the south side, I built my Hathor shrine
When I was born, Hathor suckled me.

Senmut and I set thirty-two sixteen-sided
columns and square pillars
with Hathor capitals—
her woman's head with cow ears.
The even numbers, the female.

I show myself suckling milk
from the udder of my cow-mother;
with my little husband Thutmose
offering her milk and wine.
Senmut carved his own likeness
in a small alcove in my sanctuary—
kneeling, arms raised in worship.

My father Amon-Re spoke to me
from his sanctum in the temple at Karnak

and commanded me to search out the way to Punt,
to the terraces of myrrh.

On the walls of my temple I showed
how five fine ships sailed northward down the Nile,
were carried across the wadi to the Red Sea,
bringing jewels, gold, weapons
to exchange with the natives of Punt,
who lived in houses built on stilts.

The black queen—enormously fat—
came to greet my ministers; a small donkey
carried her. My scribes and artists
recorded everything they saw.

The natives exclaimed, How did you reach here,
this country unknown to men?
Did you come from heaven,
or did you travel by land or sea?

My ships brought back fragrant wood, resin,
myrrh trees for Amon, ebony and pure ivory,
green gold of Emu, cinnamon wood, incense,
kohl, baboons, monkeys, dogs, skins of the
southern panther and several natives
who were curious to visit us.

My people rushed down to the landing steps
and cheered the ships as they came to shore.
Everyone gasped to see the marvels
as they were unloaded from the ships
under Senmut's watchful eye,
everyone rejoiced to see the fruits of peace.

In the fifteenth year of my reign
I began to raise these obelisks to my father Amon

From the rose granite quarries at Aswan
Senmut brought two long slabs
lashed end to end on the deck
of an enormous barge
towed down the Nile
by thirty oared ships.

My two seamless monuments at Karnak
rise over all other temple buildings.
From any point in Thebes,
looking up, I can see
those huge polished
rose granite shafts
covered entirely with silver-gold electrum,
their glittering tips
quarrying light
straight from the hands of the sun.

RUTH:

Tamsen Donner, who lived a hundred and fifty
years before me, came to me in a dream.
She wanted me to write her life, to restore
her lost journal.

I followed her footsteps from Springfield Illinois
to the California mountains where she perished.
As I traveled, I felt the presence
of the twin oceans on each side of the continent—
the Atlantic, where we both were born, and the Pacific,
the end we both were dreaming toward.

The book fell into three sections:
Prairie, Desert, Mountain.
The structure of a life: early promise,

middle-aged hardship, the final struggle with
mortality. I was witnessing
Tamsen's confrontation with loss and death,
her daily ingenuity in surviving
cold, hunger, cannibalism, in saving
her three children.

At the precise center of the book, on page
thirty-seven, I knew, when I constructed it,
that the Great Divide of the American continent
was the architectural divide of the book,
the line between hope and experience.

SAHARA WIND

A hot blast blows in from the western desert
palmtrees bend and thrash

thick sand covers the crops in the field
grit fills our eyes, grit in our teeth

feluccas crash against the eastern shore
flick out of the river like toys
lie shuddering and torn
against the landing steps

the desert attacks, shrouding
the courts and steps of the palace
veiling the temples and obelisks

erasing all our monuments
with tents of sand

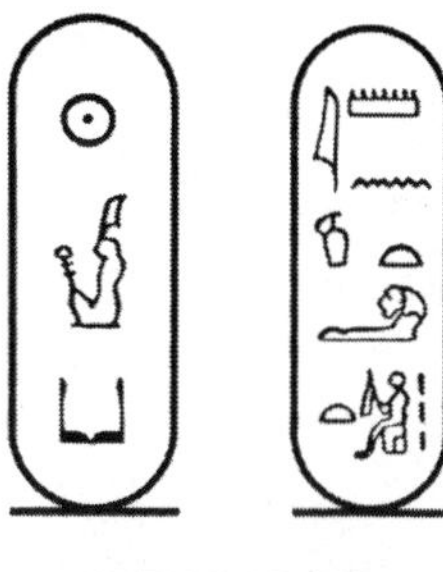

DIVISIONS

HATSHEPSUT:

I began to hear jealous rumors.

My eldest daughter Meryt-Re
whispered to me as she dressed my wig
with perfumed wax and blossoms
that in the worker's cave
above my temple—a cave
carved out of the rock cliff
where the workmen rest and drink beer
in the noonday heat—
someone had scratched a picture
on the wall:

a woman without breasts
wearing the pharaoh's wig,
a clear black triangle
between her legs—
she is bending over
and behind her
a man takes his pleasure.
He is wearing the leather hat
of an Overseer.
They laugh and say it is
Senmut and Hatshepsut.

Others say
that since I wear the royal beard
I also conceal
a three-pronged phallus
to satisfy Senmut.

My nephew Thutmose has outgrown his priesthood.
I had hoped his wish for power
might be deflected—
but now he has become a warrior,
as I feared.

He says:
I will fell my enemies beneath my sandals;
the earth, in its length and breadth,
West and East, will be subject to me.

I will deprive my enemies' nostrils
of the breath of life,
I will take them captive by their hair
I will be as a crocodile to them
I will be as a fierce-eyed lion to them
piling up their corpses in the valleys,
bringing home hundreds of thousands of their dead hands

I will conquer Palestine, Phoenicia, Syria;
I will capture Kadesh and Megiddo
I will demand tribute of slaves, grain and gold
from Assyria, Babylon, and the Hittites.
I will slay and punish them, trample them
under my feet, tangle the long hair
of my kneeling prisoners around my imperial staff.

I will take back my throne from this arrogant woman,
Hatshepsut.

FESTIVAL

The priests of henna paint my hair
and what my flesh must learn to bear

to keep observers unaware
the crafty paintbrush will apply.

Conceal the wart, conceal the mole,
Disguise the dimness of the eye.

With purple lids to veil my goal,
enameled nails to guard my soul

and perfumed arms to play my role,
what spell can make the great queen cry?

SPELL

spine of hedgehog
ground up fine
claw of dog
hoof of ass
seven dates
set to boil
in a flask
of olive oil

HATSHEPSUT:

Thutmose looked at my temple
with its banners flying,
its hundreds of painted statues,
he looked at my sphinxes, images

of myself as king,
myself as the god Osiris,
my royal beard, my name
inscribed on every marble,
my ka locked inside—

and he shouted to his soldiers
that he was the true pharaoh,
that he would drag my likenesses
out of their sanctuaries,
pound them with hammers,
sear them with fire,
scatter them in a pit,
so that like Osiris
I would be dismembered;

he would gouge out my name
from my sacred inscriptions,
erase my face
so I would be forgotten,
my name torn from the list
of holy kings.

King-Queen, who has seen my face?

Can milk from these breasts, Queen Hathor's gift,
unlock the hate, dissolve the ice?
Can all my kingly power lift
the curse or even name a price
to let me live past flesh and bone?
My enemies now call it base
beardless to hold the kingly place.
None care to see my face.

RUTH:

A young student, I brought my poems
to a professor who taught writing at Harvard.
He said,
"Surely these poems are meant only
for my lady's boudoir."

I believed him:
no one wanted to read about
a woman's life.

Later, when I was pregnant with my third child,
I came to study with a famous poet.
I brought him a poem about birth
in a rhyming imitation of John Donne.

He waved the poem aside, sneering
that it was "musical."

I didn't realize then that he was revolting
against his own music.
But it was clear he was revolted by me,
by my big belly, my female voice.

Later we found him crouched on top of his desk
babbling and raving.
Nightingale.
Toad.

DESERT

Devouring sand, waiting for whatever wind
writhing from shape to shape, folding dune
under dune, eating the feet of the granite colossus
her knees, her huge thighs, her erect kilt,

erasing her waist, her breast, her arms holding
the imperial flail and staff, blotting out
her strong neck, her girlish mouth, sealing
her breathless nostrils, blinding her eyes,
lying curved against her neck, her head
transforming her mammoth woman form
into hills of silence

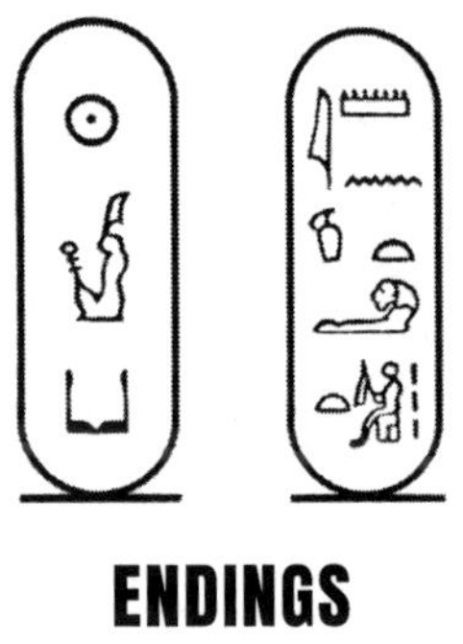

ENDINGS

RUTH:

Hatshepsut, my friend,
how can we make a bridge between us?

For you death is a continuation of life:
you will eat the same bread, beer, wine, geese,
celebrate banquets and festivals,
your shawabtis will fish in the river, plow,
gather grapes in the vineyards for you.

For me, death is the end.
I'm racing to leave behind
a few words arranged in a pattern
that will touch the living.

I've seen your Southern City,
the green strips of clover
on each side of the blue river,
the deserts east and west
and beyond the deserts
the mountains.

I've seen your one remaining obelisk at Karnak.
Your nephew did not dare topple it.
He built a wall around the lower half,
but it towers over every other monument,
the highest obelisk ever built in the Black Land.

I've seen your beautiful feminine temple
lying in the lap of the cliff.
Thutmose gouged out your name here and there,
erased your face in places, but left
enough untouched out of fear of the gods
so we know who you are.

I've seen the mudbrick houses of the farmers,
the blindfolded water buffalos turning the water wheels
the women washing their clothes in the river,

but your palace is missing
and the life you lived there.

We are both women
who have loved men
and other women.
We have recognized the male in ourselves,
the female in our lovers.
We delight in our children.

Standing in the hall of the museum,
when I saw you as pharaoh in your beard and wig,
when I saw you as sphinx with the strength and magic

of that lion-woman,
when I saw you with your royal kilt
stiff before you
as though you hid a phallus beneath it,
and your bull's tail
dangling between your legs
and when I saw you in your likeness
as a delicate girl
with a slightly prominent nose
seated on her throne—
girl and pharaoh side by side—
I recognized myself and you—
the Two in One.

Hatshepsut, how did you come to your end?
What happened to you and Senmut?

Speak to me.

HATSHEPSUT:

In year sixteen of my kingship
soldiers from Thutmose's growing army
invaded the temple at Luxor
and killed my vizier, Hapuseneb,
High Priest of Amon.

I knew this was the beginning of my end,
those clamoring for war
would bring an end to peace,
Seth would kill his brother Osiris once again

Senmut came to me
begging me to be careful
of everything I ate or drank.

But he himself was the target.
Thutmose invited him to his camp
to discuss new terms
for sharing power with me,
and savagely cut him down.

When they brought his body to me
I felt that my heart
had been hacked out of me,
my arms and legs torn off.

In the Great Place among the cliffs
behind my temple
I had long ago selected a natural cave
for his burial,
high up, out of the reach of thieves.

My workmen dug out the rock
slanting down through the limestone,
down through passageways and corridors
to the first secret room.

On the walls of that chamber
I had painted careful directions
for transporting his body
with its ka and its bird-headed soul

to Amenti, the land in the West.
I was not afraid,
I put him in the care
of Amon, of Hathor, of Isis.

For his earthly body I had prepared
a sarcophagus of red quartzite
like mine, with Isis standing at each end
and the healing eyes of Horus.

I knew his heart would weigh
lighter than the feather of justice,
that he would become a star in the polar night

RUTH:

I came into a room and found my dead husband
sitting against the wall,
looking younger, more boyish,
with smooth unwrinkled skin.

I cried, "I thought you were dead!"
"No," he said, "I'm here."

Full of tears, I said, "Are you going to stay around?"
"Yes," he said, "I'll be around here."

"What are you working on?" I asked him.
"Philip," he said.
"Oh, Philip of Macedon?"
"Yes," he answered, "I've already written
three hundred and eighty pages."

When I went back to look at the place
where he had been sitting,
it was empty.

HATSHEPSUT:

After Senmut's body was split open with a flint
and the cavity of his body filled
with linen, cinnamon, dried onions,
and perfumed with cedar oil,
he was placed in his sarcophagus.

May the first son of Horus
the jar with the human head
guard his liver
guard his spleen
from the Eaters of Blood

May the second son of Horus
the baboon-headed one
preserve his lungs
preserve his breath
from the Eater of Shadow

May the third son of Horus
the jar with the jackal head
guard his stomach
from the Breaker of Bones,
Breath of Fire

May the fourth son of Horus
the falcon-headed
keep his intestines
from the Eye of Flame
the White Tooth
the Burning Leg

THE BOAT OF THE SKY

The plane has just taken off.

When I see the tiny skyscrapers,
the streets of the city below us,
I am afraid of the smallness
of our lives,
so full of violent
hopes, wishes, connections,

so many dried peas
rattling around
in the tin can of the galaxy.

Riding above the weather,
there is no weather up here,
no whale-streaked ocean,
no bearded heads of wheat,
only a round vacuum of night
with the sun always
on another horizon.

HATSHEPSUT:

Senmut never lay in his tomb.
His body, while it lay in the House of Life,
disappeared.

For six years I continued to reign,
still protected by my priests and retainers,
while Thutmose, growing stronger,
waited.

He boasted of expanding the borders of Egypt
to include the whole world.
The people became greedy for power,
booty, foreign slaves.

One by one my priests, my followers,
fell away. My Senmut was gone.

So when Thutmose, now large and glittering
in his armor, came to visit me
in my solitary bedroom,
I accepted the poisoned cup gracefully.
I knew I had no choice.

I could see that now at the age of sixty
I had done all I could—I was leaving behind
a reign of peace and beauty.

I believed my name and works
would live after me.

CROSSING THE RIVER

desert	meadow	river	meadow	desert
brown	green	blue	green	brown
thirst	bread	wine	bread	thirst
granite	wheat	fish	wheat	granite
heart	mouth	breath	mouth	heart
tomb	lotus	seed	lotus	tomb

HATSHEPSUT:

I passed through the sky,
I walked upon Nut
I came to my mansion in the Field of Rushes
my riches in the Field of Offerings

I crossed the Winding Lake,
the Lake of the Thousand Water Birds,
the Lake of the Jackal, the Lake of the Rushes
and the Lake of Dawn

With my boat of the sun came
nine baboons (who open the doors of the Great Soul)
twelve goddesses (who open the doors of what is in the earth)
nine gods (who worship Re)
twelve goddesses (who lead the Great God)
Twelve fire-spitting serpents

EPITAPH

I wrote on the walls of my tomb:
Proceed in peace, in peace, to the horizon,
to the Field of Reeds, to the World that is Under

I wrote on the walls of my tomb:
O you who live and exist,
who love life and hate death,
offer to me what is in your hands.
If nothing is in your hands, speak the words
with your mouth (the word can create):

A thousand of bread and beer,
of oxen and geese, of alabaster vessels and linen,
a thousand of all pure things—
and may the wind from the north cool you
with its soft breath.

RUTH:

I watched Hatshepsut walk down the tunnel,
tall and quick.
She didn't look back. She turned a corner
and was gone.

I suddenly felt empty and had to sit down
where I could watch part of a wing
and the tail of her plane through the window.

I thought: now she's in a big steel womb.
May it rock her safely through the sky
and deliver her without pain
to the shore of the peaceful ocean.

Then I went up to the roof of the parking garage
and saw the plane lift from the ground
like a great pterodactyl, nose first,
and climb into the air.

The sky was gray, it was beginning to drizzle,
but I knew she would be lifting above the clouds

HATSHEPSUT OSIRIS

She sailed past the twelve hours,
led by her protectors,
the Flesh of the Sun, Lady of the Barque,
Maat, goddess of Justice, holding her feather,
Osiris, Sekhmet, the Great Illuminer,
and the Dung Beetle, holding the cocoon of the world
between his legs.

She slipped across the meridian.

Each sliver of dawn
pulled her to the sun.

SISTER PHARAOH

Hatshepsut, old girl, old friend,
man—woman, bearded Pharaoh,
we women too tied on beards
and said we were kings.
We brought lullaby rules of commerce
to the state,
we raised temples and wrote hieroglyphs
and erected obelisks.

Hatshepsut,
you crouch in the silent hall of tombs,
trying to be a riddle.
But I can see through your beard.
Beneath your terrible crown of Upper and Lower Egypt
beneath your archaic stone smile,
your milk has turned to powder,
your breasts are two inches of dust.

RUTH:

I followed Hatshepsut
into the western desert
where the circle of the horizon
locked me in its center.

The white disk of the sun
sucked out my moisture, leaving
my body dry and hollow.
No sound. No wind.
My heart rang in my ears.
Space and time vanished:
nothing but frozen distance
inside my skin and outside me.

I lost my history:
three children who had come and gone,
two wrenched from me unborn,
the dead husbands,
my gentle lost mother,
my father, that aged traveler,
even the final harbor,
my last and best beloved,
all stripped from me.

Until I noticed a footprint
inch-deep among the pebbles,
a single footprint following
other footprints back
to the eastern rim of the world.

And I understood:
I had once started a journey
and had not yet reached its end.

EGYPT

A ramp of light is put under your feet
—Book of the Dead

The pyramid from eye to brain
rose up from the primeval brine:

a shaft of light pierced through the dark
and cracked apart its granite heart

Although the hungry thieves of time
intrude upon the hidden tomb

and strip away each faculty
and smash the lintel's final room,

the pyramid from eye to brain
defies the weather of the skull,

insists on perfect symmetry
and baffles the ephemeral

ISADORA DUNCAN

To Dance Is to Live

This is an account of the extraordinary life of the pioneer dancer, Isadora Duncan, told in her voice and using some of her own words. In the narrative passages I have tried to reveal some of the major events that shaped her experience; in the more impressionistic lyric passages I have tried to reconstruct her interior drama, the feelings and convictions that drove her genius.

Born in San Francisco in 1877, Isadora Duncan was sent as a young child to ballet school, but discovered very early that she could not accept traditional ballet. She was convinced there was another way to dance—free, unfettered, with bare feet and loose clothing, listening to the imperative of classical music. She was as rebellious in her private life as in her professional one. She believed in love and motherhood without marriage. She suffered many personal losses: the failure of her love affair with Edward Gordon Craig, the drowning of her two children, the disappointment of her hope in the Soviet experiment. She was killed on September 14, 1927, riding in a Bugatti sports car in Nice, when the fringes of her shawl caught in the shaft of the right front wheel and strangled her.

She takes her place with the other women I have written about in the past twenty-five years, each of whom exemplifies a central tenacity for survival that has instructed me: the rage of the suppressed Lizzie Borden; the heroism of the pioneer woman Tamsen Donner; Hanna Senesh's stubborn obsession to rescue Jews in the Second World War; the Egyptian woman pharaoh, Hatshepsut, who demonstrated in her unprecedented reign of twenty-one years how male strength and female compassion can be combined. Isadora Duncan, the inventor of expressive dance, experienced a tragic life and death, but her passion and sensuality, her zest for life were never extinguished.

In 1989 Iris Fanger, dance critic for *Dance Magazine* and the *Boston Herald*, and director of the Harvard Summer Dance Center, asked me to write a script based on the life of Isadora Duncan, to be performed by the gifted choreographer and dancer, Julie Ince Thompson. The commission to write about Isadora Duncan reminded me that I had been intrigued by her many years before when I was a young poet in my early twenties. I had come upon a passage from her *Autobiography* and copied it into my notebook, for I felt an immediate identification with her. It now appears as the epigraph for section IV.

I spent a year reading everything I could find by and about Isadora: her *Autobiography*, her essays about modern dance ("The Dance of the Future"), the teaching of dance, her letters, and the many biographies written about her by her contemporaries, friends, and scholars, including the recent *Life into Art: Isadora Duncan and Her World* edited by Doree Duncan, Carol Pratl, and Cynthia Splatt, with an excellent text and many photographs.

Isadora was an omnivorous reader, a self-educated woman, devoted to the poetry of Walt Whitman, the writings of Nietzsche, and interested in every aspect of modern art and music. In the archives of the New York Public Library at Lincoln Center I looked at the films of her students and imitators. It was disappointing to find that there is no full-length film of Isadora dancing, only a short film of a few minutes.

What we do have are volumes of critical reviews in all languages describing her technique and her charismatic presence on the stage; and hundreds of photographs and drawings of her by contemporary artists—Arnold Genthe, Antoine Bourdelle, Auguste Rodin, Josep Clarà, her lover Edward Gordon Craig, Lucien Jacques, and Abraham Walkowitz, who created many pen and ink drawings and watercolors of Isadora dancing. Between the critical descriptions and the drawings and photographs, it is possible to reconstruct many of the choreographic gestures that Isadora invented, although nothing can adequately describe the effect of her bodily presence on the stage, according to contemporary observers.

In San Francisco, where she lived as a young girl, I read the clippings about key events in her life in the Isadora Duncan Archives at the San Francisco Performing Arts Library and Museum. I discovered over and over what I already knew—that she was a charming, brilliant, obsessed, passionate, foolish, flamboyant, and loveable woman.

The first performance of "To Dance Is to Live: Isadora Duncan" in July 1990 at the Freshman Union Studio Theater at Harvard University was followed in 1991 by three performances at the Kresge Little Theatre at the Massachusetts Institute of Technology. Despite the enthusiastic reception by the critics and the superb performance by Julie Ince Thompson, I felt dissatisfied with the script itself and knew it was not yet ready for publication as a book-length poem. In June 1994 I went to Yaddo, the retreat for writers and artists, to rethink the book. Now, free of the stage and audience, I rewrote the manuscript, letting Isadora's poetic voice come through: her lifelong love for Greece, her love for her dead children, her undying libido. The lyrics almost wrote themselves. Using the framework of her external history, I interspersed it with lyrics depicting her internal state of mind. The narrative and lyrics work like recitative and aria, a technique I have used before.

Most of Isadora Duncan's life was spent in Europe, where she found audiences more receptive to her departure from traditional classical ballet, but she is a profoundly American phenomenon. In the beginning of this century, with her prophetic vision, she saw America dancing.

Since her death in 1927, there has been a continuing preoccupation with her life and work, carried forward through her first students and their students, down to the third and fourth generations. Her daring defiance of tradition in both her professional and personal life; her independence and strong sense of individual freedom remain an integral part of the American pioneer spirit. I want to express my thanks to the corporation of Yaddo, where I wrote the final version of this book; and to dancer Julie Ince Thompson, whose friendship and insight have been inspirations to me.

Ruth Whitman

I.
1877-1904

I am an enemy to ballet, which I consider a false and preposterous art.
—Isadora Duncan, *My Life*

To dance
I must first find

my center of emotion.
Without that center

I cannot move. I stand
still as a statue, hands folded

between my breasts, hands touching
my solar plexus.

I stand before the mirror
watching for my life

to stir.
Then from within

I can start to move
outward

from the crater of power
where dance is born.

In Vienna
I watched the leaves
of a palm tree
flutter outside my window.

I learned
how to create
the same light trembling
of arms, hands, fingers.

This fluttering of mine
was often imitated

by other dancers
who neglected

to study the source,
to watch
the leaves of the palm tree

Grown people have forgotten
the language of the heart.
But children understand,
I need only say to them:

  Listen. The music.
  You feel
  something waking up
  inside you:
  you slowly lift your head
  raise your arms
  and run
  to the light.

To dance is to live.

Life is the root and art is the flower

My children
were like swallows
circling freely in the air
watching caged canaries.

They danced without mirrors,
listening to their inner music,
moving together with the great rhythm
that runs through the universe:

the metronome of tides
  the waves of the sea

the wingbeat of eagles
    the bounding of deer

the heartbeat
of small animals

the quick flicker
of a finch

pulsing in your palm
a cat's heart

a child's   vulnerable
and rapid

II.
1905-1908

Aphrodite and the sea are the two greatest influences on my life.
—Isadora Duncan, *My Life*

Aphrodite, your plundered face turned to the window
sea anemone,
what scalpel blazed that plane from hip to belly.
tell me,
how tender flesh becomes immortal stone.

If seas of years had carved and burnished you
pallid
amid salt my inquisitioner had found you
unafraid
you too might find your blood turn alabaster:

my pride is a pride that lives in things
fishes breed
sun bears flowers and sometimes raging
overhead
two figures join to echo my desire

their shadows fall across me in my sea
salt sweat
salt waves salt blood and aging stone
there is yet
time to lie in brine, change, and be born.

A cold December in Berlin.

I had just danced the Chopin preludes.

Ted came into my dressing room
and sat still and speechless before me,
his eyes brimming with love.

I understood.

We were two artists
meant to share
the same fire.

We met in his empty studio
and lay together on the floor
covered with rugs
my fur coat
our mattress

for four days we celebrated
our wedding.
No one knew where we were.

we come to
the slow music of fitting together

between his neck and shoulder
fields of clover

the fur on his belly
sunwarmed wheat

his engine of delight
finds its way

to the cave and core
of my being

beyond marriage
prehistoric

the dance of the first goddess

He has a pulse there
under my hand   a sweet bird
fluttering   my life

I am starblossom burst

out of stem's
volcano

I am leaf
bud flower

bearing the
round secret

full with its
separate

heartseed

the unborn live
in a land where olive trees
glean in arcadian air
where hilltops hover
like swimmers under water
soft on the nape of time

wake up!
    goodbye is hard
though flooded with moonlight
voices call where once had been
ancient sleep
the libidinous air is sharp
and stinging to nostrils

move quickly
    laughter will hurt
the sun is too bright

move quickly now
desires, the hungering bough
of earth will trace
its stigma on your face

Daughter
I bring you
yellow hyacinths
great window spaces
of sky

little one,
fresh from the stars,
fill my empty heart

while womb and guts ran through
their repertory of bruise and ache

my anchor groped deep
in its tiny enormous sea

my spine held me up like a mast
my bodysail snapped and buckled
in the human wind

III.
1909-1913

My life has known but two motives—Love and Art—often Love destroyed Art, and often the imperious call of Art put a tragic end to Love.

—Isadora Duncan, *My Life*

beating with firefists
    dreams streaming down my face
        I scream in my cupboard

break proud fragile bone
    whose wrist did not intend
        with stolen key

to lock those thunderous eyes
    cry rage shout
        the cupboard is empty

is dark is fiery
    and I
        have lost my bed

my rain   my hope of grass

A tall man,
blond, aristocratic—
Paris Singer—
appeared in my dressing room
with a huge bouquet of roses.

"You don't know me,
but I have often admired
your wonderful art.
I admire your genius, your courage
your idea of a school.

I would like to help you.
What can I do?"

He brought me and my student
to his mansion on the Riviera.
The children danced
under the orange trees
in their light blue tunics,
their hands filled with blossoms.

Singer wanted to marry at once
but I refused.

In the villa at Beaulieu
on the first of May, 1910,
a morning when the sea was blue,
the sun burning
and all nature bursting,
our son Patrick was born.

The children—Patrick, Deirdre—and I
agreed to lunch with Singer in Paris,
a happy outing for all of us.

After we dined, I sent the children
back to Versailles in a car
with the nurse and chauffeur.

I went to my studio to rehearse.
An hour later the door opened
and Singer came in, weeping.

"The children—the children—are dead."

"What are you saying?"

The car stalled.
The chauffeur got out to crank the motor.
The car gave a sudden lurch
and plunged
into the Seine.

The driver
beat his head
on the pavement
in despair.

When the police lifted out the car
the nurse was holding the two children
against her breast
trying to keep the water
from reaching them.

They were still warm.

My heart stopped. The earth fell away.

lost in midnight, black midnight

two small black coffins
sit in the snow
black on white, black on white

a white room spins around me
three black ravens
beat against the walls

black on white, black on white
three black ravens
over two coffins

black birds flashing
on the blind white walls
white snow, black birds

black black black black black

How shall I dance again,
how stretch out my arms
except in desolation?

Only a shadow left,
what shall I do with it?
All my life gone, all my work

I see my Deirdre,
filled with joy, skipping
across the lawn

and small Patrick
toddling after her,
both trying to dance with me.

After the death of my children
I could not bear to ride in a closed car

Once, driving from Berlin to Paris,
I felt I was drowning,
my nostrils smothered in water.

I beat against the window
until they let me out.

My hair turned white.

I cut it off and threw it into the sea.

IV.
1914-1924

It has always been the experience of my temperament that no matter how violent the sensation of passion, my brain works at the same time with lightning and luxurious rapidity.

—Isadora Duncan, *My Life*

Death's certainty
    falls blight   and then
        that great coupling force again
stirring in the leaves

I thought I had moved to a place
    of gravestones and steles
        but I notice the earth
is full of yellow crocuses

I hear sparrows quarreling over crumbs
    motions of air singing
        longlegged boys and girls
fall fumbling knee to knee

In Moscow Lenin came to my performance
of Tchaikovsky's Pathetique
and shouted "Brava, Miss Duncan."

When I brought out my fifty little students
in their short red tunics,
the crowd went wild.

In the freezing bare palace
they gave me for a studio,
there was no heat that winter.

They let me choose a fur coat
from the thousands they confiscated
from the nobles and landowners.

A vodka party one cold winter evening
the bolshevik poet Sergei Esenin—
blue-eyed golden haired—

burst into my life.
I thought finally, again
I had found someone to comfort me.

A stormy love. He was often drunk,
always depressed.
I learned a little Russian.

He had less English,
but speaking with kisses,
volcanos were more eloquent.

He was afraid of being possessed,
yet he wanted to possess me.
He was jealous of my fame.

The old story.

He slept all day, caroused all night.
eating drinking, dancing,
reciting poetry.

He was twenty-seven. I was forty-four

At Ellis island in New York
they detained us, suspecting
we were Communists.

I was furious. If I had come
back to America as a great financier
they would have celebrated me

but since I came
as an artist
I was considered dangerous.

When they finally released us
I gave three sold out concerts.

But Boston was a disaster.

I danced the Marche Slav,
wearing a red scarf around my body
at the end I snatched it off,
waved it above my head and shouted

"This is red! So am I!
It is the color of life and vigor
You were once wild here
Don't let them tame you!"

Mayor Curley banned me
from performing again.
Only Boston

saw fit to greet me
with this puritan vulgarity.

Jealous of my dead children,
he said, Forget them. They are gone.
I will be your child.

It was over.

I sold my house in Paris,
furniture, books, pictures, mirrors,
to pay for our return to Moscow.

When we arrived, he left me,
taking all my underclothes
for his sister and mother.

I will not
be here
when you surface

when that boyish head
rises out of the waves
(the smooth arm,
the difficult passion)

I will not be here

I will be learning
    to sleep
    to bear my own
    breasts' burden,
    to think of each day
    as closed

stay under
talk to the fishes

don't make
a trail of seaweed
to my bed again

V.
1924-1927

I see America dancing,
beautiful, strong,
one foot poised on the highest point
of the Rockies,
her two hands stretched out
from the Atlantic to the Pacific,
her fine head
tossed to the sky,
her forehead shining
with the crown of a million stars.
—Isadora Duncan, *The Art of the Dance*

Nothing lasts.

When I think of
all I have lost,

I see again and again—
nothing lasts.

Memory, what is memory?
A cracked decanter
with all the wine leaked out,

dry, empty,
unable to quench my thirst.

When I remember my life—
once an orchard
bursting with ripe apples—
I feel like
a parched leaf.

In Nice
a handsome Italian
owner of a red Bugatti

invited me
to drive with him.
He was a young Dionysus,

his strong thighs
straining against the cloth
as he sat beside me.

I could see
the vine leaves
in his curly black hair,

as though he had just
stepped out of a
Greek vase painting.

Now in a blaze of light that cannot tint
those smooth Pentelic cheeks
harness the shaking lust

such shaking cannot stir or mar still stone

high is the heart of stone   geometry
rests lightly on the brain
the veined and marble brain

guiltless of blood, of dying, of desire

my words beat against the solid trunks
of marble trees
of wooden goddesses

beat like chimney swifts with nervous wings

Driving at top speed
inviting death—
all debts are paid,
Nothing can touch me.

Rushing through the air—
I am dancing
strong, free, solitary as an eagle
sweeping over

a blue mountain, willing
to die, hoping
to join my children
gasping under the river.

Over the mountain,
under the river,
what will it be for me?

A silk painted shawl
two yards long
sixty inches wide
to shield me against the cold

a long red shawl that dances
with an embroidered yellow
bird across twenty
blue chinese asters—

I wore my shawl that night
sitting beside my Greek god
in his red Bugatti,
flying to the moon.

I will become
bits of clay
shark's teeth
the earbones
of long dead whales

I will lie with
the sift and sediment
snowing down
from tides of ice
from skeletons
of forgotten animals
refuse ashes bone

I will lie beneath
the flakes and chips
of brief summers
the long cold
the remnants
of failed love

First come the long-ankled girls moving in solemn
twos across the page, bearing their boughs and
baskets some holding wreaths and ribbons their
pendulum tunics moving in forward rustle
from hip to knee to celebrating feet

Then come the smaller ones
with the bringers of grapes
come flutes and drums
and thigh-spanking smocks
their hair short and their spice
impudent faces making
room for herself
priestess   dancer
who floats
    springs
        leaps
            meteor-soars
through the star-sitting
slow caravans of sky
                and arches in the air
                    with her pillow
                            ribbon—billowing
                               garments for wings
                                for spring
                        in an arch
                    to her eager
                waiting at the
            tail trail end of her fireflight
she pours herself into his silver goblet
tipped chipped bells ringing at the broken edge

THE POET HERSELF

BLOOD & MILK POEMS

Poetry for me starts with the sensuous image recollected at its intensest moment. I believe a poem should be sayable and immediate as a child.

Each of these poems came from an instant of experience when a sense of identity flashed out, when a part of the self was born.

Bearing a baby, writing a poem: both enter into life as beings not quite my own, but nourished by my blood and my milk.

—Ruth Whitman

CONTENTS

I. The Silver Skeleton

- The Tightrope
- The Demolition of Four Houses and a Life
- Elevator
- The Flowering Skull
- The Chameleon's Song
- Round
- Stone Bridge at Tiverton
- My Murder in the Mesa
- Song for Mozart's Death Day
- How We Never Touched Shore
- The Witch of the Wave

II. Stealing Forsythia

- Stealing Forsythia
- Song for a Vigil
- The Spendthrift
- The Old Man's Mistress

The Peacock Screams
Pan
Moses' Fire
Regina to Kierkegaard
A Web for Odysseus
Aubade
Nuns on the Beach
Windmills
The Night Fisherman

III. Birth and Second Birth
The Lost Steps
April Vixen
Poems for Rachel
The Sea Flower
The Phoenix
The Tiger
The Bat
My Daughter the Cypress
Birth Day
My Sister Blood
Her Life Was in My Hands
Antiphonal
Touro Synagogue

I. THE SILVER SKELETON

THE TIGHTROPE

I might have been a monkey in a right tight suit
Curling my toes around the silken wire.
High high
Up in the sky . . .

They gave my hand this parasol,
My head this silly hat,
And waited down below for me to fall.

This is like the elevator chute
From my old sleep,
The dark, the down,
The sharp-fanged hollow wall.
Debris of all my nightmares,
I will
Not will not fall.

But up is just as steep.
There above the roof
Up slants precipitous,
The icecap of the air.
And I,
One foot to balance high,
Must either fall or fly.

There.

THE DEMOLITION OF FOUR HOUSES AND A LIFE

They took away the chairs, and then the floors,
all the domestic clutter of our years.

At first we thought the stripping down was kind,
but found it rasped the bare bone of the mind.

They lopped our arbors, tore our infant grapes.
We saved the freshest leaves in sign of hope.

We carried lilacs to a foster garden,
but blight and demolition was our burden.

All fell beneath this year's reforming hand,
house, knocker, windows, leveled to the land.

Stairwells looked to stars, dry skeletons
where buttons, voices, books once stocked our brains

Pristine was all. The eating monster came,
ate chimneys, bricks, and doors, his monstrous game,

till we looked out and saw the ground scraped clean.
After such slaughter, what could we begin?

ELEVATOR

This sudden box has boxed me in my life,
Airless, I watch the leapfrog numbers play.
It's a sly trick. They want to make me think
I'm moving to perfection, but

They're wrong. I'm merely standing still.
The floors themselves are moving up and down
While I stand loyal to my gravity.

Down and up the steel girders slide.
All those bricks and not one out of place.
They do this out of ignorance or pride.

I'm standing still. You see it by my face.

THE FLOWERING SKULL

Monger of melting snow, the lovegod death
Cried up my avenue, fresh melting snow,
Who'll buy my melting snow?

Young hair will fall, ripe pear will crawl with beetle,
Doors rot and latches rust, tall lilies fall,
All tearless, windless fall,

My jagged heart, pinned at the root upon
The very hone, my season's jagged heart
Hoards death and distance. Heart

To hawker of the snow: I'll trade you death
And distance for the promise under snow,
The infant season stirring under snow,
One season's rose for all your melting snow,
I'll trade you, trade you snow for melting snow.

THE CHAMELEON'S SONG

Within my darkening range
I change
I traffic with the world of air,
Dim and fair,
A tinted pebble on a beach,
A painted leaf, I picture each,
And echoing, I bend as grass
Each universe I reach and pass.

But who, but who can range
Before his mirror in the sky
And recognize with flickering eye
This I so clever?
I walk the palette of each day,
Passion and pain, my red and gray,
Brown fear, green sleep, all these I keep
And lose the color of forever.

ROUND

I keep my clocks a little fast
so time won't take me by surprise.

Lest crows tread harshly round my eyes
I keep my clocks a little fast.

I push ahead the hands of past
before the future tints my hair.

I race the hours through the air
so time won't take me by surprise.

Before the spider bygone dries
I cobble cobwebs on my last.

I keep my clocks a little fast
so time won't take me by surprise.

STONE BRIDGE AT TIVERTON

Where once the late bridge stood, a leaning buoy
Dips in the water. Seawrack laps the town.

I can remember sunny days when gulls
Sang over stone that spanned this channeled sea,

But no approach. The stone leads slyly out,
Then stops. All water hallows me.

My master builder would not box my youth
Beneath his girders, lest the bridge cry out.

What was it, lack of practice, lack of faith?
I only undertake to tell the truth:

The pinions fell, consigned to memory.
I write this perishing to his renown.

MY MURDER IN THE MESA

No brakes. We rushed
Through the dark till a fence mushroomed
Up like a corpse from its grave, sudden and whim

Hurled up at us from its sulphurous pit.
You bucked, buckled, would not hit,
Quickly summed the infinite, and dove into it,

Rolled with the stars, roof caving through ribs,
Knees knocking giant boulders,
Palms stinging with pitch and cactus;

Rolled through the purgatory of bent metal,
Courted every thorn, pebble, nettle,
And came out into the heaven of caked blood.

And I danced in my agony,
Surprised, alive, brave to be lost
So that you would have someone to save.

SONG FOR MOZART'S DEATH DAY

When the World closes, let it close.
The wind still blows
the jester knows
desire still winnows.

I saw the skeleton die
but then with guileless eye
had not yet taught the creature how to dance,

dance with his singing pain,
dance in the ice and rain,
dance on certainty, caper on mischance.

Cut off the dragging flesh
it blinds my feet.
The bed will cheat
and misery repeat, and misery repeat.

HOW WE NEVER TOUCHED SHORE

And from the birdless sea we rode at last
to land with a three-chambered, harbored shore,
with dominoe streets and geometric fields,
small hairpin posts, and in the night a dog
who cleaved the darkness with a coneshaped bark

Such sound and order mocked our rootless keel:
what man had made, free of the sea, and mild,
his neat domestic hearths, his foolish tiles,
his fruit, his fanes, his nesting hens that sang from this the
    unschooled night and foreign stars
teased us at anchor's length.
                    The distant piles
shivered before the untamed sea who turned
once more, once more toward acres null with salt
our ship's beseeching bow and weary back.

THE WITCH OF THE WAVE

a prescription for a figurehead

That's how my carver made me:
Breasts thrust against the hammer of the sea.

Against is my element:
Driven against salt spray, wind, the jaw of the whale,

Against ice, spindrift, I plow my body's death.

Wrenched from mortal wood
I suffered the pain of birth.

With each chip
That fell on the sawdust floor my forest fell from me.

To this the birth and loss of any voyage is nothing.

The head must be carved in such a way it will
not hold water.

The body, curved in eagerness for flight, must fit
snugly to the cutwater, fit the curve of the bow.

So did he bend my tree.

Now I spring at the tide, haul crews of whalers
Anvil against the wave.

When I plunge in the storm, I rise like a diver, sheering
All water from me.

My hair steams with foam, my paint gnawed
By the maw of salt.

Tethered to the world's weight, I raise the hull,
My face high to the gale.

Gulls know me. Dolphins
Dabble in my wake.

Splintered and beached,
Shipwreck is not my end. I bequeath my lucky bones

To some young sailor
Bound for his next horizon.

Touching a fragment of me in his pocket,
He touches pain, danger, phosphorescent joy, knowing

I bribe the ocean for his safe return.

II. STEALING FORSYTHIA

STEALING FORSYTHIA

I came back with the sun smeared on my hands
A yellow guilt
Pulled from my neighbor's bush,
Ten yellow branches
Moist with guilt and joy,
Caged in a green vase on the piano top.

Each time I pass my green and stolen prize
I feel again the greening of my years.

I would steal light from any bush,
Rob any blaze from heaven for my vase,
Just as I danced once on your wooden floor,
Naked and sudden,
Whirling you in a waltz,
Or did you whirl me,
Shaking the yellow spring
From rafters winter-stained with penitence?

That's the way I'd always have my guilt,
Sudden, high, a theft of fire, a dance,
A secret flowering of forsythia.

SONG FOR A VIGIL

The bells all suddenly are nine
Be light my leaf the dark is bold

Love hung all night on a sagging vine
His grape a burr, his leaf a spine,
But now the clocks are ringing nine

Love shook all night in heavy cold,
His song a cry, his kisses old,
Be light my leaf the dark is bold

He comes with feet as bare as mine
And helps me stamp the bitter wine,
For all the clocks are ringing nine.

Be light my leaf the dark is bold.

THE SPENDTHRIFT

Bankrupt November spends her vacant leaf
And throws the thieving wind her latest penny.
Who sheds the phosphorescence in this place?

There stands the harlot tree who beckoned eyes,
Poor as a private stone, dropping her garments,
Her final rainbow garments, one by one.

For now the truth is out, the bones are out,
She drops her lace, network of hair and laughter,
And drives the instant to her lover's face.

THE OLD MAN'S MISTRESS

The two old heads
on each side of his young deathbed, mistress and wife,
met headon. He asked for the Bible.
Perhaps it was to prove he was right, after all.
But his curly hair proved it, and the women
who loved him, and his graygreen eyes, and now he was
dying,
by choice. The thing he insisted on,
choice.

Cancer, pogroms, ignorance, gangrene,
he chose the thing he was to die of
It could have been too much love.
He chose a broadhipped blondhaired mistress
with Scandinavia in her eyes, far from
the racket of his four sons in the tenement,
far from the immigrant Wife who scrubbed his stairs,
far from the Russian soldiers who took his oldest
brother to Moscow to be a goy.

She heard
the lullaby in his voice. She had slapped
her old husband, twenty years before,
for his feudal lechery, and left.
That was her choice.

And then she chose him, Jacob.
He let nothing come of her womb.
She wept when she saw
me, his granddaughter, and her would-be

greatgrandchildren.
But she baked bread
and scrubbed his sweet body in a bathtub
set in the Connecticut grass,
and learned a few Yiddish words,
and outlived him.

I am my grandmother
with her four sons, her outliving patience,
her patient hate.

I am my grandfather,
loved beyond usual lot,
stealing his delight.

I am my grandfather's mistress,
tending the alien land he left,
with no face for the face she loves,
dying
alone with her lovely bones, her only choice.

THE PEACOCK SCREAMS

A hidden peacock in the yard at night
Burns like a moonlit fish, an emperor crowned,
And waits to Hash his gold embroidered tail,
And waits to spread the palette of his eye,
And prick my dark with iridescent fire.

But dark was once when bright Ionian boys
Dove for pearls ill midnight water. Now
They dive for shipwreck.
Salt has closed their eyes,

So bury all my peacocks deep at sea,
Their color is the shape of sailors drowned.

PAN

My friend fears a midnight satyr. Child
smile, wise hands, he begins,
while in his ears a forest hissing

Grows. And when he looks down and sees
his body furred, his calves goat-tufted,
blood runs stone, for I'm his prey.

Sweet friend, begin again, begin again.
The mild hills wear no hidden horror.
These woods lie safely in the lap of cities.

But now he hears his own feet galloping
hooflike. The demon bites him in his blood,
and trembling sick he thrusts my arms away,

Hiding his horny hands, his sudden leer,
hiding the secret jackal in his blood,
begetter of sweet-faced children.

MOSES' FIRE

Kindled by a burning bush, beneath
My skin crept flame. My unsuspecting acres,
Tipped by God, yearned blistering toward sun.

Customary winds could not fan me.
Under the earth my source a hidden bush
Burst my veins and wide beneath the skin

Spread blood to scorch and char the roots of grass
That eating heat sped through my ribs and knees,
Burning like bulls beneath each tent and tree,

Parching the waves until they fell aside
And drove my sinews through their utmost sea.

REGINA TO KIERKEGAARD

Be bronze, be bronze, for now I know that I
Must beat my sparrow wings against you, deep
Bronze in the sun, the bright light of your craft
Must bruise my eyes and spin a burning net
To trap god's birds and flesh them skeleton.

I would have bound your terror with my hair,
Counted your grief, consoled your history,
And brought you sons. But now my farewell beats
Like idle feathers on their imagery.

The gull's breast falters back, the bronze ship sails
Its polar sea, breath's enemy, death's blood,
My reeling wing now falling far from shore
Must plunge behind your deep discovering keel
And watch you sing toward islands of despair.

A WEB FOR ODYSSEUS

Ten come spring ago I jackknifed
Into the trap of liberty.

But the suitors flock like crows to
Carrion while the harlot dozes,

Dreaming her warp:
                    "a proud beggar
Will knock, not looking for ease

Under my breast's shadow, but striking
Claim in my ribs' convent,

Selling his capital for love, building his
Tall anger to bind our wooing.

Then will the birds be silent."

AUBADE

When sleep kaleidoscopes and every tree
Rings out before a cannonball of sun

Sharp music shatters for the birds to sing,
Breaking their bits of glass upon the street,
Green glass, mean clatter, lovers' mourning bells

Your kiss invented me, but I forget,
So constellate my sky with stars again:
Planets burn brief beside our tides of blood.

Mean birds, to give the tattling sun report
And clamp day's manacle on dawn our sport.

NUNS ON THE BEACH

Strewn on the sand, a pride of nuns—
Apart from the herd, adrift on the beach,
Undone to their chins, with legs laid bare—
Spread out their wintry souls to bleach,
Smiled the sun their orisons,
And hid their bandaged hair.

What is the sea to a convent cell?
Sparkle and gulls and toes in sand.

The pride of nuns had a swimming race—
The buoy's gong was a Warning bell—
And each with her wimple round her face
Played leapmermaid hand in hand.

And I felt out of place.

WINDMILLS

Don't think of windmills flailing their arms,
but think of a watcher for wind,
always standing in a flat country,
green and low, with a bay
diamonding in the distance.

Think, even if obedience is obsolete,
of wind-bitten stormsnapped Wings
openarmed to time, but still,
Without sails for the miller's dowry,
without millstones dusted with wheat.

I could have lived in a windmill once.
The farmer would sell it for nothing
if I would move it off his field.
I thought of sitting with weatherbeaten sides,
a mark for the land,
waiting for wind.

And I saw an old woman windmill,
her wings neatly manicured away,
busy with a brandnew diesel heart,
filling plastic wombs with processed bread.
She had no need for winds.

But I would be a wooden tower for time,
with arms open, out of date, watching

salt flake my clapboards, watching frost
eat me, watching birds with twigs,
watching for a wedding with the wind.

THE NIGHT FISHERMAN

A landbound shadow came at night
Riding a diamond light.

The curfew water stilled my fear.
His rainbow spear

Faster than fish, a prince of steel,
Undid my keel

And savage splinters culled from air
Spitted me fair,

Until I danced upon his strength,
Up-arched my length,

And burst like joy beneath his eyes
In jeweled surprise.

III. BIRTH AND SECOND BIRTH

THE LOST STEPS

Snow fell when my young grandfather arrived,
Behind him Moscow, Eden, Athens, Rome,
Bareheaded, eighteen, and a wandering Jew.

Snow covered up his footsteps leading home.

Defiant of history, he laughed his way
Through Passover streets, under each arm a loaf
Of leavened bread. A forgetting snow that day.

***

The first snow was the laying on of hands,
Blessing and naming, while Eve looked up to see
The white erasure hide her Adam's land.

How she had come, how gone, when Jahweh smiled
Blew drifting in her brain. She turned again
Back to her dishes and her hungry child.

And those old men rocking round their ark,
Beautiful in their beards, prayed all that fell,
Manna or snow, be Jahweh's favoring mark.

And Leda knew, when feathers fell like snow,
The thunderous wings of God in bright sunrise,
And threw her arms around his swansdown neck

And served him in his passionate disguise.
But in God's ravishing, Mary had wrung
Her hands beneath the bird who brought the sky

To cover her lament. Not knowing why,
Except she thought she saw her baby hung,
Shrunken, from the rafters of the world.

Was that my garden where I sang innocence?
Was that my cross that nailed the patient Jew?
Were those my thunderous wings? Was that my swan?

I cannot bend my knee.
All, all is gone.
I live on the charity of history.

Part ark, part swan, part cross over her hair,
My daughter stands before a holy fount.
Snow falls before my eyes. I cannot see.

I cannot bend my knee. I would not dare.

APRIL VIXEN

Where sweet fern suffered the fox of desire,
Where vines had tangled the sought for fought for hair,
There with small nose,
Black, invading,
A fox little fox with a long combed fire
Of fur rose
And shook her fire in the bright noon fading.

Sweet in her jungle the scents were green.
Orange and green fell cool and moist on her lair.
A dagger of sun
Struck through trees,
A sun whose flowered haft would lean
And blade would run
Between the garden's golden knees,

Bright daffodil knees whereto a fox,
A plumed and white-tipped vixen came to bear.
Joy pierced her belly
From ear to tail
And dropped among the fern and phlox
In a mossy gully
A bright pelt who must learn to wail.

Within the cool of the latticed shade
Her nose recounted her seven who whimpered there,
Through fern and rue

Her bright black eye
Counted the cubs the season made.
What will we do,
O what will we do in the day when the pod blows dry?

POEMS FOR RACHEL

The Sea Flower

To the changeling coral and pearl
The moon is a huge purple plum.
But the shadow under the kelp,
When his time has ripened to come,
Prays through the wave's fierce furl
And the seaweed's solemn ballet
For the moon's sweet harvest help
And the bitter power to pray.

The Phoenix

A flaming phoenix came to rest
Beside my tiny nursling's nest,
Womb-warm,
Womb-blessed,

He snapped his wings of fire and cried
The world is full of claws outside,
And tall,
And wide,

The sky is turning golden red
And I have come with flames outspread
And Hallelujah in my head
To toss you from your easy bed,
To toss you from your bed.

The Tiger

And when the hours danced upon her face,
Bright time the tiger kept his ravenous cave
And waited for her hunger, her lament.

Small spousal star, who could not count his days,
Your flesh then felt the minutes in his claw,
And memorized, before his wrath was spent,

How he must garnish aeons with your tears
And dangle you beneath his brazen paw
To satiate his cubs, his hungry years.

The Bat

The bat's dark wing over her innocent face
Whirrs, falling,
While the hooded cradle
Waits to embrace her fallen, fallen in sleep.

Tender and perfect, the mouth of my innocent
Under sleep's dark wing
Trembles, falling
Through wells of air to the dark ocean of sleep.

Sleep, birth, and desire,
Down, the mind's body through space
Falls, falls,
And clutches the traitor air,
Remembering feat and the ancient fall from grace.

Sleep, desire, and death,
Both aged and innocent
In the year's falling,
The falling years, all in terror of time,
Fall and falter in sleep, and the wings of the bat
Beat forever over the brink of the sea.

MY DAUGHTER THE CYPRESS

Sleep, little daughter, I'll plant you a tree
Even as grandmother planted for me,
One tiny sapling more for the hill
Where two little cousins are flourishing still.

Sleep, sleep, dream of the sea,
Your cradle's a caïque, your tree, your tree
Will be a mast to take you from me
Grown for the boy who fells you free.

Sleep, sleep, the tree is yet small,
An infant tree, not three years tall,
It mocks its sisters, flutters its boughs,
Hush, hush, it rains, it snows,

Summer suns lengthen your hair,
You grow tall, you move with care,
And from the sea bright blue and white,
A sailor whistles in the night.

But sleep, sleep, not yet, not yet—
The hull is carved, the mast is set—
Sleep one more night in Arcady,
My little girl, my cypress tree.

BIRTH DAY

Tenant of the terrapin,
will you go your way, I mine?

If I do a lumbering waltz,
and bank you like an airplane—

if the sides of your tank
tip and bank,

hang on. Don't complain.
If I wake before you do,

And catch your elbow in my side,
if I rise while you lie,

you can deter me if you try:
but I will launch you into space

some sudden horizontal
Atlantic afternoon,

and you will swim from your fishless bowl
find the stars in your faceless sky,

And be my moon.

MY SISTER BLOOD

Once I was sister to that lioness.
Proud she was proud in her haunches,
Her breastbone was tawny,
Her jungle eye hooked mine.

Now I must think of her thighs,
How the down trembled,
Stretched on a rack devised
To farrow her cubs:

Beads of sweat lay on her island face,
Smooth with pain.
I held her iceberg hand,
Touched the sun in her thigh,

The cub was not mine.

Now she has littered clear
To the edge of the jungle,
Now she's a queen
Whose voice reverses the aspen

Leaves like rain.
All paths have suffered her step:
No cave is too deep,
No pain too dark.

But turning in sleep,
I meet her again,
Shaking,
Eye to eye,

And stroke the violence from her golden thigh

HER LIFE WAS IN MY HANDS

From Sappho to the girl upon the moon
Sitting three centuries from now, I burn
With hot winds from the
Gutters of the earth.

We three were swimmers poised to dive
In catastrophic seas
Where down beneath the surface of those eyes,
Where worlds pull, where dead stars yearn,
My wrecked and whitened timber
Lies embraced in fern.

And she who from the cold sphere gazes down
Weeps to see me swim through outer space,

My very veins translated
To pregnant universe.

And she who gazes up through tidal trees,
Against the ocean's palm that weighs me down,
Cries me to rise, still dreaming to remember
The flooding terror of the moon's embrace,
The birth to come, the sting
Of comets on my face.

ANTIPHONAL

that first pang of air
daggered me fish to man.

Child of my dark, you
And I were almost one.

all the walls fell away.
nothing held me

Now my body and I are
Almost two, part

but the giant light,
and I fell, or flew

Catapult for your despair,
And, for your anger and alarm,

then drew my brandnew breath

Part suckling heart.

and screamed.

TOURO SYNAGOGUE

As to an unknown lover I returned
To my father's land, a shifting land, now jeweled
And satined like a bride, a holy ark.

A stranger to his house, I heard my talk
More friendly to the twelve Ionic trees
Than to the tribes of Israel, more shy

To celebrate this birthday than to die.
White and perfect, starred with candlelight,
The sacred chamber held a secret stair.

The heart's escape leads out to everywhere,
Nowhere, but dreams still find a certain black
Connecticut hill.
            My grandfather stands tall

And wraps me in his cemetery cloak,
Encircles me against the nightmare chill,
Till gowned in fear I follow with his ghost

Through village, town, down through the midnight past
To a second son reading by candlelight
Forbidden books that set his future free,

To an immigrant tender in his blasphemy,
Bold, repentant, joyful against death,
Rich in gesture, eloquent as earth.

Ignorant of all, I catch my breath
To hear the sharp crack of the shattered cup.
Driven to live, I grope to gather up

The windless torch of love, my tribe's rebirth.

THE MARRIAGE WIG

It was the custom for the Jewish bride in eastern Europe to shave her head—as a sign of modesty, or submission, or to make her beauty less distracting to her husband; she then wore a marriage wig (*sheytl*) in place of her own hair.

—Ruth Whitman

CONTENTS

A Spider on My Poem

I

Tall Grasses
Spring
Listening to grownups quarreling,
Persephone Travels Back to Hell, as Arranged
Rachel Waking
Apples and Barns
Running Upstream
In the Lobby
Cutting Rapunzel's Hair
The Nun Cuts Her Hair
A Daughter Cuts Her Hair
Cutting the Jewish Bride's Hair
The Marriage Wig
Ripeness
reunion
David's Breath
Summer Thunderstorms
The Wax Doll

Sitting for a Picture
The Act of Bread
She Doesn't Want to Bring the Tides in Any More

2

A Sound in Cambridge, Mass.
All My Bicycles Are Emily Dickinson
Lava Mold of a Girl Overcome at Pompeii
Sister Pharaoh
Sunrise in Athens
Dancing at Delphi
Noonday in the Plaka
One of the Kings
Public Images

3

Her Delirium
Almost Ninety
Bicycling Downhill
A Burned-Out Engine on the Southeast Expressway
Found Out
The Mark
Dead Center
In the Smoking Car
I Bite a Stone
Old Houses
I Become My Grandfather
Departures
All Presentiments
You Outlive All Your Diseases Except One
Uncle Atlantic
Swimming in Salt
I Laugh in Russian, Kiss in Yiddish, Bleed in Greek
Shoring Up

A SPIDER ON MY POEM

Black one,
I was going to frighten you away,
but now I beg you,
stay!
You're what I need.
This poem needs real legs, faster than the eye.
And a belly with magic string in it
made from spit,
designed to catch and hold whatever flies by.
Also, the uninvited way
you came, boldly, fast as a spider,
till you paused all real in the middle of the page
Everything I need.
Please stay.

1

TALL GRASSES

Now too I hold my arms up
when grasses grow higher than waist-high
and the shadow still runs out of me
        crying, a child of six, lost in the grasses,
        and I taste the tears of green saliva
from a bent blade scratching my thigh

The green is too high. Like the hostile fingers
the day I saw my mother cry
in the mirror, saw her lost in her weather,
        lost in a field of hurricane,
        lost in a jungle of blades like knives
where the grasses grow too high

SPRING

When I was
thirteen I
believed that
the mailman
had sperm on
his hands and
if he touched
me I would
be pregnant
if he brushed
against me
in the hall
from my pores would sprout twigs branches leaves
buds blossoms unfurling I'd be an apple
tree in my white wedding dress swelling
the room until flowers exploded into the street
and rose up filling the sky blowsy with
fruit to come

LISTENING TO GROWNUPS QUARRELING,

standing in the hall against the
wall with my little brother, blown
like leaves against the wall by their
voices, my head like a pingpong ball
between the paddles of their anger:
I knew what it meant
to tremble like a leaf.

Cold with their wrath, I heard
the claws of the rain
pounce. Floods
poured through the city,
skies clapped over me,

and I was shaken, shaken
like a mouse
between their jaws.

PERSEPHONE TRAVELS BACK TO HELL, AS ARRANGED

So long as this old subway keeps going,
I'm all right,
but it's the sudden stopping, the pause
in the middle of no air, nowhere
that gasps me.

Traveling back to a first rape,
cold and self-kidnapped,
I feel blunt and dulled.
It seemed truer, the first violence.

***

Snatched up in my father's Packard, his ancient troika,
crouched by his side,
we went plunging through the curving
Vermont hills
at what I thought was a fast clip, forty
miles an hour;
learning winter, forced to surrender
to one direction,
I learned the high glee of being driven,
ridden by a man.

The road ate itself up like a snake with its tail
in its mouth,
the world was a great perilous snake of a
roller coaster.

***

Now in my smart new winter coat,
orange, the color of sunsets,
and a hat made from a lamb
slaughtered half a world away;
packed lightly in one suitcase
so I won't need a porter,
I buy passage on his bankrupt line.

My gratitude to the black guts of the earth,
my thanks to this submachine taking me into the tunnel.
I brush kisses from my fingertips to all bats, roots, moles,
all blind and upsidedown things
squatting and squinting in the waiting dark.

RACHEL WAKING

She's in a well,
the walls covered with
slippery moss between
wet stones.
Under the water asleep,
holding her breath.
The clock strikes,
shooting her to the surface.

Her nose and the top of her head break through to air.
She scatters the scum lazing on the surface, the dragonfly resting,
the flat leaf of autumn.

She climbs,
sliding up the slippery walls,
dreams clinging to her ankles.
She wants to fall back.

But up there standing in crisp grass, Jacob
waits by the well, leaning his elbow against

the day, tossing idly in his hands
her brand new morning.

APPLES AND BARNS

There was a time of apples and barns
Pastures and lawns, parsing
Latin parsing kisses in the sweet

Smell of hay.
            They brought us back
From the heavyappled orchard, shamefaced,
In the back of the hired man's truck.

I watched the apples rolling down the sorter,
Small from big. Parsing apples,
You must look for yourself in barns.

Remember the pasture near the orchard,
The good smell of manure and boysweat,
When I blew over you petaled like a flag?

We said we'd be buried there.
I looked for myself in orchards, pastures,
Barns, I looked for myself among

Brown shoulders green eyes.
I remember your white boythigh.
And I came to an allnight barn

Freckled in moonlight, heavy with hay.
Leaning across fields and pastures,
You leaned on me. I began to be parsed.

Infinitive. The apple to be.

RUNNING UPSTREAM

waterfalling up
        those flights of stairs to you

my breath hooked in my throat
        a goldfish trapped and leaping

the bait you spilled in me
        was kiss beneath the skin
        I waited at the top.
Then you reeled me in.

IN THE LOBBY

In the lobby while people shook hands
and flashbulbs of friendship popped like smiles,
while you said hello and hello to everyone
who didn't matter and I stood stylishly by
pretending I didn't know you
suddenly
I took my machine gun and,
dressed as I was in maroon velvet,
mowed down the popular lecturer with
his witty charm and good wife,
his friends, clingers, all parasites
and passersthrough, all those related to me
by birth, marriage, and death,
until finally I could see the ceiling.

The walls were absolutely bare and solitary.
Across the tiled floor only you were left.
You smiled, took my arm, and we
began to go home together

CUTTING RAPUNZEL'S HAIR

Rapunzel, locked in her tower, learned
to let down her hair and become
a ladder to her secret self.

    And the witch,
    climbing the secret every day,
    knew a prince would soon follow behind her.

Rapunzel, Rapunzel, let down your hair,
open your windows and doors,
let in the sun. And beware.
Loosing your hair is telling
your magic name.
Winter is watching you.

    The angry witch
    lopped off Rapunzel's braids
    and blinded the prince so he couldn't find her

Some say it ended another way.
But now what girl would dare unbind her
magical, her sorry hair?

THE NUN CUTS HER HAIR

The nun
bald as
a uniform
offered her
hair to
her endless
Bridegroom.

And He
caressing as
air as
the sea
remembers winter
remembered
her hair.

A DAUGHTER CUTS HER HAIR

Once upon a time
a cat princess,
wanting to grow up,
cut off her golden hair,
and as it floated to the floor
babyhood
dropped from her,
yellow years curled gently with the dust

CUTTING THE JEWISH BRIDE'S HAIR

It's to possess more than the skin
that those old world Jews
exacted the hair of their brides.
    Good husband, lover of the Torah,
    does the Calligraphy of your bride's hair
    interrupt your page?

Before the clownish friction of flesh
creating out of nothing
a mockup of its begetters,
a miraculous puppet of God,
you must first divorce her from her vanity.

She will snip off her pride,
cut back her appetite to be devoured,
she will keep herself well braided,
her love's furniture will not endanger you,
        but this little amputation
        will shift the balance of the universe.

THE MARRIAGE WIG

If you're going to marry, make sure you first know whom you're going to divorce.

—Yiddish proverb

1.
The Mishnah says I blind you with my hair,
that when I bind it in a net
my fingers waylay my friends;
that in a close house I shake loose
the Pleiades into your kitchen.

How can I let you see me, past and future,
blemishes and dust? Must I
shear away my hair and wear
the wig the wisemen say? Will you
receive me, rejoice me, take me for your wall?

To any man not blind, a wig is false.

2.
Once upon a time I wrote a boy
into my calendar of weddings. We lived
in a gargoyle house with many eyes.
Snow furred the street lamps. Inside
we had our wine, one pot, an innocent fire.

Now the gargoyle house is gone. On a tree
is the orphan number, forty-nine, meaning
49, a house, a marriage, a time
scythed clean, crunched to powder, flat
as a grave, as though we'd never been.

Let me apologize for that lost number.

3.
Let me apologize for all the faces
I've worn, none of them my own.
See me in my glass. A ghost looks back,
a witty ghost, who counterfeits my mask,
wearing a marriage wig made of my hair.

Inside, I'm threaded on a passion
taut as a tightrope. Strip away the hair,
the tooth, the wrinkle, the obscene
cartoon that decades scrawl—
underneath I'm naked as a nun.

I wear that nakedness for a disguise.

RIPENESS

You wake up feeling
like an oven
where bread
has just been baked.

All night the yeast rose
and at dawn
you baked the bread,
a round full loaf.

REUNION

After the division the two parts of man, each desiring the other half, came together, and threw their arms about one another eager to grow into one.

—Plato, *Symposium*, translated by B. Jowett

when your skin is strapped
to my bones, when I breathe
with your breath, wear your small
of the back, smile, eyelashes,
I'll be home again:

but I might cry for your marrow,
parching for your tongue,
and you might still turn away,
fearing the smart of my going,
so slowly grows our grafting—

until your sex takes mine,
finally, as it was
before the beginning, before
the pregods envied us
and split in two our one

DAVID'S BREATH

let's celebrate the
breath and airs
of love. David's
mouth, pastures of
honeysuckle, the nape
of his baby
neck, crops of
clover. Leda's hair
newly washed, a

thicket of balsam.
Under your arm
a decanter of
spices, the slope
of your torso,
newly cut wood.
And your sex
spilled over, like
barnfresh milk, like
warm brandy, like
David's breath

SUMMER THUNDERSTORMS

She walked bravely down the country road
every late afternoon

but she was frightened before it began. Protean
mountain shadows had moved

around her all day, a young bride
whose mother had now grown old.

Womb shapes gathered over the mountains, tongues of
electric snakes licked

the sky, just as she came back to the house,
lit the fragile lamp,

and began to get the meal. The house had stood
two hundred years, but brides

can't believe they'll live in history.
When the roof seemed to split

with the first crack of the daily storm, her throat
became cement. The table

was only half set, the potatoes just
boiling, but she sank
sank again into the sky's cauldron.

THE WAX DOLL

Simple the eye
that sees the moon
lurch down the sky
and crack the pool
if snakes should go
a midnight journey
and mad dogs howl
she'll only say
she gave a finger
nail away.

She's wax beneath
the sorcerer
who fingers and
transfigures her
and when she tells
her secret name
then every toad
will croak the tale
how belly swells,
wits curl,
and shame curdles
a real girl.

SITTING FOR A PICTURE

The painter
narrows his
eye, measures
along his
finger, looks
at her up-
sidedown then
backwards in
a mirror.

Not touched the
girl on the
couch begins
to wear his
grammar. Per-
spective flat-
tens her curves
buttock brow
she becomes
more than her
self, catch for
a palette.

She gives off
faint power
like perfume
or buddha
she sits in
his eye like
an apple.

THE ACT OF BREAD

Some practice is required to knead quickly, but the motion once acquired will never be forgotten.

—"Water Bread," *The Boston Cooking-School Cook Book* by Fannie Merritt Farmer, 1898

That happy multiplying
should have lasted all night.
But long before dawn
my batter crawled up the walls.
The trouble was, I let my secret
passion run into my thumbs:
into my own
flour yeast water I plunged my lust
up to the elbows—pounding the white
buttocks of my children, turning
their rosy heels; kneading the
side, loin, groin of him
to whom I long owed this caressing.

But before I could give form to desire,
invented flesh outran me.
It towered in my biggest bowl,
flowed over table shelves floor
till I scooped it up, frightened at my power,
and tried to hide it in a paper
bag. In an hour
it burst the side, climbed
out the window, through the door.

If I had baked that dough,
a crumb would serve as aphrodisiac:
one slice of bread
would people a continent.

But in panic
I carried it outside, bucket by bucket,
and gave it to the cold November morning

SHE DOESN'T WANT TO BRING THE TIDES IN ANY MORE

Every time she tugs the sun across the sky
some old wound
comes apart at the seams.
But housekeeping by the clock means keeping
every star prompt. She puffs along,
blowing a strand of graying hair out of her eyes,
but she gets each planet to its place
on time. She bruises a hip
moving all this furniture around.

She steers clouds, fans winds, and slices
or mends the moon, according to the day.
Worst of all is bringing in the tides.
One hand brings them in on one side,
the other pushes them away;
while her knee
keeps the tipped earth spinning on its axis
precariously.

No wonder she went away and sat down on a sand dune,
wishing she were grass.
If she sits still long enough,
rain will come to her.

2

A SOUND IN CAMBRIDGE, MASS.

Every late evening in the silence before sleep
there's a crisp latch
opening in the darkness, the creak of a door
and two sharp steps
out to a porch, a balcony, and a voice
calling two notes.
They're the first two notes of an opera, an aria
to a lost cat.
She sings them over and over like a bird,
a bob-o-link,
only I never can hear the words that she sings,
perhaps Sam-bo,
Plu-to, Ju-no, a trochee, ending in o,
she sings it
always the same, never higher or lower,
the same breathless
expectation, the same lyrical patience.
And the cat
on a fence, in a garden, leaping at shadows, chasing
a velvet moth,
hears his own personal two-note violin
and comes home.

ALL MY BICYCLES ARE EMILY DICKINSON

Perfectly oiled, her tires tight with twenty pounds of air
delighting in her moving parts, she mows
a narrow ribbon up the gravel. In low,
aware of every separate pebble, we make smaller
revolutions, fighting gravity all the way.

Out on the flat, we shift to second, raising our eyes
and seeing the bird's-eye map of leaves, striated bark
under the blue proscenium. Our spokes
make a girlish click click as we lope down
the wide highway, watching everything.

Now in high, we start to take off. Leaning my soles
on her pedals, I lift slightly off her seat,
letting the wind take us. I name her
Emily. And now she remembers how once
God pumped his floods of warm diamonds into her.

LAVA MOLD OF A GIRL OVERCOME AT POMPEII

Her house is roofless
and the shoals lie shallow
in the alcove of the hot mountain
where every keel scrapes rock

Drowned a girl surprised
beneath the rain of stone
the hot deceit
she lies in her unlucky shell
ankle knee waist high
the damage rose
until the flood bit
breast throat eyes

Weightless stone
harvests her hands
sea moss salts the once-
breathcaught, the burned
and tattered girl who floats
facedown and swaying
in the eyeless sea

SISTER PHARAOH

Hatshepsut, old girl, old friend,
man-woman, bearded Pharaoh,
we women too pasted on beards
and said we were kings.
We brought lullaby rules of commerce to the state,
we raised temples and wrote hieroglyphs
and got the men
to erect an obelisk for us.

Hatshepsut,
you crouch in the silent hall of tombs,
trying to be a riddle.
But we can see through your beard.
Beneath your terrible crown of upper and lower Egypt
beneath your archaic stone smile,
our milk has turned to powder,
our breasts are two inches of dust.

SUNRISE IN ATHENS

I go to close the window.
Framed in my eye
like Aphrodite just out of the sea
the Parthenon stretches her pearly arms.
Roseglow
tips her.

A donkey sobs a wailing
hello to the morning,
bellowing in great griefstricken breathcatching
brays, in and out like a heartbroken harmonica.

Shawls of lacy yellow, white, lavender
blow wisping around her shoulders.

The hand that claims her every day,
the golden sun, comes down
and grasps her firmly.
I slowly close my shutters
against the heat.

DANCING AT DELPHI

Ribboning down the unpaved highway
from Delphi to Arachova,
a skein of men and women
full of cheese, wine,
Saturday night love,

lifts you off the ground.
Through their bodies,
into their fingers,
the earth leaps upward
into you.

NOONDAY IN THE PLAKA

Walking up from a bulletpocked house—
the smell of urine, dust
rises from the crackedlazy
sidewalk, fresh
bread from some
kitchen and crisp
entrails frying.

Up the sheet metal street,
each jagged house is
pinged by white light.
The organ grinder plays *o sole mio*
on his gingerbread organ, then

the death dance
from Zalonghou.

ONE OF THE KINGS

Child,
the globe turns
tipped on its axis
half night half day.
At this moment
a lovesick assassin
is taking a wife in
Ghana; hit by a stray bullet
a mother of twelve
lets out her last
bubble of breath
in China; in Egypt
a future inquisitor
is crying his first
sharp cry of birth.
Here in our classroom
under the slanted roof
we're playing a pageant.
A crowd of little faces
tied in handkerchiefs
dyed seven different colors
move up the aisle toward
six-year-old Mary
and her doll. We recognize
the shepherd by his
crook and toy lamb.
Annunciatory angels
in coathanger haloes
search the audience
for their mothers.

Now come the three kings
bearing gifts.
The blackskinned one
eight years tall
moves through us wearing
a crown on his closecropped head.
Over his shoulders the purple
mantle spreads, sprinkled with
golden fleurs de lis. He walks holding
the flask of imaginary
frankincense. He moves
handsomely toward
the little stuffed symbol
unaware
of the torn god crying
betrayal and massacre.

PUBLIC IMAGES

THAT WOMAN HOLDING OUT HER HAND
is lying under
rafters, sand, stone,
bricks, sticks
of wood, a giant
girder, a mountain.
Only her head and one hand
are free.
Her face holds
continents
of pleading.

THE BOYISH POLITICIAN
naive and human, his
tie askew,
seems to be explaining.
His jacket is torn,

his collar all in motion.
They have poured cement
into one shoe
making his foot
immobile.

AN APOLOGY TO THE LIBERATED INMATES:
my clean underwear
makes it difficult for me
to understand you.
At what point did you
stop filing your nails,
stop planning what to have for dinner?
Peeled from my house, my skin,
would I be
raw like you
sick like you
an angry
harp of bones?

OUR NEXT DOOR SURVIVOR
lives above the waist
strapped on a bed
among lilacs, tulips,
suburban cherry blossoms.
Her legs belong to those
black woods where
Jewish children
march, trying not to
cry at the guards,
at the sourfaced trees.

THE LATE ASTRONAUT IN THE BOSTON GLOBE
grins foolishly at the unmanned
camera. Behind him
the earthglobe dangles.
His shoulderblade

blots out the map of Africa,
his earlobe overcomes
the China sea.
We've caught him,
tipsy in space,
walking nowhere.

Let's give him
burial toys—
two planets,
one for each hand,
let's paint
an Egyptian eye
to steer his ship
as he passes
our old sky.

3

HER DELIRIUM

The old lady
(a child of seven)
cried in her sleep
Stop beating me!
Zu hilfe!
Zu hilfe!
In the dark cellar
her sons had murdered . . .
And the policeman was punishing

The bright light
slid down the white bed
and the little girl

saw her wrinkled arm,
her withered knee.
Which is me, she cried,
which body is mine,
and why are they beating
an old lady of eighty-nine?

ALMOST NINETY

The last time I kissed her
I held a thin sparrow
her bones were that hollow

Where did she get the juice to turn
her eyes, to laugh at her greatgrandson
singing her jingle bells?

Now for my little dry wren
a cardboard box could serve as nest.
Too frail for feathers, she took my kisses,

waving come back, come back again.

BICYCLING DOWNHILL

To all things God is possible.
        Tipped at an angle for angels,
            Leaning on my breakneck ankles,
I try to pin the dirt path with my eyes.

Nervous pebbles, mounds of sand,
        Twigs fly slanting up my wheels;
            My rigid wrists, grown to handlebars,
Hold me counterpoised against the road.

I'm holding back while hurling down,
        Tensing past each hump of moss, each
            Rock, each bole of tree,
Each yellow leaf. A tiny toad

Becomes a frantic stone, avoiding me.
        Birds flute past my windy ears,
            The slow sky spells me out,
More tilting than my spilling down.

Plunging, I abandon brakes, no hands,
        Whipped by my gravity, beating
            The dust, devouring hesitation,
Letting the reins go, the final reins.

A BURNED-OUT ENGINE ON THE SOUTHEAST EXPRESSWAY

My pretty seagreen manslaying automobile
raced lightly up the long hill, scarcely
        grazing the macadam.

Her heart purred under her hood, the even hum
of all her joints played fugue and counterpoint—
        until she missed a beat:

She drove delicately, trying to hold back
the first rasps of disaster. The pistons were out
        of time, something was dragging

under the tailpipe. A wheel had gone soft.
The dry clashing of injured bearings.
        Jammed in mid-course,

her slain parts clattered, then stopped.
I climbed out of the car, pale and empty,

feeling in my belly—like sudden old age—
        the ruined dry engine.

FOUND OUT

a fractured villanelle

There's a strange man parked outside my house
I don't want him to see me spying
So I watch him sideways
from the window,
screened and blurred.
                All I can see
is a shoulder, a white, a grub-white sleeve.

He's sitting, parked outside my house.
He doesn't move.
            I let my jewel
of a rapeable daughter out of the door
and watch him sideways from the window.

He doesn't move.
His car is red.
He's been parked all day outside my house.

Trapped inside my head I think:
he's singled out the very thing
I'm guilty of.

            I watch him.
Parked outside my house.
Sideways.
He's waiting.

THE MARK

Grandpa, when you
lay dying, your throat
wrapped in bandages,
I came to see you
after school.

You wrote kindly
on a scrap of paper,
What's new? and I,
blindly, Today
I got an A.

You smiled at me
for that schoolgirl boast
You already knew
what I couldn't see.

And I'm ashamed,
still ashamed.

DEAD CENTER

for John Holmes

            A thin fox
sidled by with his stingy shadow.
Bees hung in air,
each like a chandelier,
hot pine pinched my nostrils.

You sat up in bed
wrestling with the fox's silence,
it isn't time, it isn't time.
I looked at your face with the sharp regret

a mother feels for her child
sleeping after the day's war.

They broke flowers on your coffin,
knowing you weren't there. The sun came out
and all your faces flared for a moment:
you weren't there.
I'll beat my poem into a trap
for the stingy fox, to prove
that you were here.

IN THE SMOKING CAR

That hatless chewed woman sending me messages
with her eyes, what does she know about me?
That I've had my last child, that my
clocks are stopping? That love still comes to me
like birthdays or Christmas, and a brushed kiss
can be a whole concert?

She is grayer than I, more toothless,
but she grins like a sister.
Do my sins show?
                    What deception
does she see through me?
I shrink from her wrinkles, her sporty air,
her certain knowledge, older than cats,
that I am pretending, pretending, pretending.

I BITE A STONE

I had this dream where I told you to go away.
I don't know what the end of the poem will be,
The dream said it. It wasn't really me.

Was this a kind of self-discovery
To have this dream (I always wake to stay)
Saying I don't need you, go away?

I gasped, coming up from webs of sleep.
I tried to brush the sticky threads away.
I don't know what the end of the poem will be

Something about a young girl with a deep
Need for mother twenty years ago.
Like most necessities, it didn't keep.

I cannot see where, waking, this will lead,
Nor why I told you I had lost my need.
I had this dream where I told you to go away.

I don't know what the end of the poem will be.

OLD HOUSES

I wear this house like a barrel
to cover my struts
and I see:
        the plaster's getting veined.
        Tender clapboards won't stand
        too much more rain.
        Inside
        the wallpaper's crepy
        where the storm came in.

Looking out from inside
it's hard to tell:
will a coat of spanking paint
make the trim seem new again?

I've seen other women preen
to the image in their eyes,
picturing moviestar lips,
a dashing lilt to the head,
        while in the mirror
        looking back
        an old mask
        props up its wrinkles
        with a kissed out mouth.

But I feel like a virgin in the dark.
I hear my voice like a child's
enter the telephone
and come out no older.

        How come this new me
        is looking out of an old house?

I BECOME MY GRANDFATHER

Grandpa, I
want to tell you
simply:
that picture of you,
the handsome one with
curly gray hair,
amorous eyes,
arms folded in satisfaction—

I have looked
at you since I was
a little girl:
my grandfather.

Today I thought:
he's like some friend of mine,

a man I could love,
a sweetheart.
And reckoned
I'm now older
than your picture
by one year.

DEPARTURES

The buses stand in slips like ocean liners.
I scan the driver's face for signs of kindness.

Rachel, now taller than I, once asked
(before she had breasts, when she thought she was Snow
 White):

How does a man look to a dragon?

And answered:
the man is very small,
the dragon doesn't care about him at all.
He'd crush him with his toenail.

Brave as an eggshell,
I've come to see her off.

A bulky girl stands by
with stonehenge ankles.
Sorrow seems to fill her like cement.

Rachel squeezes into the monster Greyhound,
clutching her suitcase.
I stand in the shadows.

Beside me a tiny Puerto Rican couple
are waiting with their children.

The boy and girl are chalk-faced, hollow-eyed.
They never cry.
The mother looks sixteen, too young to worry.

She holds the little boy slung on her hip,
while under him a spread of urine slowly
stains her skirt.

    Last night, love, when our bodies meshed most deeply,
    I touched your face and knew,
    across a highway of nightmare,
    your sudden absence.
    Traveler, you slipped away
    as we lay side by side.
    Come back.

The driver slams his door and starts the motor.

Stonehenge stands alone like stone, crying.

Wrong bus for the Puerto Ricans.

    As the Greyhound backs away
    I blow it an anonymous kiss
    and think I see,
    through the moving dark,
    an answering hand.

ALL PRESENTIMENTS

All presentiments
of dying are
true. The angel
blows in the window and spatters
your bedsheet with
east wind and rain

and you pull your
comforter, ocean,
up under your chin.

YOU OUTLIVE ALL YOUR DISEASES EXCEPT ONE

1.
Give me anything of value, the nurse said,
watches, rings, teeth, whatever
is removable, also your eye, leg, hair
no I said and there are no
hairpins on me either, nothing,
nothing, I am stripped
down to my self,
plucked like a chicken, punctured for oblivion
in anonymous white worn backwards,
wheeled like secondhand goods to a stall.

Strapped under arc lights I see
a dark doctor who says he writes poetry
in Arabic. I sympathize with a kind
anaesthetist who can't find my veins. I halloo
my own doctor who like santa claus
with a black goody for me sends me
raw, split,
sailing into cushions of mercy.

2.
Name me the parts
of cars, pistons, spark plugs, axles,
tires, doors, roof, radiator, categories
of fallibility that will be eaten
by collision, rust, attrition, age
and lie

abandoned by a used car dealer
in a hospital of wrecks.

Grass pushes through that speedy engine.
A lazy beetle
on the steering wheel
turns imperceptibly with the earth's
turning. They have lost their counterpoint of motion
Gaping like lepers
the old cars freeze
in insufficiency: sky, weeds.

UNCLE ATLANTIC

He sat me on his stony knee,
put his great foggy arm
around my shoulders.

I said:
Uncle.
Hello.
I need.
        I'm glad to see your vast gray
fastnesses
are still here.
I can't see any seagulls
in this rain
but I know
fishes and seaweed
are sleeping in your beard.

Teach me
calm.
He taught me.

SWIMMING IN SALT

Like fluid of
the human body
sweat or sperm
or tears, you're
cleansed by it,
nourished, fertilized. Walking

lightly in water-
space, you come
up from its
sharp unbreathable, pores
diamonded,
immortal.

I LAUGH IN RUSSIAN, KISS IN YIDDISH, BLEED IN GREEK

I laugh in Russian, kiss in Yiddish, bleed in Greek.
Laughter up through the knees, full in the breast,
rich with potatoes and grass, as though
the world would never wither; kisses full of birds
and babies, tongues of morning rivers
running to oceans of light; blood
straight from the womb, the marble veins,
mountains and Attic plains bled dry,
the sea robbed of its rosy islands,
blood as the future's monument, thighs
of laughter, kisses to mark my trade:
        twist water, thrust fire,
        wring the truth from the walls
        and people the instant earth.

SHORING UP

1.
On a clockless summer afternoon
in a cradle of seahaze
cupped in the palm of a dune
a man sleeps, defenseless as all sleeping creatures are

Medallion.

I wear that graceful icon
pinned inside my forehead
to ward me against certain disaster.

2.
Last night's explosion blew
the starfish high.
I looked out and saw
sharks swimming in the sky;
the shaken sky
shook my bed.

I pulled in my knees,
saw a hill in Greece
where two small boys
fished in the air for birds.

They cast their lines in the thick gold air
and reeled back finches and starlings.
The cameo sea grinned
as though posing for eternity.

3.
Propelled by old guilts,
cast up on a rocky shore,
I lean propped on my images.

The man sleeps, his buttocks curved like a child
carved on an ivory gem, his fingers
opened out, his tender arc
suspended in my eye.

THE PASSION OF LIZZIE BORDEN

New Poems

TRANSLATING

(for Jacob Glatstein)

The old man was cold.
King David, they said,
we've heaped piles of clothes
on your bed, but your feet
are still icy, night after
night. Let us find you
a girl, a young
Shulamite, intelligent,
kind, who can spread
her warm bones
over you. . . .

            Abishag's
black hair lay
like a shawl on his throat,
her breasts and belly
and her rosy thighs
rode his flesh
shyly all night.

He did not enter her.

But as they lay,
slowly warming,
his voice found her ear,
and since he was sleepless,

he told her what
he was thinking:

how a slingshot had won him
a great lopsided battle
when he was a boy;
how he slew his ten thousands;
how his soul was knit
to his lover Jonathan;
how he answered Saul's
hatred with mercy;
how he danced unashamed
before the Ark
with songs and lyres
with harps and cymbals
and made his wife angry;
lusted alter
married Bathsheba;
got himself children,
was betrayed
by a son, a son;
how songs still came
to him. . . .

And Abishag,
after all those hours
of listening, the world
in his voice,
rose in the morning
full of spermatic words.

BREAD LOAF 1941

1. R. F.
We drank beer, cheered
Schwartzkopf, rolled

in the mown meadow
and wondered
which poet to marry.

We played
on our plateau, heedless
of Hitler. And the
granddaddy
of us all,

shaggy as a bear,
wagged his white head.
His despair
was so wittily said,
we didn't care.

2. On Theodore Roethke's Lap
There was only one motion,
down, racing down the mountain
in a beatup Chevrolet

crammed with a zoo of poets
and fat round Ted,
the lowflying slug.

We clutched each other
inside that black box
feeling our way by guess

and by gosh, whizzing down past
devilmaycare trees and a brook
at the bottom of the gulch

calling its cool persuasion,
early death for nine young
geniuses, thirsty for beer.

Ted's large knees under
me, the smallest and youngest,
felt soft and warm.

"Remember?" I asked,
years later, "after your
papa's waltz?"

"I always got a hardon," he answered,
now almost at the bottom of the mountain,
the waters loud in his ears.

3. Rebuilding the House
        On the flat lawn of silence
we will take each red brick,
    each yellow clapboard,
        and put back nail by nail
    like a film clip in reverse
a demolished Queen Anne house.

        The Olympic highjumper floats
    in the air like dandelion fluff
backward to his starting point.
And we will take each syllable,
    each movement of the mouth, tongue, jaw

        no, before that,
    the breath from the chest cavity,
    the smallest muscles to expel air, sound
waves, voice, word
and build the house that held the
first marriage room the poem.

IN THE VATICAN MUSEUM 1952

Through a glass box, behind an Attic vase,
love face, habitually misplaced,
how you turned up like a clown
in the museum in Rome,
looking through to us
at the same vase
in the same case in the same room,
far from Cambridge, Salt
Lake City, all your warring
and contrary places.

Awkward body born from a candy machine,
you appeared and disappeared, sad
smile on a mummer's face.

Young and naked in March
we all plunged together
into the cold Rockport quarries—
and you disappeared.
            I found you

gaping over a halfeaten banana
at the Spreading Chestnut Tree on Brattle Street
We captured you in our furnished room
over a bottle of chianti.

You disappeared.
        Love,
in and out of windows, we
took a bus to Salem
and lost you again
among the seven gables.

            Antic face
in the Vatican, how

did you come to be jumbled among
these antiquities?

AMONG THE GREEN MANSIONS 1936

At the tea our mothers arranged
we two sat bored, you
in your fourteen-year-old
braids, me in my
prim chignon,
until we discovered
we both really lived below the neck
among the Green Mansions.

Afternoons by the river we waited
(you sitting on the wall,
an ocean liner waiting to be launched,
I a toy boat with nervous sails)—
scribbling poems of longing
and sudden rape—
like W. H. Hudson's jungle bird
glinting her breast
among the torrid trees.

PLAYING DEAD

Locked in a motel
of mummy light,
fake air, we breathe
plastic.

Thin dreams
flick across the walls.
Voices quarreling from the next tomb

keep us
not quite asleep.

A splinter of morning
enters through a crack.
We pry at the slit
until an untamed
tiger of sun springs in,
pushing the door open.

We have the answer
before the question.

FOR DAVID SACKS, ODESSA 1881–BOSTON 1965

Once in his jaunty middle age
his wife had caught him again behind the door
kissing the girl from downstairs. . . .

Driving to the hospital we lied,
They're going to make you well, you'll
dance at our wedding.
                    His arm
was still smooth as a boy's. You could hide
your fingers in his thick
eighty-four-year-old hair. Natty
even in his hospital johnny,
he basked in a flurry of nurses.
But he no longer wanted to eat.

. . . Fighting years of cooking smoke,
counting children, pennies, sugarbabies
from the candy store she kept for him,
she locked him
            debonair as Odessa
in his room.

UTTERANCE

Miss Muffet,
perceiving the spider
beside her,

screamed.
She moved the tiny muscles
in her adam's apple, dropped

her lower jaw, and forced the air
in waves
out of her mouth

to my eardrums,
a minute thrumming.
She knew, as her animal ancestors

before her, that sound
carries well, will turn a corner,
can be heard in the dark.

I think I hear
through a musky orchard
the silent abdominal

language of bees
playing violins
to the bass sonatas of whales

circling the sea.
I'm threading these songs
on syllables of wonder, remembering

bekos, the Phrygian word for bread.

A NAP AT SUNION

Peeling away the layers of clouds,
dollying in with my dream camera,
I see

a girl
curled up naked
sleeping on a rock.

She has climbed down the spiney hill
to explore an ancient cave
chill with the smell of shepherd's urine and Poseidon

She swims in the sea near a ledge,
never thinking of the octopus watching her.
She floats

toward adolescent islands
nippling the horizon.
And then she sleeps

while the horns
of the god's temple
rise over her.

DIGGING

centuries from now in the soil
of his city, the antiquarian will change
his story, partly guessing how rain
wore down the mountain
and how earth heaved up its double.

Layer on layer, the land doubles
back on itself. But all his digging

will not reveal the mountain
worn away or the soil
multiplied, or how rain
marries out his features. Change

comes atom by atom, an exchange
of smooth for rough, double
for unique. Each drop of rain
pocks the world's surface, digging
minuscule trenches in the soil
of mountains.

And the mountain
changes,
moving through air, water, soil,
like a juggler with a double
set of oranges. Digging
reveals he is not wholly lost, becoming rain

The rain
pours down the mountain,
wearing away the scholar digging
through each change
of lifetime, through each double

city under soil,

wearing away the soil
itself. Pebbles rain
down, doubling
the ground he walks on. Mountains
of change
open beneath his digging

Digging in the soil
of his city, he exchanges himself for his double:
atom, mountain, rain.

ZION

Grayfaced,
groping through the day,
I come to touch you breast to breast
and spring up, replenished, rosy
with your quickening.

Touchstone,
your body is my Israel,
your shoulder my wailing
wall, your face the bible
of my wandering.

THE THIRD WEDDING

On the way to her second wedding
dressed like a Christmas package
tinseled and laced with ribbon,
she caught a look at herself.

Her heart crashed with terror
under her champagne dress.
She shook from her shoes to her careful
veil.

    Where was the minyan
of ten good men? The cup
under the bridegroom's heel?
The canopy of flowers?

When guests turned to the altar,
she shed her mistaken skin
and rose clear of the building.
No one noticed her missing.

She gathered ten years for a minyan,
plucked a canopy of planets,
brought her body like a cup

to the bridegroom long denied
who drew her to his side,
his rib, his final bride.

FOUR POEMS OF COMFORT AND DISCOMFORT

1. After the Abortion

Your knees, Uncle Doctor had said,
Watch those knees.

                    Traffic,
tuned to Schönberg,
floated through
the August window.

I tasted flat peroxide
and death.

On a certain betrayed afternoon
I realized
the bubbling was my own blood.
Half a lifetime later,

twenty miles away,
I leaned my head on my hand
and aged.

2. On the Way to Mount Auburn Hospital

Inside pain's white
balloon I tasted
every pebble and pothole

the narrow red truck
jerked over

The fireman beside me
with the vague family face
was saying something blurry,
but his hand holding mine
was dry and clear

3. Derailed
that time the train
    heeled and yawed
I braced my angry back

against foot-
    loose evil, my long expected
adversary

His dark flank
    passed over
me

Stumbling to the broken
    door
I discovered
    I had lost my shoe

4. Bellyache
The night she had a bellyache
  she fitted herself into
    all his corners

    and spaces, wearing
  him like a bandage
against her little pains.

Curling behind him
  holding his sleeping penis
in her hand

she tried to become
part of his
architecture.

RISING TO THE OCCASION

Up! As Archilochus said,
soul, you must, despite all
annoyances, and this
vile island you live on, shaped
like the backbone of an ass:
despite this, up, wash, dress
and out.
Soul lies wallowing with a cold in his nose.
His head aches. Fever. Loving enemies
come running with pills, chicken, exotic
remedies. All night there's a chill in the room
Fever. War.

Up! Beneath the island,
vomited up from ancient
volcanoes, there hides a grievous
fault. But splayfooted soul
will rise. His juice will spurt
again, again through a
dry stalk.

WHEN THE CHILD AT YOUR BREAST IS A METAPHOR

1.
At the pool

the young mother in the yellow hat
follows along the edge,
on land,
watching her tadpole child in the water.
Every muscle in the mother's dry body
swims, as her child paddles across the surface,
not drowning. She can't keep her hands
from stretching out. She moves
her feet along the edge,
dancing a pas de deux of terror
and separateness.

2.
The child's voice on the telephone
wavers and breaks
as the rainstorm breaks on the line.
Thunder slams the house.
His words,
jigsawed by lightning,
fall
apart
while rain
beats in the open windows
blurring the words
in her ear.

A CRY

A man is howling like a dog.
Is a dog crying like a man?

In your backyard universe
where clusters of birds sang like roses and
crows rowing through the thick air
have dropped their triangular cries,
someone is in pain.

A dog thinks he is a man.
Or a man is skinned to his animal.

K.516

From your graveyard
on the moon, three
hundred thousand
miles away, you
look back
on your leafy toy
(diminutive, savage
as a child, round
with baby fat
and dimples)
and you think of a pulse
in the throat of Constanze
in 1782,
a mote in the mote
in the eye of death,
and out of your cinders,
across your rubble of birthdays,
you jig her a rondo
allegro, the broken
wing of a fly.

PAINTER

What's riches to him
that has made a great peacock
with the pride of his eye?

—Yeats

He sees into yellow balloons
        of sun.

Dives
into turquoise. Swims
under layers of blue.

Turns and walks
around the trunk of a tree
flat on the wall. Drops a cat

between the sleeve
and the rib
of the portrait.

Sees space.

Six oceandeep miles of it
in a narrow room.

Sees.
And holds Cezanne's apple,
like love,
the round of it.

LAYING A FIRE

The fire starts when two logs meet.

They barely touch.

Close enough to draw juice from the embers,
enough apart so every tongue moves
freely.

In a little while time changes the relation.
One loses in the fire more than the other.

I'll step back.

              You
move an inch forward.

MEDITATION

Traveling back forty-five light years
through the middle of
your forehead;

tumbling over the edge of the medieval
ocean until you are
merely a

point of light in a black universe,
an absolute elsewhere,
an ovum,

a picture of an ovum on a black page
magnified a billion
times;

feathering off from cushions of sun,
you wake up laughing,
your laugh

tickles the edge of the galaxy,
waiting to be born,
to be

LAMENT FOR A YIDDISH POET

Jacob Glatstein, 1896–1971

1.
I want to fasten you inside my head.
Where else can you go now?

I'm sending you my strength,
I said on the telephone.

The telephone wires were laughing at us.

Words are all you left me:
they stroke my cheek, thrust under my hand

like kittens. I heard you shouting, you were angry.
But now I know you were frightened

and didn't want to die
here, at the edge of the desert,

where you struck voices out of rock.

2.
They put you in a pine box
under a star of David
and a few red roses.

The room was breathless
as a grave,
busy with worms.

You stood at the door watching
the coffinbirds peck at the poet.
And quickly left.

3.
In the air, on the wide sky,
you write from right to left,
dark and sunny,
sending me messages.

Adam and Eve
are lazing in a pool of blue,
waiting to begin.

Where are you?

With a Word,
with a flock of words dense as starlings
you wheel across the sun,
naming the first creatures
in a cantata of light earth sea.

4.
You kissed the face of despair.

I may live to be a hundred, you said,
but I will be dead for centuries.

The faces of all the children, the dead,
the burned, the living, the murdered,
the unborn, are lifted up,
are waiting for your kiss.
For the mother-tongue of rain.

CASTOFF SKIN

She lay in her girlish sleep at ninety-six,
small as a twig.
Pretty good figure

for an old lady, she said to me once.
Then she crawled away, leaving
a tiny stretched transparence

behind her. When I kissed her paper cheek
I thought of the snake,
of his quick motion.

PASSOVER 1970

1.
Athens and Jerusalem   cities of my being   the faces
on your streets are my face   the houses   the rooms inside
the houses   the beds inside the rooms are places   where I
was born   made love   took in your seed

2.
    A child of many wars,
    how is it my tongue
    speaks only the vocabulary of peace?

3.
Now it is time to move out of the narrow space.
The I is the starting place, never the arrival.
The journey outward begins now

4.
Inside Agamemnon's beehive tomb,
the stones,
square and heavy,
fit cleverly together.

The king was laid inside,
a bled shell
once warm to the hands
of his wife.

He was practical,
he traded

his child's life
for fair winds, for war.

Thieves have emptied his tomb.
He did great harm.
And was harmed.
Words   Stones   A cool air

5.
When I was pregnant in the Athens prison, the colonels
beat the soles of my feet with sticks. I asked them
to be careful of the baby. They laughed and said
Another one like you? Soft and arrogant? And beat me more
Afterwards I lay, unable to walk, weeping in my cell. In
  the dark
I felt a sudden gush between my thighs, and knew
    that I had lost my child

6.
    Tigers roam the streets. A crow
    snuffs out the sun.
        Babies
    tilt with hairpins at the president,
    who scoops them up and stuffs them
    in his smile

7.
Pharaoh's horses were closing in behind us.
We shouted and dodged in the dark, stumbling down
  to the beach,
shoving aside even our fathers and children,
trampled, half-drowning, cursing our foolish escape
  from Egypt
when Moses said:
    Stand still, my people. I must think what to do
    Stand still. I will not let you perish.
    O Lord, you created the earth

and the water that covers the earth—
how can I, a mere man,
separate the sea,
reverse your plan,
and give my people a safe path
to the other side?
Help me.

8.

Leaving for war, the husband ties his shoes
tightly, confirming the miles between
her bed, his chair.
        Masada falls.

Lilacs fill the air.
Surviving lovers, barefoot,
multiply.

PERMANENT ADDRESS

CONTENTS

Holding Up the Bridge
- Liftoff
- Word
- Arrow
- Yom Kippur: Fasting
- Soup Cools from the Edges First
- Holding Up the Bridge
- A Questionnaire

Human Geography
- Seven Variations for Robert Schumann
- Bubba Esther, 1888
- My Greatgreatuncle the Archbishop
- Maria Olt
- The Language of Hills
- The Grilled Window, Jerusalem
- Mediterranean
- Human Geography
- Watching the Sun Rise Over Mount Zion

In the Country of the Whitethroated Sparrow
- In the Country of the Whitethroated Sparrow
- A Phoenix
- After
- Apple
- Fog

Rooms of the Ocean
- Rooms of the Ocean
  - crossing Tiverton bridge to Aquidneck Island
  - Second Beach

Bishop Berkeley's Rock, Middletown, R.I.
yellow
Purgatory Chasm
the moon over the sea
August storm
Sachuest Point
a veil fell just now
December sunset
the beach in winter
the light the face gives off
Singing

HOLDING UP THE BRIDGE

LIFTOFF

You will make a myth
out of the ordinary
rising beyond your skin
into a new country

breaking the thin
filaments of gravity

You cannot elevate
without the hand of wind.
The strong
air stalls in your lungs.

You hesitate
on the brink of land.

And in this instant all
the sorrows of obstacle

pause and dissolve.
You lift—

    and, barely moving, skim
    the impossible sky.

WORD

A fur muscle ran across the road.

Only when I saw the pointed tip of it
waving, did I think *chipmunk*.

Sometimes we move inside our bodies
as inside a stranger. The sack
hangs loose, inviting us to think
I can be anyone, go anywhere, do anything.

But once your pen touches paper, all
choices become one, the word as single
as the chipmunk moving in one spasm
from green to *green*.

ARROW

The aiming:

you aim at the center of the eye
you gather all landscape around that single point
    if a bird-ribbon flies across the edge
    if a cloud teases the sun
you gather all to the one point

there is only one

The letting go:

you are let go
you are no longer grasped
empty air surrounds you

you no longer lean against the bow
your hock is free
you are free
you are in danger
remember the center

all of you remembers the center

The flight:

you are moving along an invisible track
(you make it yourself)
straight as your spine is straight

you move forward
air whistles past you
you are speeding towards

    you are gathered
    you are pointed
    you are free
    you are in danger

the center
of your eye

YOM KIPPUR: FASTING

The appetite
stirs. On this one day

of the new year
the head becomes light,

without embroideries
of tongue or hand.
Saliva drying, your body
is a transparent cave.

You can see
through the skull into the brain's cavity
You are a harp for whatever wind
God wants to play.

His music sounds sharper. There is no
barrier between his thought and you.

SOUP COOLS FROM THE EDGES FIRST

Here's the only praise
you can give yourself:
words will obey

you if you listen to them, let
patterns emerge. Otherwise,
nothing will come out as well

as you wish it. Except, when eyes
are not watching, there will rise
deep explosions of joy

from the middle of the earth,
in the dark, mind you,
where the heat still lies.

HOLDING UP THE BRIDGE

The diver under the bay
reports the concrete block
holding up the bridge
is cracked and crumbling.

A narrow road
arches over the water space,
dips towards the shore.
One end of the bridge
goes down on its knees,
Cars and trucks
tumble off like toys.

No.

The diver is lying. Inside
that concrete block
my bones
are holding up the bridge.

Three times the builder tried
without the sacrifice,
three times the bridge
shuddered and collapsed.

And then he knew:
only the bones
of his young wife
could placate the girders.

She came, bringing his lunch, singing,
the birds warned her:
that was at Arta,
hundreds of years ago.

A QUESTIONNAIRE

Describe your early education.

At six, standing on the low stone wall
beside my grandfather, I was taller than he.
Wearing my white beret, hair cut short,
with leather leggings to my knee, I put my hand
on his shoulder possessively
and sang him his lullaby, a *moloch veynt*,
an angel weeps, an angel weeps.

What is your permanent address.

A flat rock in Central Park
where an innocent policeman
found me with my first sweetheart.
Under Cambridge clocks chiming each quarter hour.
Beside the sea.
Beneath Mount Zion.
On Boston's broad Victorian bosom.
Across the pond where you are standing, laughing at me

Male or female.

Both. When I saw the Greek Hermaphrodite
I recognized myself and you, each
two in one. Now I know why
the Masai warriors grow brave
by drinking blood and milk.

Are you married.

Yes, many times.
I marry my first loves
over and over. Like coming home.

Describe a crucial event in your life.

At twenty, I died and was born again. For a while
I died every day. One day when I was dying
beside the sea, which ignored me,
when my guts ran empty and I started sinking
into that bottomless hollow
beneath the bed, I suddenly heard
(through the window, in my head)
the notes of the *Appassionata*
calling me back into the world.

List your awards and honors.

Three children.
One, a yellow tearose.
Two, a winedark peony.
Three, a young fox, heart's desire.

Give a brief statement of your plans.

To fly.
To swim across the pond,
To tell what I know,
To love you harder.

HUMAN GEOGRAPHY

SEVEN VARIATIONS FOR ROBERT SCHUMANN

1.
I want to explain about the broken finger.
It is all appetite.

Voracious, exuberant, world-
devouring appetite.

When I was five
they found me at dawn beside the piano
playing chords and weeping.
Even when they boxed my ears
for putting a thumb on a black key
it did not diminish my appetite.

I used to place the music
upside-down on the music stand
and laugh at the strange intertwinings
like upside-down palaces
reflected in the canals of Venice.
The notes stare at you
with strange eyes—eyes of
basilisks flowers peacocks maidens.

At twenty, determined to be a virtuoso,
I knew I must risk stretching myself
to the snapping point.

I made a pulley to strengthen
and stretch my hand.

The pulley held one finger up
while the rest played.
I heard the finger snap. I thought
the pain would make me faint. Vertigo.
A crippled pianist.

Who will attempt to reassemble the burst bud?

2.
My mother called music The Breadless Art.

It was my ring finger.

Little Clara, fifteen, eyes enormous
in her delicate face,
played Hummel for me. It was as though
champagne flowed from her fingers. She stroked
my hand, told me not to drink too much beer,
not to turn day into night,
and to write to her.

I write letters of the alphabet
only under compulsion:
I find my real language
in sonatas and symphonies.

She is my hands. My A-major.

I'll fill a balloon with my thoughts
and send it by a kind wind: I'll harness
the butterflies
to dance my two-sided soul to her.

And Clara in answer
will play my new Etudes, saying
she knows no other way
of showing me her inmost heart.
She dares not do it in secret
so she does it in public.

A kiss on the stairway.
A blue dress.

3.
I had a dream of walking beside a deep pool,
I threw my ring into it,
I longed to fling myself in too.

The need to write is so great,
if I were on a lonely island
in the middle of the sea,
I couldn't stop.

When I published my Opus One,
I felt as proud as the Doge of Venice
when he married the sea—
I now for the first time
married the whole World.

When I wrote my Spring Symphony
my state was like a young mother
who has just been delivered—
light and happy
yet sick and sore.

Clara—now woman, wife, mother, mine—
finds me sometimes very grave.
But I do not allow her to watch me
or practice her piano
when I am composing.

4.
There is a ringing a kettledrumming a trumpeting
inside my head. Heights beckon me,
they want me to jump,
Sharp knives terrify me, death is on every side.

Only at night, shored against Clara's sweet body,
now full with our third child,
does the raft stop rocking.

5.
Silence.

I cannot lift my arm
to conduct. The players before me
seem far away.
I see them
through veils and dim windows.
Their instruments
are crumbling to dust
like old newspapers.

In Venice they asked Clara, after her concert
"And is your husband, too, musical?"

I hear one note constantly in my head,
one single merciless note,
tuned to A.

They told me a young man had come to call.
Thin, shy, he sat down to play for me,
At once I knew—a genius, a young eagle.
I called Clara to come and hear him.
This is Johannes, I said,
he is the one
I have been waiting for.

Clara is pregnant with our eighth.

6.
The single note is opening like a flower,
a melody of petals in E-flat major
whispered to me by Mendelssohn, Schubert,
they want me to write It down,
no,
the angelic voices
now have the faces of tigers, hyenas
who want me dead, who want me dead—

It is raining, it is Carnival,
the ring finger, the ring, I must
throw it into the Rhine, I am sinking beneath
the green mystery, I hear
the secret music.

7.
Locked in this safe place
I sit in the cool garden
making lists
of German towns and cities.

It is two years
since I have seen my Clara.

It is hard
to move my tongue. Or hands.
But now she is sitting beside me and she
is lovely. I would like
to give her a flower. Or a butterfly

Brahms is standing behind her.
She is pouring me a glass of wine
and offers it, her hand shaking.
A few drops of wine
spill on her hand.
I lick the drops from her fingers.

BUBBA ESTHER, 1888

She was still upset,
she wanted to tell me,
she kept remembering
his terrible hands:

how she came, a young girl
of seventeen, a freckled
fairskinned Jew from Kovno
to Hamburg with her uncle
and stayed in an old house
and waited while he bought
the steamship tickets
so they could sail to America

and how he came into her room
sat down on the bed, touched
her waist, took her by the
breast, said for a kiss
she could have her ticket,
her skirts were rumpled, her
petticoat torn, his teeth were
broken, his breath full of
onions, she was ashamed

still ashamed, lying
eighty years later
in the hospital bed,
trying to tell me,
trembling, weeping with anger

MY GREATGREATUNCLE THE ARCHBISHOP

The cossacks snatched him from his mother
at the age of five
to serve in the Tsar's army.

He was farmed with a family
who found him so docile, so bright
they forced him to enter the church.

One day he passed through the shtetl
where he was born Borisov,
and he heard the sound of a melody,

mournful and familiar.
It haunted him, why was he so shaken by it?
He grew up and became an archbishop.

In the middle of a foursquare
Gregorian chant
he wept to remember

the old Hassidic notes:
di-dona-di, di-dona-di.
They drew him back, back to Borisov,

to the house of his kidnapping.
I am the brother of Yitzie Orkos, he said,
I have heard of my nephew, Yankev Leyb

(that was my grandfather),
he too wants to be enlightened, he has
secretly taught himself Russian,

let me take him, let me educate him;
I have no children of my own.
But they refused,

they denied him,
they were afraid.
It was the time of pogroms.

What was a Russian Orthodox archbishop
doing in their Jewish house?
They sent him away.

MARIA OLT

On a hillside in Jerusalem
under the hammer sun, she lifts

a little carob tree, the tree of John
the Baptist, and sets it

into its hole. Solid as a house,
she is called Righteous, a Christian

who hid Jews in Hungary. Her hair clings
around her broad face as she bends

with the hoe, carefully heaping the soil
around the roots. She builds a rim of dirt

on the downhill side and pours water from
the heavy bucket. She waits until the earth

sucks the water up, then pours again
with a slow wrist. The Workmen

sent to help her, stand aside, helpless.
She straightens up. Her eyes are wet.

Tears come to her easily.
The small Jewish woman she saved

stands beside her, dryeyed.
Thirtyfive years ago, as they watched

the death train pass, faces and hands
silent between the slats, the girl

had cried, I want to go with them!
No, said Maria. you must understand,

if you go, I will go with you.

THE LANGUAGE OF HILLS

The slope of that hill
is saying something to me,
something diagonal, stony as music

What is it saying?

Horse.

A bony horse
is grazing on its lip,
white bones on tufted brown.

Does it say *sheep*?

Sheep like stones? No,
but a shepherd moves restlessly
across its haunch.

It says something else;

Weight.
Sky.
It hoists an old city on its spine.

Now I hear:

Trash spills down its shoulder,
bullets, blood,
kicking up the tan dust.

I stumble among the stones,
hearing
footsteps.

THE GRILLED WINDOW, JERUSALEM

Beyond the grilled window:
yellow suns on a bush,
churchly cypresses, mud, rosy stone,
a tower that talks to angels.

On this side:
books, spoiled paper,
tongueless lectures. Hatshepsut
is finally at peace with her
double sex. The Persian lovers
twine around each other.

Radiance leaks through
the diamond-shaped spaces.

I'm on both sides
preparing
to Walk on the ancient hills.

MEDITERRANEAN

1.
The sun is a gold coin slipping into
an envelope of sea.

2.
The sea is a mouth
that opens at the horizon.

Everything in the sky
falls into her.

3.
She is hungry for the first fruit
of evening.
She draws him into her,
a round harvest.

4.
She is swallowing
an orange.
She is sucking it in
slowly,
whole.

5.
He slips down her throat,
a pocket of fragrance.
His orchards burst open.

6.
Tomorrow he will rise
crescent by crescent
above the dusky hills.

7.
A saffron air washes his absence.

HUMAN GEOGRAPHY

The mother rock is black basalt,
hard, handsome.
Walls are made of it, ancient
synagogues, the house of
Saint Peter's mother-in-law.

Climatic conditions:
a rush of new milk,
brief rains, the slow
grinding of wheat,
disappointments.

Bits of rock fall.
Each passing heel
grinds them. They are whipped
by the *chamsin*, dried
to fecund dust.

From this my children rose.
They were crops, they were trees
They will squeeze
geengold liquor from olives
ripening by the black wall.

WATCHING THE SUN RISE OVER MOUNT ZION

Orange fish are swimming
over the roofs.
The air is tinseled
with scales of gold.
Someone is coming.
All the harps cymbals violins
drums horns cellos
sing
    one blinding note.

The tower is on fire.

It is today.

IN THE COUNTRY OF THE WHITETHROATED SPARROW

IN THE COUNTRY OF THE WHITETHROATED SPARROW

1.
two long calls
and three triplets
from a sky of blueberry blue

        now   now
        it is now   it is now   it is now

on an emerald division of earth
we two have come
to a halfmown field

lying circled with pine
we breathe with a sharp first breath
new hay clover sun on bark

and the whitethroated sparrow
two-thirds through our harvest
cries   now   now   it is

2.
    over the darkening harvest
the sky curves heavy
    with silent birds

we come from a room
    secure in lamplight
where a trio of Schubert

    waterfalls us
into the shaking thunder
    long hands of lightning

reach over the pines
    thrust above the meadow
and weave us garlands

    behind us Schubert sings
over stones glinting through
    great sheets of light, it is now

3.
A million kilovolts eat
the dark. We're inside
an electric gale,
watching the white

bones of trees appear
and disappear. The night
is flying metal,
each piece a radiance

of stones, grass, the pillars
of the porch. The neon
sky cracks on and off,
blowing me like wind

against your mouth,
Where I am struck to ash.

4.
Time is the mountain that watches over the meadow
Circling the loved shape in a wedding dance,
we look for a path in thickets of maidenhair,

assault the pinnacle blazed clean by fire,
stretch our lungs in unaccustomed air,
climb across rocks, streambeds, logs,

past trees in second growth, up granite slabs,
muscles in back and thighs reaching
to take the moment, ratify the day.

Breathless above the stunted trees,
above the tangle looking out towards valleys
of promises, somewhere in the pines

below (but seeming high above), we hear
a voice speak prophecy, the sparrow sings
plainly in sheets of light over the peak

not yet it will be it will be it will be
nudging us gently down, where we must live.
Time is the mountain bending over us.

5.
spaces of sun and shadow
are painted on the grass
again
unlooked for
the season of harvest
in the play of light and morning
your loved shape
moving towards me
through the trees
almost rounding the path
renewed there
coming coming almost
here
the pines dark with longing

6.
a stretto of birdsong:
one cry scissors the air

across the dawn
a crow hones his call

on the granite sky:
two one-notes

echo each other
question and answer

rapid as rain falling:
a cricket adds his bass viol

and the whitethroated spar
hidden in pines

waiting for sun
to zigzag through leaves

lets drop half his song
two long calls and a pause

A PHOENIX

When the embers have fallen away,
she turns towards him—

against all
expectation,

all design,—
holding time

between her breasts.
How does he know

he is being watched?
By the silence?

By a change in the air
behind him?

He thinks something hostile
bristles the hair on his neck,

but it is she
from an empty beach

parting the air
around him.

AFTER

The sand was tender,
motherwarm to my feet,

the cleft in the rocks
dazzled my eyes with absence:

the sun pressed down, and the sea
as it rocked in my arms

shamed language
and the language of comfort.

APPLE

Love, on your grave—flat
and strange in the dry grass—
I place a stalk

of red and yellow
everlasting
and prop it
beside your name.

Apple, you called me,
thinking of a girl
round and succulent,
thinking of pink and white
petals blowing their honey
breath over us
that first nuptial summer.

Tomorrow I will bring you
small Rhode Island Greenings,
new red Macintosh
to moisten
your dry sleep.

FOG

SHE *HE*
I come to your shore longing
you don't notice
for the shape the rise of your land
how sunlight sieves
your special rounds and levels
through me you come
but you pull your blanket over your head
a large shape
hoping I will think you
that parts and breaks
all flat all gray
my brooding you are
a separated mist
all troubling

no shore no trees no sky no water
                    waterfall
you pretend that you never
                    all whirlpool
tugged me under your cover
                    you don't see
or drew me down to your contours
                    how I become lost
that you never entered my crevices my
                    in you
long cave and shook me
                    you are final
back to my beginnings
                    I am germinal
you hide from me
                    stop moving
pretending to be blank
                    rest in me
look at me

ROOMS OF THE OCEAN

ROOMS OF THE OCEAN

crossing Tiverton bridge to Aquidneck Island

where the Sakonnet river becomes the sea
a flank of water
stretches pewter to the horizon

the morning sun has sucked the sky white
leaving below a blanched gray disk

under the bridge
the river curves northward,
stained a deep irrational blue

I come to the edge where the island begins

a strip of silver foil
a dagger of ocean
glints just beyond Saint George's tower

SECOND BEACH

once on your edge
in your adolescent embrace
I read my summer hunger

I brought my loves to you
one by one
testing them against

your indifference you
my first love and my last
still hiding your secrets

BISHOP BERKELEY'S ROCK, MIDDLETOWN, R.I.

A natural sphinx—
head and shoulders—
thrusts out of the landscape
and stares at the great bowl of ocean before it:

its jaws, once filled with soft soapstone,
have been pried ajar by time:
                in that maw

where timothy grass grows in puddingstone,
Bishop Berkeley sat, where you and I

are sitting now:
we climbed up, as he did,
through tangles of cat-brier (the long talons
trying to hold us back),
through thickets of blackberry:

we sit in the mouth of the sphinx,
looking down over wild pear trees, wild black cherry
over feathery locust buckthorn, over the half circle
of farm and ocean that makes the world:

the Bishop sat, musing on Reality,
waiting for sails to bring
King George's gold for his Academy:
but the sails never came:

we sit cradled in the lion's jaw,
imagining sails, surveying
the promising false horizon:
behind us dwarf ebony spleenwort

clings to the roof,
blackstemmed fern growing against gravity,
against all nature, nourished by
random drops of rain, reflected light:

beneath us the rock is a palette
of orange and black patches, strange colors in a cave
spiders hold their kingdom here, weaving their traps
from the upper jaw to the lower, undisturbed

YELLOW

the sun lowering through the porch windows
rinses everything I look at with little suns
the metallic skin of the ocean
the western air opening wide
reels me into its yellow mouth
as it swallows the rocker, the book
I am reading, the watery golden panes

PURGATORY CHASM

a deep cleft
in a cliff of puddingstone:
once a stripe of quartz between boulders
cracked open when the sleeping ocean
shifted: the surf
nagged out the rift
splinter by splinter

into this breech
two Puritan lovers leapt
(the legend says),
hand in hopeless hand:
and a suitor jumped across,
dared by his mocking mistress:
black prints in the stone
prove the devil once passed by

now boys and girls climb down
between the lips
to gather rosehips
or sit reading on a steep
shelf in the sun
or stand on a rump of rock

watching the sea
boil in the abyss

THE MOON OVER THE SEA

still brightens the flesh of
lovers, still sets them in
a magic country, still
makes a myth of their brief
gestures: their bodies are
wiser than their minds: they
climb up the ladder of
the moonlight, then let go,
spill themselves into the
buoyant the shining flood

AUGUST STORM

the gulls are
breasting
a southeast gale

the wind holds back
their weight
with its palm

stiff winged
they stand
on the wild air

resting against
the wall of wind
rain

is starting to fall
staining
the waves

slate gray and white
foghorns of autumn
begin

SACHUEST POINT

on this small tongue of land
shaped by the surf
where the Sakonnet river
merges with the sea

a salt water farmer
built his house
two hundred years ago:
his windbeaten meadow

lay covered with timothy
dwarf trees
bent to the blow
steady from the southwest:

here on the lip
of the continent
his neighbors were wind and stars
birds and field mice

***

generations
passed across his fields:
in nineteen fortyone

the warring world
made this spit of earth
a target base

soldiers drove their trucks
over the timothy
piled cement blocks

strung barbed wire
across the rocks and grass:
but we climbed

around the beach
slipped past
the target range

and swam in our secret cove
naked
to the sound of guns

***

after thirtyfive years
fat shadows of owls

glide over the meadow
over crumbled cement,

over shards of glass:
flocks of scoters

ducks geese
rest in the coves

dancing the cadence
of their long migrations

their bed
of spindrift

moves with the pulse
of the open ocean:

the farmhouse stands
blind

its face turned
to the sea wind

A VEIL FELL JUST NOW

between me and the white ocean

one of the shutters of evening is closing

the blind hands of tides
are feeling their way
below the cliffs and mountains
beneath the forest of water among
the weeds and eyeless fish
along twilight canyons to the

underside of light

DECEMBER SUNSET

the room is blinded with sunlight
burning silver foil pingpongs off
the ocean the sun already
past its zenith the surf busy
flooding and unflooding the curved

beach the north wind catches the spray
and hurls it towards the open fetch
of sea my sun about to set
but first I'll send fingers of light
to outline the clouds caress the
firepool over its basalt bed

THE BEACH IN WINTER

in this round gray February afternoon
a dish of silver tilts into my lap

along the edge
I trace the stiff

white lace
where spindrift

lifted up
and froze

THE LIGHT THE FACE GIVES OFF

your aura
when the sun bounces against you
gives me back a sea of flints

even under the shadow
of dwindling boulders
you fling me shimmering nets

without the sun
without the white relief
of your breaking

in night's unclosing eye
I know your face is gathering
is gathering its light again

SINGING

1.
three spears of sunlight
lay across the floor

each stream of pointed brass
pierced her throat

2.
she built a tower with her voice

it grew upward
until flocks of chimney swifts
flew in and out of its arches

3.
twelve sandpipers
skittered behind the long lip
of the tide,
peeked at the seaweed:

then skittered back
up the beach
legs trilling
just beyond the wave's bite

4.
sailors rose through her voice
from their drowned boats
drifting up
through the sharp blue of her throat

5.
a chorus of gulls
turned and wheeled
over the full-lunged sea:

the sea sang
basso profundo

it had no doors

6.
they sang together:

she moved
breast first
across the curve of the globe

she arched over
the hidden geography
of the ocean floor

she sailed across
its peaks and resonant valleys

singing

LAUGHING GAS

New Poems

CONTENTS

I

Eightythree
Seven Stones
The Promise
The Awakening
Falling, 1924
Anna Pavlova
Writing in the Dark
Fool's Thread
Clara Schumann
The Meow Woman, Thailand
Uncle Harry at the La Brea Tar Pits

II

The Drowned Mountain
1. The Mountain
2. Sachuest Beach, 1941
3. The Wedding
4. Basic Training, 1942
5. Coming Home During the Second World War
6. The Young Scholar, 1952
7. The Shepherd
8. Sunion
9. The Ruins of Tiryns
10. The Divorce
11. The Minuet
12. The Drowned Mountain
13. Snow
14. The Mating

III

Cruelty
Messengers
Cracow
Losing a City
A Gesture
In the Jerusalem Bakery
In Nazareth
Foreign Tongues
Net, Lake, Sieve
An August Morning
Chamber Music in Early December
Your Call
Word as Window
Cold
Old Love
In a Mirror

I.

EIGHTYTHREE

My mother sits on a towel
on the toilet seat. I dip a cloth
into lukewarm suds and wash her face and neck,
her dry, crevassed neck.

She says, "Sometimes I feel as dark and alone
as before I was born."

I wash her arms, her elbows, the crooks of her elbows
her underarms.

"That feels good." she says.

I wash her back round and fleshy, the tired
breasts, her belly broad and generous as an old
Renoir. I wash her buttocks, those large apples.
so like my own.

She says, "I'm no good for anybody.
not even for myself."

I wash her thighs and knees, her gnarled toes,
pat her dry, rub her all over with oil.

She says, "Am I your baby?"

SEVEN STONES

for MHB (1896–1982)

1.
She is not sitting in her chair
not standing at the window
not playing Chopin on the piano
as she did every evening
when I was eleven.

I danced to please her,
awkwardly, but she believed
that I was Pavlova
and that we were both
immortal.

2.
She was afraid of thunderstorms.
When she was a child,
worrying at the window
for her absent mother
who never returned,
weather stabbed all around her.

3.
A garden house
in a deserted resort. New Jersey, 1930.
My mother. young and darkhaired,
reads a story to my little brother and me
about a frog and his transformation
into a man.
Later I see her crying
among the lattices of the summer house

4.
The hurricane of 1954.
I lead her to the back of the house
Pretending she must wash
my baby's diapers,
afraid she will see
the wind breaking the trees
the murderous ocean
flogging our front windows.

5.
In the shtetl in Russia
everyone knew
death has no reflection.
Her ancestors
covered their mirrors with sheets,
left little stones on the grave,
for remembrance.

6.
I look in my mirror and see her
with bobbed hair and bangs
in a slim long skirt, faintly
smiling. proud and frightened,
holding me, her firstborn, in her arms.

7.
She comes into the room
wearing a blue and white striped blouse,
her dark hair soft around her face.
I think: I must introduce her
to this assortment of shadowy friends
and I hear myself saying, "This is Martha"
as she speaks to me,
some special advice,
some knowledge that will surely untangle
the knot of my life. Her words
are a round breath, a gift of petals.
but I can't catch them, I can't hear her.

THE PROMISE

Last night I found her
waiting alone
in the middle of the lobby
in a strange hotel,
wearing the brown coat
I keep folded in my closet.

She was standing
like a child
lost in a department store,
ready for tears, frightened,
and I threw my arms around her
and held her to me, saying

You will never be lost!
You will always be found!

Waking, I knew my promise
defied the gray ashes

already dissolving in earth,
the late summer cricket
singing, losing its strength,
waiting for me on my doorstep.

Winter is coming. I hoard
the warmth of the sun on my face,
the caress of the ocean
as my aging body
cuts through the water
and comes out shining with salt

and the warmth of motion,
and I swear to her,
as long as I breathe,
whether or not she waits
on my doorstep of sleep,
she will always be found.

THE AWAKENING

An angry horse is facing me,
coming straight at me, eyes wild, the long nose
distorted. On his saddle sits a woman
sprawled backward, her arm lifted in terror
as the stallion gallops out of the frame.

I stared at the scene
in the half-dark of my mother's room,
unable to sleep, sure if I closed my eyes
the crazed horse would burst
out at me through the glass.

A French etching: *Le Lever*.
The horse's head the lifted arm of a servant

standing at the foot of her mistress' bed;
the horse's eye her eye in profile
looking back at her mistress.

She is pulling back the curtain to disclose
a half-clad woman beginning to rise,
her breasts exposed, not knowing her bed
is the back of a horse. By her side
a lover kneels, kissing her hand.

She is reluctant to wake. If I squint my eyes
slightly, I can see the wild horse.

FALLING, 1924

Steep marble steps in an old hall.
My brown wicker perambulator
hangs on the top step,
back wheel slipping at the edge,
front wheels dangling in space.

Engine stalled. Motionless. Until

ass over elbow in a whirr of
blankets, knitted booties. pillows,
a smothering hat,—
                    brown wicker
shoots past me.

            A rocket
of birds bursts from the trees,
scatters over the sky
in long spurts of motion
as I fall through the marble air.

ANNA PAVLOVA

for my daughter Rachel

Prepare my swan costume.
—Anna Pavlova's last words

1.
I'm old,
almost fifty,
but can still dance the swan.

Without the swan
there is no Pavlova.

2.
On the way to the Marinsky theater
her mother said, "You are about to enter
fairyland."

She was eight years old.

She watched the princess dance the sleeping beauty.
She held her breath.

3.
At twelve
She learned to keep
the middle and little fingers
of each hand extended.
her right hand a mirror copy
of her left.

At sixteen she danced Giselle.
her gauze wings
lifting her from the ground.
The audience stood and cheered.
threw roses. bouquets, wreaths.

4.
My hands are not beautiful,
the fingers a little too thick.

But my ankles are strong,
my arch high.
and have toes of steel.

When I stand on one toe
the sole of my foot
is an absolute vertical.

The flame spurts up through my feet,
out through the tips of my fingers.

5.
An admirer sent her
a pair of swans.

Jack is her favorite.

His large warm
feathery body
sits in her lap,
his neck curved around
her neck.

Strong Jack,
he could flatten a grown man
with one blow of his wing.

He came to her wild,
flew chest first into a chimney.
and broke it into pieces.

When they found him, twenty miles away
on a strange lake,

they brought him back
and she clipped his savage wings.

6.
I want to be a feather
carried on the least wind,
poised on a breath,
my head proud on my long neck
my body light, arched,
a whisper of motion.

7.
Arms folded over my breasts,
I float across the stage.
At the brink,
wings outstretched,
I reach towards the horizon,
ready at any moment
to fly.

WRITING IN THE DARK

In her sick bed, in the dark, she laboriously made words on scraps of paper.

—David Porter, *The Modem Idiom*, speaking of
Emily Dickinson

Across the old quilt
my hand gropes
for the stub of pencil.

Blindfolded, I feel my way
over the scraps of islands
I've sewn together:

the old checked tablecloth,
mama's blue dimity,
my gingham pinafore.

I know my life by feel.
Ah, here it is:
my paintbrush, my wand,

my sword. They think
I'm singing the old hymns.
They don't know

how with one stroke
I cut through the fiery bandage
that films my sight

and run through the garden—
my old enemy, the zero,
snapping at my heel.

FOOL'S THREAD

She sews with thread too long for comfort,
out of laziness. impatience, eagerness

to get the task done. Often the thread
swirls and gnarls tight as a spring.

knotting back on itself. Quick at unraveling
tangles. she frees the needle for seam or button

or hem. She refuses to use a thimble.
Her finger keeps the prick mark for days,

but she is proud to confront the chore
without disguise, naked, face to face.

She pulls the optimistic needle through the cloth
while the long tail of the thread

follows snarling behind.

CLARA SCHUMANN

Along the rocky path in the pine woods,
away from the city and her testy father,
she walked behind Robert,
holding the tail of his coat lightly
so as not to disturb him.

Each time he came to a rock
she tugged at his coat,
a playful warning
to keep him from tripping.

I do not want horses or diamonds,
she wrote, but I wish to lead a life
free from care: I am happy
in possessing you, but I shall be
unhappy if I cannot work at my art.
You will need quiet for your composing.
Children will come.
Am I now to bury
my own music?

He strolled, lost in his thoughts,
gazing at birds freckling the sky,
noting the clouds' notations,
while she stumbled across
the rock she had warned him against.

THE MEOW WOMAN, THAILAND

after a photograph by Walter Kaufmann

The brightness in her eyes
comes from a light inside her,
something she is remembering.

An old safety pin
strains her jacket
across her ancient breasts.

Her nose is like my Slavic grandmothers,
flared at the nostrils,
flat and passionate.

Her stubby fingers, like my grandmothers
and like my father's and mine.
are blue and translucent.

She smiles, crinkling up
her wrinkled leather face.
She knows me.

UNCLE HARRY AT THE LA BREA TAR PITS

Against the iron fence surrounding pools
of black asphalt bubbling and boiling up
through geologic layers; against the fence
where this hot tar surprised and swallowed
families of mastodons forty thousand years ago
(their bones now tangled with birds, camels, antelopes,
hundreds of dire wolves and dinosaurs);
where, nine thousand years ago, a young
woman came stumbling across the treeless plain
of Los Angeles, and slipped or was hurled

by a jealous lover into the sticky black lake—
Uncle Harry poses in a jaunty fedora,
his elegant profile turned toward the camera.

> He says, life has cheated me.
> When they shipped me to America
> in 1907, I lost my friends
> and I lost the Russian theaters
> where I stayed every night
> until one or two in the morning,
> adoring the actors.
>
> A childish prank ruined me.
>
> I was the smallest of the gang,
> so they hoisted me up
> to hang a black cloth
> over the Tsar's double eagles
> in front of the prison
> while sailors from the Potemkin
> were rioting in the streets.
> Cossacks were clubbing Jews
> left and right. I saw a woman
> running with a baby carriage
> in front of the horses' hooves.
>
> My father said it was Siberia for me,
> or America. I boarded a broken-down
> ship in Leeds, bound for Boston.
>
> Later I wandered here,
> still an exile,
> to Elysian Park in Los Angeles.

The feather on his hat is motheaten,
his coat torn and stained.

but he has turned his plucky collar up
like an unemployed actor from Odessa
who knows he is still handsome.
He is ninetythree.

Behind him a lifelike mastodon
made of plaster and acrylic
lifts her tusks in terror
as she struggles half-submerged in tar,
While her mammoth baby
hesitates behind her
on the edge of the black museum.

II.

THE DROWNED MOUNTAIN

for C.U.W. (1916–1979)

1. The Mountain

A meadow in Vermont, on Bread Loaf Mountain.
I watched you walk with a dancer's quick walk
along the path on the edge of the meadow.
Your shoulders were bent like a scholar's
but your legs were the legs of a dancer.
Your jacket, thick for a hot summer morning,

hiked up on your shoulders. It was the morning
after we spent all night on the mountain
talking in the innocent moonlight, dancing
on the grass. Not wanting me to walk
on the wet ground, you carried me in your scholars
arms, home at dawn across the meadow.

Smelling of hay and clover from the meadow,
I woke late that August morning
and found you waiting for me, a grave scholar
who knew a mossy cradle on the mountain.
We lay there in the wood. Not a creature walked
by us. Half undressed, learning the dance
of darkness, beside our cooling beer, you danced
hesitantly, as you did in the meadow.
I knew then I would never walk
back without stealing your morning,
without dancing down the mountain
with you, my poet, my curly-headed scholar.

The summer virgin captured the grave scholar.
reluctant or not, and we both danced the dance
of darkness, thigh to thigh on the mountain.
In the full moonlight, back across the meadow,
we found a barn where we could stay till morning
When the sun was high, triumphantly we walked

back to the ordinary world, where poets walk
and talk in the stilted language of scholars.
But we had learned the dialect of morning;
we had made the star of Venus dance
like a burst of meteors over the meadow,
a wedding beyond time on the mountain.

2. Sachuest Beach, 1941
A smell of salt and wild roses all over the island,
red and white roses, the colors of paradise.

We lay, wrapped in one blanket, under the puddingstone
rocks
on the West end of the beach. The waves came in
slanting

while your mother bent over the fire charcoaling
hot dogs and hamburgers for the others. But we

were oblivious, drunk on salt air, kisses, our own
salt sweat.
You were twenty-four, I was nineteen. When everyone
left,

the moon rose over the phosphorescent water, a ribbon
of gold
that moved with us as We swam. Bubbles of fire

exploded around our shoulders, between our thighs.
We rose together. Mermaid. Merman.

3. The Wedding

In your best friend's car with a borrowed ten dollars
we eloped to Newport, singing over and over
the trial by fire and water from The Magic Flute.
My father cursed us over the phone and threatened
to sit shiva for me as though I were dead.
Your mother howled in the backyard, crying
that you were still a child. My childhood lover
pursued us with a gun. My mother forgave us.

In the morning you sat writing a composition
for your class, describing love and marriage
in Latin, while I went in search of breakfast.
The streets of Cambridge were glistening,
my heart ready to burst like a ripe peach
with love and terror.

4. Basic Training, 1942

I lay stifling on the sheets
in a rundown rooming house
in Miami Beach;

you, buttoned up in stiff khaki,
    your curly head shaved
        close as a convict's,

were marching a mile away
    with the typewriter brigade:
        artists, actors, musicians.

You were the only poet.
    You held your gun awkwardly
        while the sergeant

barked and snarled at your heels.
    Sunday we swam among the palms
        in an ocean tepid as a bathtub.

Under a sky askew with unfamiliar stars,
    your friends wept on my shoulder
        for their lost music, their wrenched lives

Before I left, I ran along
    beside your platoon, shouting
        Look at the sunset, darling!

and every head turned to see
    the sun collapsing
        behind a bloody horizon.

5. Coming Home During the Second World War
The train from Denver to Chicago,
from Chicago to Boston. Our 4-F friends
were waiting in the Oyster Bar
at South Station. We drank our way

across the street to the Essex Hotel:
giant martinis for twenty-five cents.

At Hayes-Bickford Cafeteria I threw forks
and spoons in celebration across the counter.

When the subway lumbered over
the old Salt and Pepper bridge
to Cambridge, we greeted the river,
shouting Charlie! Charlie!

I crumpled up on my hatbox near the kiosk
in Harvard Square; you dropped my typewriter.
unable to stand any longer,
laughing and crying.

We woke
the next morning in someone's livingroom.
sober and jobless, and went out
into the bright Harvard autumn
where headlines reported the rumor
that Hitler was slaughtering the Jews.

6. The Young Scholar, 1952

In the Athens cemetery
the stones lie crumbled
all around us
the sun blisters
the dust, sears
our young heads
as we crouch reading
the old inscriptions

You stand up
among the marble
portraits of mourning
and tense with joy
raise your hand
in the classic gesture
of stone farewell

7. The Shepherd

In Arcadia,
huddled together on a narrow bed
we conceived a daughter.

I too have dwelt in Arcadia.

I can prove it
by this shepherd's crook
made of olive wood.

Pregnant, I rode donkey back
up the narrow mountain rocks
from Olympia to Bassae,

the temple of Apollo.
An old shepherd
playing his reed pipe

asked us how much money we had
and whether we were millionaires.
You said: We're poor students

traveling on nothing.
He laughed:
All millionaires are liars.

8. Sunion

Sunbathing naked
on the rocks at Sunion
we vowed eternal marriage:

the stern temple,
inscribed with Byron's name,
our only witness.

Doubt
lurked like the octopus
under the rock,

a dark shadow
holding back
under the cliff.

9. The Ruins of Tiryns
High on the peloponnesus of sleep
a stone arch leads nowhere.

Broken stairs.

Where our bodies once touched and turned
rain gathers in gullies.

Sheep huddle in the gallery,
polishing the wall
with their fleecy sides,
avoiding that same wind
that tore
our mycenaean eyes.

A path slants down to a hidden spring:
to be used only in times of siege.

10. The Divorce
I see your harlot
wearing a black velvet
dress from my closet.

A little play,
You smile, no harm:
a salute to youth, a trifling addition

to your stable of admirers.
You have no permission, I scream,
take that off, it's mine, it's mine,

as you and she turn
and continue walking away.
Why did you come from the grave

into my dream
with your smile, your terrible charm,
unreachable as ever, alive
or dead?

11. The Minuet
As you lie dying I come into the room
where your second wife and your new mistress
are standing by the bed.

You smile at me like an angel, hold out your hand,
take mine, and cover it with kisses.
Then you stop, look at my new wedding ring,

and bowing your head on my hand, begin to weep.
I draw my hand away, and like a partner
in a minuet, move aside as your mistress

takes my place beside the bed.
The nurse comes in to adjust the plastic bottles.
She looks at the three of us and says:

You have many friends.

No, your wife says, wives.

12. The Drowned Mountain
On the lake of our childhood, the lake
shaped like the Caspian Sea,

shadowed by dark Vermont pines,
we drift in a canoe,
you and I and the boy you were.

He slips naked into the water
and you laugh and say, A Greek god!

And then we notice, under the water, under
our keel, a black shape appears
beneath the surface, the shoulder
of a lost continent, a drowned mountain.

Its rocky flanks spread far beyond
where we can see
as we paddle over its secret crevices,
its sunless peak.

The boy swims away and clambers up
on the darkening shore.

I hide from you among the pines.
A silver belt, your wedding gift,
glints around my waist.

You plunge beneath the surface
while the empty canoe drifts away,
your white heel
flashing among the ripples, your white heel
slipping through the sheets.

13. Snow
The sky flat and heavy like old
pewter; the ocean a twin of the sky,
dark gray, like the goblets they sold
to us one day in a Newport junkshop. Why
do I keep talking to you, my
love more sharp to me each year?

The winter's first morning of snow.
The steps of the house, cars hissing on the road
become muffled and still, like your breath.
Slowly the white padding grows
deep, deeper. Has your death
muffled my old rage and fear, the weather
that kept us apart? Together
we drank wine from those goblets, poor
and young.

I hardly remember winter here.
Wasn't it always an afternoon in summer.
the sailboats racing on Narragansett Bay.
picnics at Sachuest Point, the saltwater farm
where we heard gunfire practice every day?

Now you are lying under a hill
close beside Bishop Berkeley's chapel
where an eighteenth-century squire and his bride
sleep on their sarcophagus side by side after two
centuries. sculptured in stone, arm in arm
under the snow.

14. The Mating

I cross the brook
and walk up the hill towards your grave.
A humming fills the air,
a giant motor buzzing among the trees.

Is it the grass growing?
The dead murmuring?

At the crest where you lie
I see in the trees above you, along the edge
of the mausoleum, the air dense with bees
humming loudly, swarming and darting.

The queen is pirouetting with her mate,
performing her act of darkness
under the noon sun.

All our cruelties and denials
all structures of power and frustration
fall like pollen
through the early summer air,
and the simple truth appears:

a wedding, a hint of honey
in the lion's mouth.

III.

CRUELTY

This human wind spoils everything
it grazes over, leaving spittle on the floor,

on table tops, pages of books. Rolls
salty hot fog across the bay into

this room. Keeps forcing its damp breath
into my ear, an insistent junta of a wind.

It brings poison from Chernobyl, blight
from our tattered ozone. It insults

the wounded ocean, already scarred with oil,
mimicking its primal essence. It is

without mercy, like the boy carrying
his mother's heart to the sorcerer—

heedless, inexorable—who doesn't hear the heart
cry "Watch out!" as he stumbles through the woods.

MESSENGERS

In my town near the ocean
at nine in the evening
I turn into my driveway
and a baby rabbit
slips from the hedge,
runs across the lawn,
small as a dandelion
in the evening light.

In the morning
by the backdoor spigot
a two-inch toad
hops from a stone
in the salty air:

in this familiar landscape,
anachronistic, doomed,
are they telling me
the newborn will survive,
the young will keep replacing
the persistent dead.

CRACOW

The wizened man in the Jerusalem market cried,
Don't buy a dead fish, buy a live one!
A lebedike: es schvimt, es shpringt, es tantst!
Flapping his arms to show how the live fish
swims, leaps, dances.
We laughed and said, yes, a live one.

He dipped his net into a tub
and brought out a sparkling bewhiskered old man
flopping and gasping. It sprang to the floor,
unwilling to die.
Laughing, he held an ice cube
to the O of its mouth; then holding it down
on his cutting board,
he struck its head with a mallet
and cut it into steaks.

The fish was all bones,
flat and tasteless,
no matter how I cooked it.

Death, too, is a kind of resistance.

LOSING A CITY

The alleys behind the old Jewish market
twist around each other, some paved with
Jerusalem stone, some merely a dirt path for donkeys
others opening into a sunny white courtyard:
The flash of an orange tree. A box of geraniums.
A gate. A bench. A latticed window.
A few hens scratching in the rubbish.

The phantom pain of a severed limb.

Spiny hills, bitter and inexorable,
sting my feet with absence. Vanished walls,
austere behind the blandishment of roses,
rebuild themselves each night between me
and my exile. I wake, holding my arms
around lineaments that aren't there.

When can I turn the key of my privation
and open a door
into a valley
with olive trees and real brambles.

A GESTURE

The woman clasping her arms around the bearded man's
neck
and leaning on him
is his mother

his two teenage girls stand apart
stroking their long hair,
his teenage boys, each wearing
a yarmulke and a plaid jacket
punch each other half-heartedly
his wife stands aside, embarrassed but docile
her pretty legs in plain oxfords

but the mother the mother
something about her skirt
her short grayblack hair
her old belted sweater
speaks of Europe, war, deprivation
she is whispering to him
kissing his cheeks he is going away
he is going away
and she has had enough of separation

IN THE JERUSALEM BAKERY

The middle-aged woman
in the Jerusalem bakery
gives me warm honey cakes,

braided challahs, small
triangular pockets
filled with cheese and spinach,
crescent-shaped cookies.

She wears a faded dress and over it
a stained white baker's apron.
I see the numbers on her arm.
I try to enter the sadness in her eyes,
in the midst of this sugar,
this cheerful yeast, crumbly pastry.

I greet her, shalom, and hand the coins to her
as she stuffs the separate packages
into my net shopping bag. Our hands
touch, our eyes meet, she almost smiles.

IN NAZARETH

The Arab poet had written, *Little girl,*
do not come near the perilous outposts,
watch out for the barbed fence . . .

Marked as his enemy, I arrived at the hall
where he and I were to read our poems together.
A small whitehaired man
held out both arms as though to embrace me
saying, come, let them take your picture
standing beside me.

In a country where signs in every bus
warn the traveler: BEWARE OF UNMARKED PACKAGES
where we wait for an hour on Nablus Road
while robot sappers dismantle the bomb;
where police stop every Arab, friendly or not,
demanding to see his papers,

there is every shade of hate, friendship,
shame.

I'm ashamed of my fear.

Later our picture appears in his magazine,
Arab and Jew side by side,
arms linked across the barbed wire fence
in his poem. The picture is
dim on cheap paper, surrounded by
the words of a veiled language.

FOREIGN TONGUES

We sit around the table
in a Jerusalem suburb,
the bearded Russian painter,
his gentle pear-hipped wife,
and the new cousin from Odessa
with the melancholy eyes.

Each speaks his own language,
Russian Yiddish Hebrew English:

we dip our tongues hesitantly
into each other's words:
yes lo kum aher panamai
we admire the view, complain about
shadowless light on biblical hills.

A double echo of voice and stars
arches over our syllables

and for a moment
we are standing together

at the siege of Leningrad,
the blood from our wounds
turning to red icicles
on the snow.

NET, LAKE, SIEVE

for my students

Here are these mirrors,
one broken, one framed in red,
and three in neat little boxes
that hinge open.

Look at yourselves for one minute.

While you look,
cells are sloughing off,
atoms are multiplying,
the light is changing.

You with your sweet hair
clinging about your face;
you with your loving black eyes;
and you, who have dared
to reveal yourself to me,

look, look hard
into the brittle lake
of our morning.
Only the eye of the mind
can record us whole.

AN AUGUST MORNING

Motionless.
The pines arrested against a wall of sky:
each needle, blade, branch (smelling green
after last night's rain) stops, breath held.

Over this same meadow we have seen
storms flying, lightning, hot winds,
niagaras of birds. But now the season is stilled

Reversed. As, for the moment, we cease to age.

CHAMBER MUSIC IN EARLY DECEMBER

A cold Sunday morning in early December.
The first snow. All night long the sky
hung heavy with a locked-in gathering flood.
Then at dawn the first snow came.

The first snow. Looking at the sky,
Rachel, who lives twenty blocks away,
sees at dawn the first snow come,
drawing a veil between her house and mine.

Rachel, who lives twenty blocks away
with her cat, her violets, her ballet shoes,
draws a veil between her house and mine.
She unfurls the tender petals of her life

with her cat, her violets, her ballet shoes.
She bakes bread, warming away the snow,
unfurling the tender petals of her life.
Leda returns home from the masquerade,

warm as new-baked bread, despite the snow,
all curves and roses, possible with love.
Leda comes home from the masquerade.
breasts round with soft witchcraft.

curved and rosy, possible with love.
returning as the wheel of seasons turns.
Round with soft witchcraft.
fingers of sun touch our window.

Turning as the wheel of seasons turns.
aging in bed, we come together in hunger.
Fingers of sun touch our window:
We start to Perform our feast, our chamber music.

Aging in bed, we come together in hunger,
heavy with a locked-in gathering flood.
We start to perform our feast, our chamber music
A cold Sunday morning in early December.

YOUR CALL

All morning the meagre snow kept falling,
barely whitening the street:

at the window waiting for the soup to boil
I watched a dry leaf pulling on its stalk

and thought how the heart must teach itself to starve—
when your voice—like fire from a star—

burst through the kitchen telephone
and I saw light, sunlight on the branches

as I took you in. Beyond the window
in the empty bushes a sudden bird

wore passionate black and white markings
and a small red crown.

WORD AS WINDOW

I'm looking for the word that will window
your mysterious music, the lovemusic

of Mozart, full of loss, and despite the angry
pain in his belly, hopeful. The music asks

what is so delicate, desirable
as your mouth, your feet, your soft luxurious

shoulder and side, warming my terror at night
And answers: although flesh will dissolve,

here is the courage to remember; to accept
every stab of memory,—your music

radiating in severe silver streams
through my window, the word merely

the opening. To unlatch.

COLD

Suddenly she wants soft blankets, hot cereal,
tapioca. The damp chill in her spine
ignores the layers of wool she piles on herself
like a poultice.
            Where is the child
who couldn't tell hot from cold; the adolescent
who cavorted naked in front of winter windows;
the nineteen-year-old bride wading in November

in the heedless ocean; the hungry woman
coupling with her lover under autumn hedges?

They are all here, huddled with her under
the comforting quilt, trying to show her how
the heat of the mind can ease the body's ice.

OLD LOVE

Familiar, the face you now see
when you look at me belongs to
the young woman perched thirty-five
years ago on the arm of a
sofa, swinging her shapely leg,
wearing a skirt the color of
sunrise. The face is unlined, the
hair long, black, swept into a bun
or braided into a regal
crown. You don't see the cropped gray hair,
the thickened waist or the wrinkled
skin. And I look at you and see
the slender bridegroom pausing at
the door, searching the room, his hair
falling over his eyes, the eyes
bright, hopeful, caressing: you lift
me up and we slide into each
other, young and old, wrinkled, smooth,
like Mozart's Adagio, *con*
amore, tender, heartbreaking.

IN A MIRROR

Sometimes I can see the old woman
in the child, the child in the woman,
a game I play, traveling

in a plane or train, imagining
the businessman next to me a toddler
in diapers, or that mischievous redheaded
infant a woman of forty.

My ages, stacked behind me, blow past
like cards in a hurricane:
the blackeyed four-year-old
with a ball in her dimpled fist;
the fourteen-year-old bathing beauty
with barely defined curves.

But who is this Woman in my mirror?
Who is this interloper?
Looking more closely, I recognize
the dark eyes and the high cheekbones,
echoing those ancestors
ravished by the Mongols on the Russian
steppes. In the end it's the bones
that tell who you have been.

ATLANTIC LIGHT

CONTENTS

Statistics

- Statistics
- The Behavior of Birds
- Exile: Jerusalem
- Pablo Casals in Jerusalem
- Jerusalem Dawn
- Hearing a Mozart Duo at 36,000 Feet
- Ramesses' Toothache
- The Army Hospital, 1942
- January 1, 1953
- Moment of Ascent
- The Postponement

The Lost Silver

- The Swim, 1936
- The Lost Silver

Atlantic Light

- Atlantic Light
- Touch
- Little Aubade
- First Knowledge, the Smell of a Plum
- An Education, Buffalo, N.Y., 1933
- Crocheting
- Flight
- Visitation
- U-Haul
- Time Capsule
- The Skater's Waltz
- My Father's Dream
- The Accident, 1901

Conversation with Dust
Tashlik

STATISTICS

STATISTICS

History is too clean.
It wipes away the blood,
claps a rational hand
over the mouth
of a screaming girl.
It speaks in numbers.

It says 263 air raids
instead of her demolished house
it says 22 missiles
instead of her splintered bones
it says 400,000 troops
instead of her torn city.

Persephone is dragged
under the earth again and again.
But her mother Demeter
lives in the seed. She knows,
even while she weeps,
the earth will turn,

the world will reel forward,
and the destroyer, ploughed under,
will be transformed into
silent grain, sweet corn.
The earth that feeds him
will eat him again and again.

THE BEHAVIOR OF BIRDS

They are savage at the feeder,
colliding with their own kind
as well as with strangers.

Finches—gray female, redheaded
male—pushing each other away.
In this motley array of gray

a blackcapped chickadee, a scarlet
tanager, a blue and white jay
make a lovely abstract design,

sweeping and darting, but entirely
intent, each on his own appetite,
inexorable, unruly, like us.

EXILE: JERUSALEM

Give me a place to stand and I'll move the world.
—Archimedes

Spring again. And no place to stand.
Images of street life—buses, beggars,
an old man sleeping on the sidewalk,
an Arab woman squatting among her baskets—
are written in an alphabet I haven't learned,
syllables of meaning in a wordless desert.

Over the dusty hills,
beyond the sappers dismantling the bomb,
beyond the fury of stones,
across the gardens of oranges in this
sacred airless well,
the sea is speaking,

a universal turquoise language
I understand, but can't hear.

PABLO CASALS IN JERUSALEM

Aged to the essence of himself,
his pure ka stroked the strings.

A voice the colors of wood
sang like fruit in the cinnamon air.

At ninety-six his hand fell,
his wisdom closed.

Of his cello,

his old companion, he had said: here is
my friend. I love him and he loves me

He makes beautiful sounds
for my sake.

JERUSALEM DAWN

Let it in!
Throw open the shutters!
Unlock the door!

The lion sun
just licking the top of the hill
with a tongue of fire

races over
the cypresses, the fir trees,
the pepper trees

and springs into my room
flinging his golden mane
over the marble floor,
the rumpled bed,

my empty page

HEARING A MOZART DUO AT 36,000 FEET

This cosmic
conversation
is holding
my body up.

Riding above
the weather
the viola
reminds me

there's no weather
up here,
no whale-streaked
ocean, no

bearded heads
of wheat, only
a round vacuum
of night

with the sun
always somewhere
else. The mind
misreads itself,

flesh continues
its descent

towards dust,
and I am part

of the viola's
theme: trapped
in a disparity
of aluminum and air

but sustained
by the violin's
tender
counterpoint:

buoyancy,
despair.

RAMESSES' TOOTHACHE

He has learned to believe his prowess irresistible and himself almost divine

—Amelia B. Edwards

Even as a young man,
my teeth were decaying.
They were never strong and even,
like my father's Seti the first.

My gums were throbbing
as I built the temple of Osiris,
at Abydos, flames were playing
around my lower right molar
as I directed the erection
of the hypostyle hall at Karnak.

I was a good son, a good father,
although I couldn't always

remember the names of my
hundred and eleven sons
and my sixty-nine daughters.

When I was free of pain I enjoyed
playing with my children
and my pet lions. My beautiful wife
Nefertari was always a pleasure
to behold. But Kadesh was the worst.

Even before the battle the pain began
in my upper jaw and seared up
into my head, making me roar at the
Hittites like a crazed beast.

My soldiers thought it was courage.
Both sides claimed victory, but I knew
it should have been ours alone
if I had been free of pain.

No other Pharaoh built more massive
statues of himself or larger
temples than those I built
from Abu Simbel in Nubia, the southern
border of Egypt, to Tanis on the Delta.

I had been a handsome charming boy,
but at thirty I began to lose my teeth
and by forty I wished all those
aching molars would disappear.

I named my chariot horse Mut-Hotep.
meaning the goddess Mut is satisfied,
But she wasn't satisfied. She exacted
feverish gums, flaming pain, a throbbing
jaw that swelled as large as my largest
monument. Only my ka knew that my

funeral vestments would survive
as well as my naked leathery body,
outlasting war, breath, teeth.

THE ARMY HOSPITAL, 1942

He never saw
the South Pacific or Italy
or splashed onto the beachhead at Normandy
He cried every night at the thought
of pulling a trigger.

They put him away
in the army hospital in Denver,
unlocked ward. I came to see him
every afternoon, a bottle of muscatel
smuggled inside my schoolbag.

We wandered among the haystacks
on the dry plains of Colorado
beneath the frowning Rockies,
drinking and playing, like the
forgetful children we were.

Coming back at sunset curfew,
we heard from the locked ward
on the third floor, the angelic
voice of Private Jussi Bjoerling
singing La Donna e mobile.

When they finally let him go,
he took his mustering-out pay
and bought me the last twenty-four
pairs of prewar silk stockings
in the Denver store.

JANUARY 1, 1953

Three naked Florentines
rushed into the icy Arno,

and came out laughing, triumphant
having washed the old year away.

Each felt as immortal
as baby Achilles

dipped by the heel
in the River Styx.

This was the year
when Stalin's death

convulsed Calabria;
when black-plumed horses

crept through Rome
to muffled drums.

At mid-century
three beautiful Florentines

swam for luck
on New Year's day.

MOMENT OF ASCENT

for Edwin Honig

You know that moment.

A tiny shut-in world
suddenly tipped askew,

the earth like an apple
falling off a plate.

Only your breathing,
deep regular inhalations,
will allow the plane
to continue rising.

You are an arrow
pointing towards
a chaos of clouds
that perhaps you will enter

if sunlight waits above
this rainfilled air,
you know you must keep
breathing, breathing.

THE POSTPONEMENT

Somewhere metal was splintering,
  glass crunching inward;
a tent of darkness
  stretched over my head.

Anubis adjusted his scales,
  Jackal Anubis,
to see if my heart weighed
  lighter than a feather;

the Angel of Death
  scanned the Book of Life
to see if my name
  was inscribed on the page.

My head flew against steel,
    my body was wrenched and tossed
Who postponed the weighing?
    What did the Angel see?

At the edge of the Black Tent,
    moving towards the light, I saw
a woman sitting stunned

    in a crumpled car
on the side of the road,
    holding a key in her hand.

THE LOST SILVER

THE SWIM, 1936

Even the most uncompromising champion of the rights of women must admit that in contests of physical skill, speed, and endurance, women must remain forever the weaker sex.

—*London Daily News*, Aug. 6, 1926

I just knew if it could be done, it had to be done, and I did it.

—Gertrude Ederle, the first woman and the first American to swim the English Channel, Aug. 6, 1926

First Hour
Leaving Gris Nez in a dawn
brilliant with stars,
a slight westerly breeze blowing,
she steps into the water.

Second Hour
Johnny Weissmuller said,
She swims more with her arms
and less with her feet
than anyone, man or woman.
She would swim just as fast
if her feet were tied together.

Third Hour
She walks briskly into the channel
until it reaches her waist,
then launches off at a steady pace,
twenty-eight strokes to the minute.

She has rubbed a coat of
lanolin an eighth of an inch thick
on her bare skin and over that
a heavy layer of vaseline.

She has smoothed another thick layer
of grease on her red wool swimsuit.
She wears a rubber skull cap
over her bobbed hair.

At six-thirty a.m.,
wearing a motorist's goggles,
she faces the white cliffs of Dover,
and heads into a squally rain.

Fourth Hour
She's a small chunky girl with powerful shoulders
breasting her way through the icy waves
between Calais and Dover.

This stretch of water once was land,
a bridge of land where grass grew

and migrating families
walked across the miles
from unnamed France to unnamed England.

The south Atlantic drove a wedge northward
into the land bridge and formed
a narrow gulf of water.

The sea's tongue
licked at the chalk and earth
until it became this strait,
this narrow womb-neck
reaching
from the Atlantic to the North Sea.

Fifth Hour

By noon the sea becomes choppy.
She ignores her trainer's pleas
to slow down, although she drinks
a cup of beef broth at one o'clock
while she treads water.

She asks her father, who is on the tug beside her,
to play "Yes, We Have No Bananas"
"Sweet Rosie O'Grady"
and "The Sidewalks of New York"
on her phonograph.

She keeps stroke with the beat.

Burgess, her trainer, shouts
"Go slower!" and she answers,
"If I go slower, I'll sink!"

Sixth Hour

President Coolidge cut himself off entirely from world affairs today. For the first time since he became President, he passed the day walking about his Vermont acres, repairing fences and pruning trees.

—*New York Herald Tribune*, Aug. 6, 1926

Seventh Hour
Nine miles from Dover
punishing seas begin to swamp her,
a drenching rain pours down.

Cupping the bitter water in her hands,
ploughing ahead with her shoulders,
keeping a steady eight-beat kick,
she starts to tack on a zigzag course,
forced to stretch
the twenty miles between the coasts
to thirty-five.

The British coastline
becomes more and more distant.

Eighth Hour
Her father holds her, a child of eight,
splashing in the surf on the New Jersey shore.

She suddenly finds, as he lets go of her,
that the water will hold her up like another hand,
she can move fast and strong
in the friendly element.

Ninth Hour
As she battles a foreign arm of the same sea,
cold and unfriendly,
the water still belongs to her.

I've made up my mind to swim the Channel
or sink. I don't want to drown
but I'll feel like drowning if I fail.
They'll have to take me
out of the water unconscious.

Tenth Hour
The tide race bites into
the chalk cliffs and towers,

eating away the old channel,
now a tempestuous gray gulf.

She swims through three tides.

The first pulls her too far north,
the second south, away from her goal,

and the third pushes her
back toward the English cliffs.

The steep sea with its overfalls,
cloudy and muddy as it rushes north to the Arctic
paws at her body;

the wind-scarred sea that hates the sailor
parts before her tired arms.

Fog blows into the headlands and harbors
as warm air caresses the channel's frigid skin.

A mist rises, fatal blindness for a swimmer.

Eleventh Hour
She thinks about her father's promise:
if she succeeds this time—after the failure
last year, when she had to be taken

out of the water, swallowing half the channel,
if she succeeds this time—
he'll buy her a red roadster.

She thinks of speeding along the highways,
unfettered, light, like flying, like swimming,
as she moves ahead with powerful strokes,
waves thundering in her unprotected ears.

Twelfth Hour
On Dover Strait, sometimes called
Lake Vomitorium, cliffs on both sides
funnel the wind, and waves bounce
off the headlands,
breakwater and shallows.

One line of waves
crisscrosses the other,
making humps and hollows in the water,
creating fierce tidal currents
that flow into the wind.

Thirteenth Hour
She battles the contrary current.
She battles the wind.
She skirts around Goodwin Sands,
where wrecked ships have been sucked down
and harbored for hundreds of years.

She pictures the bottom of the Channel
littered with ghostly shapes of ships,
parts of ships, masts, bottles,
notebooks, tattered rags, corpses—and thinks, *Will I end up down there?*

My mother and uncles are getting ready
for my triumph, hanging flags from the family's

sausage factory on Amsterdam Avenue.
She pictures their joy
if she comes home alive.

Eyes smarting from trying
to peer through the fog,
breath rasping, ears ringing,
she aims for the inside of Goodwin Light,
hoping to touch the shingle at Deal.

Fourteenth Hour

It has been fourteen hours
since she first entered the Channel.
Her grease is smeared, her goggles
clouded over, she is hungry, her arms ache,
her ears are throbbing. Her bones are chilled.

Water smothers her face
at every stroke. Exhausted, she stops fighting
the huge waves, and lets the tide carry her in.

She sees the beach.

Last Half Hour

Keeping a steady count,
eight kicks to the stroke,
twenty-eight strokes a minute,
she pulls toward the shore in the dark,
guided by the bonfires set on the strand
to light up her finish.

Rising from the water,
wading towards the beach,
she snatches off her bathing cap,
tosses her head to free her damp hair,
and smiles triumphantly
at the crowd cheering her.

Hundreds of tugs blast their sirens in celebration

Envoi
Three thousand miles away,
in the New York where she was born,
her triumph is echoed
in a newsreel in my first movie theater.
Standing waist-deep in the water,
she raises her arm to wave
from the screen at me, a child of four,
and the unseen millions watching her.

THE LOST SILVER

1. The Earrings
They were my favorites, those silver earrings—
tiny double inverted pyramids
modeled from Italian filigree
by the Peruzzi brothers.
                    You
(here I am talking to you again,
as though you were not dead) took your
scholarship money again and again
to decorate your bride
with rich Renaissance silver, never mind
we were poor and hungry.

2. The Necklace
We sold my typewriter
to buy box seats at the ballet,
                    where I,
bareshouldered and barebacked
in a long Greek chiton that you designed
wore the silver necklace with two
tiny arches making a medallion
over my clavicle.

Queen of the swans.
At intermission we paraded around the Opera
House like two besotted millionaires.

3. The Bracelet
Was it part of playing the role
of submissive slave, wrists crossed
that made you think of a bracelet,
jewelry I never wore and still don't?

Cunningly made of tiny silver arches
in four linked medallions
echoing the necklace, it made
a heavy ornate statement, something like
the burden of being your possession,
despite the Mozaertian lightness of the gift.

4. The Upper Arm Bracelet
Talk about being a slave, a hetaira
in a harem, the bracelet on the upper arm,
lighter and airier in design
than the cuff on my wrist, pressed
inexorably into my flesh, into
my twenty-year-old flesh,
smooth tawny gold.
It took
ten more years to realize
I had lost my self.

5. The Belt
Made of curved rectangular links,
worth a queen's ransom, twenty-four
inches long, the belt spanned my waist
like two icy hands.
You preferred me
to wear it naked. No earrings,
no necklace, no bracelets. I felt

more naked than naked, framed by your
frigid silver, but still amused that this
white equator, just above my navel,
could frame your thimbleful of champagne.

6. The Anklet
It had no bells
and it never quite worked.

The sections were square,
a shape antithetical to my contours

Your invention was flagging.
Professor, father, fond teacher

of nubile girls, you wanted me to
bare my feet, but there was

no conviction. The sharp edges
scratched my skin.

7. The Tiara
Undecided if you wanted queen or slave
you crowned me with a glorious silver
tiara. An amethyst sat in the center
above my brow.
                    Part of our mythology,
a gift of terrifying power.

After the divorce I put all the silver
together in a pouch and hid it.

Did someone rob my freezer? Or toss
away the contents of my waste basket?

Cruel treasure, I never found it again

ATLANTIC LIGHT

ATLANTIC LIGHT

I've come back to the house
where the light,
pouring in from the west,
bounces across the ocean
and into my window,
lies strewn over the couch,
slides over the rugless floor,
glinting on books, pictures,
telephone, and settles on the
breakfast table.

Last night, when I woke at three
and pulled aside the shade,
the almost-completed moon
was spilling light into the bay,
over the silent road, the pines,
soothing, promising
a world other than this,
a world without anger
or crumbling flesh
or dark ambition.

The light is not the blinding
radiance of Skiathos
burning over the black and white
tile floor, filling the room with
thalassa, thalassa, thalassam,
drowning the wooden bed
where I lay dazzled, pregnant
with a daughter, a love, who later
thrust a black shadow
into my heart.

This new england light
is white and sunny,
but allows
a certain ambiguity.
Sometimes salty fog
shrouds house, road,
water, beach, dissolving
my familiar landscape
in light's underside.

But I hold to the light,
this Atlantic light
that always recurs, this
October light that haloes
the nimbus on the windowsill,
this light that promises
no redemption but is,
this Buddha light that shows me
how to be still.

TOUCH

Why, sitting and reading a book of poems
does she suddenly think of his slipping in her
from behind?
                    There was a time
when he would come in from any which way:
she was all entrance to him.

Walking across somebody's lawn
at any time of day or night,
or on the livingroom floor
when the host went to get more ice,
he would be in her.

Now he is many minds away
across an ocean of detours and delays:
why then should she suddenly remember
his slipping inside her from behind,
a touch as innocent as holding hands.

LITTLE AUBADE

Do I taste
of breakfast? You asked
as you kissed me
good bye.

No I said
you taste of clover
and asphodels. And the word
asphodel

stretched over me
all morning
like a wedding canopy.

FIRST KNOWLEDGE, THE SMELL OF A PLUM

A dark blue plum
was sitting on the piano.
The smell of it came to me,
a girl of fourteen,
after I went by.

I can feel between my hands
the rough blue upholstery,
dark blue, of the diningroom chair

I grasped,
when I first knew I loved you,

my tides pounding.
It was only after you left
that I knew,
that the smell of the dark blue plum
came sweet to me.

AN EDUCATION, BUFFALO, N.Y., 1933

The summer I was eleven I learned to ride
my cousin Rita's two-wheeler down a steep

driveway; to play spin-the-bottle and be kissed
crammed in a closet with a boy named Ralph.

Our mothers took us downtown for tea
with a turbaned gipsy who told our futures.

The gipsy took my hand and told me two things
I shall never forget: the most important

person in my life will be M. S. (my mother's
initials and those of my third and best

husband) and I am destined to become a writer.
Later we visit Niagara Falls with my mother's

lover, Otto the Hungarian.
I rush back to the car in terror

when I hear my father is expected. I catch my
fingers in the door of Otto's elegant Buick.

CROCHETING

I wish I could ask my dead grandmother:
How did you crochet? Did you wind
the yarn on your left finger while your right
hand plunged the hook into the loops,
making the peak of your famous ripple pattern
shimmering with five different shades of color?
You once tried to duplicate the colors
of an Arctic sunset for your son my father
after he came back from Greenland, lonely
and discontent. What were you thinking
as you sat still with your arthritic knees
crocheting afghans for your children
and grandchildren? Did you think about
your childhood in Kovno before the Cossacks came?
Of journeying to America, a girl of eighteen
torn and despoiled by your lecherous uncle?
Did you think about struggling to keep four sons
fed and clothed as you scrubbed the grimy stairs
in your walkup tenement on the Lower East Side
while your husband hung around with Bohemian cronies
and finally deserted you for a younger woman?
I can still see your hands fair and freckled,
moving through their mysterious motions with
hook and wool. Did the motion lull you? Was it
comforting? At ninety you said to me:
I've always been curious to see what happens next.

FLIGHT

The doctor said, count to ten.

One (a funny mask on my face)
two (know the doctor is kind but)

three, they promised ice—, four,
I can't, five, say five, and I

was flying up over the roof
with crowds of red and blue balloons
and I was sneaking up in the air
with my uncle in his scalawag plane,
looking below to the ribbon rivers
and fields of puzzles fitted together

but I never told my mother
that I flew that day, that I flew away,
a plane, a kite, a balloon, a child
beyond her worried hands.

VISITATION

the sharp crack of wood
hitting a ball: a green

diamond of grass with boys
shouting and running as I start

to race across their field.
my mother and father have just

arrived at the other
end, to save me from

this cruel holiday
where I lie awake all night

in the chilly campers' cabin
listening to the rain

fill the river; trembling,
planning what to save

when the flood overtakes me.
There they are! I run

towards them blindly, hear
the crack of the accurate bat

as the ball smashes my lip,
something sticky running

down my chin. More than
sixty years later,

when I run my tongue inside
my lower lip, tasting

the lump where the village doctor
tried to sew up the wound,

I hear the smack of the bat.

U-HAUL

My children leave one by one, each in a big U-Haul
truck piled up with their belongings, one for Chicago,
one for Atlanta, one for New Haven, clutching their
raggy suitcases, carting their cats, dogs, lovers,
favorite records, making dangerous u-turns, speeding
on the highways, backing blind out of driveways,
scraping other cars, arriving breathless where they
drink out of old frozen juice cans, keep books on
boards and bricks run out of money, get and lose jobs,
then return in a big U-Haul truck packed with mattresses
lamps, books, crates, coming back from Chicago, Atlanta,

New Haven, wiser, poorer, having collected new cats,
new lovers, new books and babies, ready to start again.

TIME CAPSULE

Driving alone with her son the future,
wrapped together in one cocoon car
they speed along a black strip
between green hills
hover just beneath
rock candy clouds
close enough to bite
he asks her
if she knows how color
comes from prisms
and if she knows
how salt got in the sea
and when she says no
no and no he says
I'll tell you

THE SKATER'S WALTZ

Rotund, aging, the father
holds his fledging
daughter against his belly.

A Viennese melody
blows them across the lake
the frozen Persian lake
of the blood red livingroom rug

Left arm propped on her waist,
right elbow held straight,

he hides her small square hand
inside his larger one.

She bends like an aspen,
while their feet slide lightly,
lightly over the palms,
the leaves the buds the fronds

the mirrored arabesques
of a lost country.

MY FATHER'S DREAM

At eighty-five
he picks his way
among the pebbles on the sand,
feet tender as a baby's.

Holding my hand
he toddles to the edge of the surf,
where once in his vigor
he held me by the waist
as I kicked and gasped,
learning to swim.

He says,
last night I dreamed I was walking,
running, dancing,
my strength had come back,
my legs were quick again.

When I woke, sure that I was
young and sound
I put my feet on the floor
but they couldn't
hold me up.

THE ACCIDENT, 1901

My father, five years old,
wandered idly in the clutter

of turn-of-the-century Harlem,
past the bowfronts

of brownstone houses,
down the avenue of trees,

collecting rainbow leaves
scattered on the sidewalk,

a bright orange leaf
shaped like the palm of a hand

glittered at him from the gutter
He stepped off the curb,

bent down to pick it up.
A wagon, drawn by a large

white horse, hurtled
around the corner, its rear

wheel severing his
left index finger.

Horse and driver, heedless
careened down the century,

leaving behind the stunned
diminished child.

CONVERSATION WITH DUST

Father, where are you?

Dust.

Can dust speak?

No, but I left words for you,
on paper, in letters, words
hanging like dead birds on the
telephone wires.
You didn't hear me.

And the end?

Laceration of hope.
Crumbling of bones.
Rage. Rage. Rage.
Whiskey and pills.

Why did you leave me?

You left me
over and over again.
I grasped
the hem of your dress
and found I was holding
spiderwebs.

But I can't forget you.
If I forget, my dreams remind me.
Wasn't that you—sanguine, dapper,
forty-five—waiting for me
in my dream last night?

Perhaps.

If you saw me in your dream
it was your wish that put me there

Are you satisfied now?

Particles of dust
can't be satisfied.
Everything
becomes something else.
I enter a drop of rain
and wait for my transformation.

TASHLIK

I went to the beach to throw my sins
into the ocean:
Pride. Ego. Anger.

I emptied my pockets of their detritus
sand, a broken
shell, a crumpled tissue

and flung them away towards
the open sea.
An east wind blowing

across the waves, past the seaweed,
blew my sins
back at me. Unforgiven,

I walked to the Esplanade
where yellow butterflies danced by twos

near the barren rosebushes
and a single sail
stood against the horizon.

BECOMING A POET

Editor's Note: In this abridged edition of *Becoming a Poet*, you'll find some poems that appeared in full in the original 1982 edition quoted as carefully chosen excerpts. This approach allows us to highlight a wide range of voices and poetic methods in a concise format suited to this *Collected Works* edition. Readers interested in exploring the full versions of excerpted poems are encouraged to locate them online, as reading these complete texts can enrich the learning experience for those seeking deeper insight.

CONTENTS

I. Climbing the Jacob's Ladder
II. Starting with the Image
III. Digging into Memory
IV. Bringing Dreams to the Surface
V. The Law of Recurrence
VI. Finding the Organic Form
VII. The Art of Revision
VIII. The Ultimate Task
IX. Communicating the Poem

I. CLIMBING THE JACOB'S LADDER
An Introduction

> What is it, then, that poetry means? Its meaning is the vindication of the worth and value of the world, of life and of human experience.
> —Erich Heller, *The Disinherited Mind*

I was sitting one morning on the porch of a cabin in the woods, where I had been given the gift of two weeks in which to do nothing but write poetry. I had left behind all my family responsibilities; there was nothing to bother me, except that no poem came. I knew I was at a turning point in my writing. My first book had already appeared, and now I was very dissatisfied with it, feeling that it was tight, formal, constricted, full of masks and symbols hiding my real life and feelings.

It was a cool New Hampshire day in July, the smell of pine very sharp, the woods full of their own quiet sounds, but the yellow lined paper beside me remained blank. I was in despair.

Then I looked down and saw a small black spider sitting in the middle of the blank page. I found myself writing this poem:

A SPIDER ON MY POEM

Black one,
I was going to frighten you away,
but now I beg you,
stay!
This poem needs real legs, faster than the eye.
And a belly with magic string in it
made from spit,
designed to catch and hold whatever flies by.
Also, the uninvited way
you came, boldly, fast as a spider,
till you paused all real in the middle of the page.
Everything I need.
Please stay.

The spider had a real message for me, which I knew before I realized I knew it. Its presence reminded me that I wanted my poems to catch the stickiness, the palpable nowness of the moment, just as the spider's web, which comes from its own body, catches whatever flies by. What I wanted, and felt I had not yet attained, was to transfer the immediacy of my experience directly to the poem.

I also wanted a greater boldness of form. I had schooled myself since I was in my teens in the complicated metrical and rhyme patterns of John Donne, in the pentameter and lyrics of Shakespeare, and in the quatrains of Emily Dickinson, as well as in the symbolism and patterns of Yeats, but now I wanted to break away. I felt that the long irregular lines of this new poem, combined with the sound patterns of *away*, *stay*, and *page*, of *eye* and *by*, were just the mixture of freedom and control that I was looking for.

Becoming a poet is not a casual accident, nor is it a sudden ascension into heaven on the wings of sheer inspiration. Denise Levertov, in her poem "The Jacob's Ladder," emphasizes that the poet's work is concrete and difficult. The stone ladder the poet climbs is described as possessing a certain beauty, a "rosy" tone that softens its appearance. Yet, even the angels must exert effort to descend, giving a "little lift of the wings." For the aspiring poet, climbing requires scraped knees, a strong grip, and hard work. After this struggle, the poem transforms—it takes on a life of its own, lifting and ascending independently. She writes, "The cut stone / consoles his groping feet. Wings brush past him. / The poem ascends."

It has often been said that poetry is the only art that uses a medium common to all mankind: words, language. Other forms of writing—fiction, essays, biography—also use the medium of language, but not in so intense and concentrated a form as poetry. Then what is the difference between the poet and other people? Poets are in love with language. They weigh and treasure the sound and meaning of words; they relish the use of language by other writers and have a compulsion, a necessity, for working with words.

I have often been asked when and why I started writing. I wrote poems almost before I can remember, but I know that at nine years of age I was reading poems in my fourth grade class, and at eleven I had sold my first poem to a youth magazine for five dollars. With that five dollars, I bought a copy of *Modern American and Modern British Poetry*, edited by Louis Untermeyer, and read it from cover to cover. I knew that I had found the company I wanted to keep.

The why is much harder to answer. No one in my family had been a writer. But my parents, grandparents, uncles and aunts were all talkers, they talked loudly and incessantly, and they constantly read books and newspapers. One of my earliest memories is of my paternal grandfather, who had a lovely baritone, singing songs to me as I sat on his knee. Words, music, and language were my first and deepest pleasures.

But how do you move from a love of language to the practice of words, arranged in a pattern on the page, a pattern called poetry? As a child, I knew the answer before I could ask the question: by reading and imitating other poets. There is no other way. In every art beginners must start with models of those who have practiced the same art before them. And it is not only a matter of looking at the drawings, paintings, musical compositions and poems that have been and are being created; it is a matter of being drawn into the individual work of art, of realizing that it has been made by a real human being, and trying to discover the secret of its creation.

In his book, *The Dyer's Hand*, W. H. Auden says: "The questions that interest me most when reading a poem are two: (1) Here is a verbal contraption. How does it work? (2) What kind of guy inhabits this poem?" It is only by asking these questions that you can begin to develop taste, critical judgment, a knowledge of craft, and a sense of humanity.

In practical terms, this means using the library, reading books and magazines of poetry, trying to get an understanding of the poets who have gone before you, and those who are writing now. You may find much to reject. But there will be someone, a voice, a subject, that stops you with the thrill of discovery. This is the first real step in the education of a poet—to fall in love with the work of another poet, to read all you can of the work, and set yourself the task of imitating it.

There is nothing wrong with imitation. I have heard students say that they don't want to read other poets because they might begin to write like them. But it is only by writing like the masters—as an exercise for yourself, as an experiment to find out what you can learn from them—that you will begin to expand your own possibilities. It is even valuable to retype a poem—for instance, a sonnet of Shakespeare's—in order to examine closely how the poet orders his words, how he turns his line, what he does with rhyme. Later, as you develop your own style, you will find that you learned something useful from everyone you have imitated, that you learned something that you will eventually absorb and digest into your own work.

One of the consequences of excessive television watching is that people are less inclined to read books for pleasure. It is hard for them to realize that if they want to become writers, they must find out where they fit into the long history of literature, by searching out and reading what has been written.

If you write in a vacuum, if you write out of nothing but your own experience and imagination and never compare yourself with other writers or develop a sense of taste and judgment, it is likely that your work will remain raw and inept. But if you understand what has happened to poetry in your own century and in other centuries, if you study the work and lives of other poets, you will begin to develop from an apprentice into a practitioner. Eventually you will become a link, however small, in the great chain of poets, past and present.

Becoming a poet means more than reading and imitating other poets, however. It also means using the mundane, concrete aids to composition that are available to you. If you are serious about the business of writing, you can hardly do without the following tools:

1. A good spiral or bound notebook (the size doesn't matter).
2. *Roget's Thesaurus* (either online or a physical copy).
3. A good unabridged dictionary (again, online or physical copy.)
4. A laptop, typewriter, or other tool for writing and printing.
5. As many books and anthologies of contemporary poetry as you can afford.
6. Sources to reference poetic forms. These can be online or hard-copies of *Poetry Handbook: A Dictionary of Terms*, by Babette Deutsch (Grosset); the more complex *The Book of Forms: A Handbook of Poetics*, by Lewis Turco (Dutton); or the delightful *Rhyme's Reason: A Guide to English Verse*, by John Hollander (Yale).

The notebook can serve several purposes. It is a central place to catch the ideas and phrases that fly by in your head. You can then draw on your notes when the time comes to write. Inevitably, poets who use scraps of paper and backs of envelopes to write down ideas, phrases, lines, even whole poems, find it useful to collect them together in one place. It is like depositing your money in a bank instead of leaving dollar bills lying all over the house. Then when you need cash, you know where to go.

The notebook also serves as a journal. Keeping a journal is an invaluable aid to writing. But it is important to remain casual and flexible about your journal and not to feel compelled to write down everything that happens, or to write in it every day. Your journal is your private repository; it should not become your taskmaster.

I have been keeping a journal for over twenty years, but it fills only five or six large notebooks. Some poets are much more prolific. You must listen to your own needs and discover what is best for your way of thinking and writing. Because the journal is utterly private, you can risk writing nonsense, free association, dreams, raw emotions. The journal helps you to center your experience, draw on it, and objectify it. It is your primary source for poems,

The *Thesaurus* and dictionary are basic tools for anyone using the English language. If you have not seen the original Thesaurus, which is not in dictionary style, it is worth reading, just for pure delight. Its inventor, Peter Roget, had a genius for categorizing the ideas that lie behind words. If you are struggling with a meaning or an idea, if you need possible alternative words for the one you are stuck with, Roget may have a solution. The *Thesaurus* provides parts of speech, synonyms, antonyms, and idioms for almost any word you can think of. The dictionary will give you a more extensive definition for a single word, in addition to its origin and correct spelling.

I include a laptop as an essential tool for several reasons. If you are accustomed to writing your first drafts by hand, these tools offer an immediate opportunity to translate what you have written into the objectivity of type. Type gives you distance, a perspective on your work—something toward which every writer is constantly striving.

If you like to compose directly on the keyboard, you have the advantage of instantly legible copy. I myself feel that the first draft of a poem is such an intimate personal event that I don't want a machine to get between me and my first flow of language. But after I have written the first draft by hand, I use the keyboard over and over again to type revisions, to polish the poem, and finally to produce a professional copy. Typing a poem helps you to see its defects. And it is revealing to type out someone else's poem, especially a poem you admire, in order to see how it is made.

The importance of owning anthologies and books of contemporary poetry is self-evident. This doesn't mean you should buy every book of poetry that comes out, even if you can afford to do so, but it does mean that to begin with, you should own a good historical anthology and a good contemporary anthology. Owning an anthology allows you to browse in it at your leisure and find out which poets speak to you. You are looking for the experience of discovery and recognition. The library, too, is an excellent place to browse, not only in contemporary books of poetry you might want to buy, but also in little magazines and periodicals to see what kind of poetry is being written and published today.

A book of forms will help you get some sense of the techniques a poet can work—and play—with.

Now, with the tools of your trade on hand, you are ready to begin.

Why do poets write? The quotation by Erich Heller at the head of this chapter seems to me a good answer: you write because you want to celebrate being alive, even the grief and pain, and because you want to share your feelings and experiences. Behind every form of creation lies the urge to communicate. Writing poetry, as well as reading it, gives you insight into your own experience, helps you feel less isolated. You are drawn to poetry because you were affected by the poems you have read or heard.

A. R. Ammons illustrates this in his poem, "Poetics," where he starts from a concrete observation: "the birch tree white / touched black at branches." He wants to understand the form of a tree in the universe; he wants his poem to reflect the absolute naturalness of the tree, to unfold its inevitable shape, a shape that comes from him but belongs to you, the reader. As Ammons observes the tree standing "wind-glittering / totally its apparent self," he describes looking for "the forms / things want to come as" and emphasizes the importance of being "available / to any shape that may be / summoning itself / through me / from the self not mine but ours."

II. STARTING WITH THE IMAGE

> In essence, the poet has one theme: his live body.
>
> —George Seferis, *A Poet's Journal*

The window in my study faces the ocean. Every morning I pull up the shade to see the salt water inlet, to find whether the tide is high or low, to look at the opposite shore with its houses and lawns, at the sky, and to my left, the open sea.

One morning I pulled up my shade and saw nothing. A summer fog had rolled in from the Atlantic and covered the entire view. There was nothing but a large gray blanket hiding what I knew was out there.

I looked at the fog and thought, "It reminds me of something. What is it like? It is like something very important to me, but what is it?" And then I knew. The fog is like the relationship between two people when one is hiding, psychologically or emotionally, from the other. It is like the lack of communication between lovers. And I began to write a poem in the form of a dialogue between two lovers, called "Fog." Here is part of the poem. The woman says:

> I come to your shore longing
> for the shape the rise of your land
> your special rounds and levels
> but you pull your blanket over your head
> hoping I will think you
> all-flat all gray
> a separated mist . . .

And the man says:

> you don't notice
> how sunlight sieves
> through me you come
> a large shape
> that parts and breaks
> my brooding . . .

The image, the visual impact of the fog on my eye immediately suggested to my brain something that it resembled—a concern about human communication that had already been lurking in my consciousness.

An image that thrusts itself into the mind almost always holds within itself the beginning of a poem, or for that matter, any work of art. That is what George Seferis means when he says that the poet's essential theme is his live body. He doesn't mean that the poet actually writes about his physical body as his chief subject. He means that the source of all perception from which images come lies in the physical senses. Everything you have felt or experienced remains in your mind in the form of images, and every image holds the seed of creation.

What is an image and where does it come from? The image is a vivid flash—often visual or emotional—of an intense moment in your experience. It is almost always based on a concrete sensuous perception. Every human being starts to accumulate a storehouse of images from the moment of birth. The newborn infant suffers the first impact of light and air, enjoys the first pleasure of contact with its mother's flesh, the nourishment of milk. Everything that the human being perceives through taste, smell, feeling, hearing, and seeing is stored in the brain for future reference.

The poet learns to use these perceptions more directly and consciously than most other people. I remember hearing May Sarton talk about the vignettes that had stayed in her mind since childhood and had become the seeds of her poems and novels. I was a young poet then, and I understood from what she said that I must be on the lookout for just such seed images.

In what ways can a poet capture the seed image as it happens, an image that often comes from the immediate experience of taste, smell, touch, sight or sound? As we live in cities, cut off from the observation of nature, as we indulge more and more in passive entertainment, our senses become dulled and unresponsive. But you, as a practicing writer, can sharpen your senses and intensify your responses and your receptivity by exercising a constant awareness of the physical world around you, by opening your attention to everything that impinges meaningfully on your mind and recording it in your journal. This doesn't mean attaching a significance to all experience indiscriminately, but it does mean valuing the ability to respond. Miguel de Unamuno describes this kind of response in *The Tragic Sense of Life*, when he says:

> There are people who appear to think only with the brain, or with whatever may be the specific thinking organ; while others think with all the body and all the soul, with the blood, with the marrow of the bones, with the heart, with the belly, with the lungs, with the life.

There are many ways to pinpoint your sensuous perceptions and evoke the images that lead to writing a poem. One effective method is to focus on a single perception, such as the experience of intense heat.

In H. D.'s (Hilda Doolittle's) poem "Heat," the speaker calls on the wind to "rend open the heat" and "cut apart the heat." This heat is so extreme, so thick and heavy, that it seems to hold up the fruit and blunt its shape: "fruit cannot drop / through this thick air— / fruit cannot fall into heat / that presses up and blunts the points of pears / and rounds the grapes." The idea of cutting the heat and of "ploughing through it" is extravagant; to put it that way is taking a risk, but the image succeeds because it helps the reader, together with the poet, feel the intensity of her experience.

> **EXERCISE 1.** *Close your eyes and try to remember a specific moment in your life when you experienced or observed extreme heat—perhaps a heat wave or a fire. Let your recollection be as specific as possible, don't censor or cross out any part of the recollection. Be as open as possible to whatever details come into your mind. Write down any word or phrase that seems to you to characterize the image of heat, then go on with specific details. Have you ever been in a heat wave? In the desert? Have you witnessed a fire? Try to remember. At the very least, you will have the raw material for a poem.*

Perhaps the most neglected and dulled of the human senses is the sense of taste. Seeing, hearing, smelling and touching are commonly more easily stimulated and remembered. One of my favorite class exercises is to bring a basket of red and yellow apples into the classroom. I start by talking about the taste of fruit, and we read together one or two poems about eating fruit, perhaps from Erica Jong's book *Fruits and Vegetables*, where she writes, "For the taste of the fruit / is the tongue's dream / and the apple's red / is the passion of the eye," or Shirley Kaufman's evocative poem "Apples," which intertwines the scent and flavor of apples with memories of her mother. Kaufman captures the act of picking apples as they "slide in my hands like cups / that want to be perfect," and recalls her mother's skillful slicing that revealed "a star break / from the center with tight seeds." The sensory imagery leads to the poignant moment of offering the fruit to her mother with "Mother, eat. And be well." The poem deepens as it links the smell and taste with the death of her mother, whose "brown eyes / empty out the light, watching / her mind slip backwards / on the pillow, swallowing / apples, swallowing her life."

I cut the apples into quarters and pass them around the room. As we eat the apples, we pay careful attention to every detail—the sound of the bite, the burst of juice, the colors, texture, smell. We go around the class asking each student to say quickly, without thinking, a word or phrase that comes into her or his mind, either a specific detail of the apple itself, or a related (or even unrelated) idea, such as myths of the apple, Bible stories, fairy tales, childhood associations—single words or phrases that may be the staging point of the poem. It is enough simply to describe the process of eating, or even watching someone else eat, as in William Carlos Williams's poem "To a Poor Old Woman." He writes,

They taste good to her
They taste good
to her. They taste
good to her.

The repetition of the line "they taste good to her" with the break at a different word in each repetition forces the reader to see the old woman relishing the taste of the plum, the one half sucked out, and finally, to sense the solace that she is feeling.

I have always had best classroom success using apples for this exercise, perhaps because I associate apples with some of my most poignant experiences. Here is a poem I wrote about a summer I spent on an apple farm in upper New York when I was sixteen:

APPLES AND BARNS

There was a time of apples and barns,
Pastures and lawns, parsing
Latin parsing kisses in the sweet

Smell of hay.
    They brought us back
from the heavyappled orchard, shamefaced,
In the back of the hired man's truck.

I watched the apples rolling down the sorter,
Small from big. Parsing apples,
You must look for yourself in barns.

Remember the pasture near the orchard,
The good smell of manure and boysweat,
When I blew over you petaled like a flag?

We said we'd be buried there;
I looked for myself in orchard, pastures,
Barns, I looked for myself among

Brown shoulders, green eyes.
I remember your white boythigh.
And I came to an allnight barn

Freckled in moonlight, heavy with hay.
Leaning across fields and pastures,
You leaned on me. I began to be parsed.
Infinitive. The apple to be.

EXERCISE 2. *Choose your favorite fruit and eat it slowly and carefully, then write about it immediately. The object of this exercise is to practice sharpening your perceptions and increasing your state of receptivity. Don't worry about writing a perfect poem—let the words* *come. Does the taste of the fruit remind you of anything? It is enough simply to describe what you observe in each step of eating the fruit.*

Once you start to take note of your own perceptions, you will become aware of how the senses overlap. An acute perception of taste often evokes the sense of sight, smell, and touch as well.

May Swenson's poem, "The Blindman," shows how intense the experience of seeing can be, especially by looking through the "eyes" of someone who cannot see. The blind man declares, "this scarf is red," and feels "the vectors to its thread / that dance down from the sun." He engages all his senses, expressing how he "knows / the seven fragrances of the rainbow" and can "hear / crimson's flute." The poem not only describes details of sight but combines these images of seeing with images of sound and touch.

Here is an exercise to help intensify visual experience. I once took an unruly class of eighth-grade boys out into a field in early spring and gave them this exercise. It was only when they opened their eyes that they noticed for the first time the buds on the trees, the faint green of the early leaves, the fact that winter was over. That day they wrote some of the best poems of the year.

EXERCISE 3. *Either indoors or outdoors on a city street or in the country, close your eyes, turn around three times, and then open them. Turning around with your eyes closed takes away your ordinary seeing and gives you a new view of familiar things. Write about the first thing that you see when you open your eyes. It will have a vividness that it does not ordinarily have for you. Think about touch. Do you notice the texture of objects in your everyday life? A ceramic candlestick, the smooth cover of a book, the stiff twigs of a dry hedge, the softness of a baby's skin? Here is a poem about a woman who doesn't notice what she touches, who goes through her life wearing gloves:*

TO A FAT LADY SEEN FROM THE TRAIN

O why do you walk through the fields in gloves,
  Missing so much and so much?

O fat white woman whom nobody loves,
Why do you walk through the fields in gloves,
When the grass is soft as the breast of doves
  And shivering-sweet to the touch?
O why do you walk through the fields in gloves,
  Missing so much and so much?
—Frances Cornford (1910)

EXERCISE 4. *In this exercise, too, it is important to close your eyes because the experience of touching is intensified if you cannot see. Close your eyes and reach out for the first object you come in contact with. Or you can choose your object first, but then close your eyes and explore it. Describe its texture. Describe the sensation of feeling, of touching. Does the texture remind you of anything else? Describe it as minutely and accurately as you can.*

It is especially valuable to repeat this exercise more than once. The more often you repeat the experience, the more you will perceive and the more these impressions will call up images in your mind.

The image, then, is a single representation in the mind based on a concrete sensuous perception, either real or imagined. There are basically two ways of dealing with the image in poetry. One is simply to describe the image itself in all its details, impressionistic as well as actual. That is what H. D. is doing in her poem "Heat." She learned this simple rendering of the image from the Japanese poets, who were masters of the art of letting an image stand by itself, letting the readers draw their own conclusions about the meaning or emotional implication of the image. Writing an "imagist" poem is a way of taking delight in the image for its own sake.

Amy Lowell is one of the best of the "imagist" poets. Here is her poem, "A Decade."

When you came, you were like red wine and honey
And the taste of you burnt my mouth with its sweetness.
Now you are like morning bread,
Smooth and pleasant.

I hardly taste you at all for I know your savour,
But I am completely nourished.

This brings us to the second way of dealing with the image, the image that sticks in your mind and absorbs your attention. That is to ask, "What is it like?" as I did in my poem about fog. As soon as you say an image is like something else, you are dealing with simile and metaphor, that is, you are comparing one perception with another.

Simile is the simple comparison: "Fog is *like* one person hiding from another." Metaphor is a more subtle kind of comparison. The word *metaphor* comes from two Greek words meaning "to carry" and "beyond." The dictionary defines metaphor as "a figure of speech in which one thing is likened to another different thing by being spoken of as if it were that other." In other words, you carry the image beyond mere likeness. Instead of saying that fog is like hiding, you show one person hiding from another and suggest the idea of fog, leaving it to the reader to make the actual link between the two.

Emily Dickinson said: "To the bugle, every color is red." This is instead of saying, "The sound of a bugle is like the color red."

What the poet always wants is to recreate in the reader the same feeling of excitement that the poet experienced on first perceiving the image. Zbigniew Herbert, the Polish poet, complains in his poem, "I Would Like to Describe":

. . . to put it another way
I would give all metaphors
in return for one word
drawn out of my breast like a rib
for one word
contained within the boundaries
of my skin . . .

He is speaking ironically, but notice that he is using a metaphor ("one word / drawn out of my breast like a rib") to describe his dissatisfaction with metaphors, as being too far removed from the experience itself.

To me the metaphor in most cases is far more effective than the simile. The important thing is to understand the generating image in all its factual, specific detail, and to describe it in the plainest language you can find. The radiance of the fact will infuse your words. Then, if you are lucky, the metaphor will emerge, just as the rainbow emerges from the right juxtaposition of air, water, and light.

At the end of a long life of writing poetry, William Butler Yeats looked back in his old age at the place—the humble, private place—where poetry begins. In "The Circus Animals' Desertion," he acknowledges that even "masterful images" arise from ordinary, often unsavory sources, asking, "but out of what began?" He admits that inspiration often comes from "a mound of refuse or the sweepings of a street," ending with the powerful realization, "I must lie down where all the ladders start, / In the foul rag-and-bone shop of the heart." This imagery captures the raw, unrefined place within oneself where poetry is born.

III. DIGGING INTO MEMORY

> It matters not where or how far you travel—the farther commonly the worse—but how much alive you are. All that a man has to say or do that can possibly concern mankind is in some shape or other to tell the story of his love—to sing, and if he is fortunate and keeps alive, he will be forever in love.
>
> —Henry David Thoreau, *Journals*

Where do you store those vivid sights, sounds, smells, colors, feelings that you have been receiving since infancy? In the part of the brain that monitors memory, you preserve every significant experience of your life. You can draw on this memory whenever you want to, by deliberately willing yourself to remember. But sometimes, for no apparent reason, a childhood memory will suddenly leap into your mind unbidden and stay there with demanding persistence. In either case, whether it is called up deliberately or comes accidentally, such a memory may be the beginning of a poem.

Everyone has memories; even young children can recount a memory, as soon as they have language to describe the past. Everything you remember about your family—your feelings about them and the events of your childhood—is a key to the kind of person you were as a child and the pattern of your life.

How do you reactivate a memory if it doesn't come spontaneously into your mind? You can call up memory by deliberately thinking back, and trying consciously to recreate an early experience. You can train your mind to dig back into your earliest years. As you do this more and more often, you will find that the process becomes easier.

But mere remembering is not enough; you must turn the memory into language. Write your recollection down in your notebook or journal as soon as you can, in words that you would use if you were describing it to an intimate friend, in language that is unself-conscious and honest. Don't be afraid to write about an event or an emotion that is negative or unhappy. Talk about a memory with as much specific detail as you can remember. If you write in generalities, the poem will not be vivid. Only by recreating the reality with as many concrete facts as you can think of will the poem find the energy to spring into life. A poem that deals in specific factual details will be likely to stick in the reader's mind, while a poem that deals in abstractions will seldom touch the reader's sensibilities.

A common event of childhood that few people have written about is the experience of hearing grownups quarreling with each other. To a small child, hearing those loud voices raised in anger is often terrifying. Here is a poem I wrote about just such a memory:

LISTENING TO GROWNUPS QUARRELING,

standing in the hall against the
wall with my little brother, blown
like leaves against the wall by their
voices, my head like a pingpong ball
between the paddles of their anger:
I knew what it meant
to tremble like a leaf.

Cold with their wrath, I heard
the claws of the rain

pounce. Floods
poured through the city,
skies clapped over me,
and I was shaken, shaken
like a mouse
between their jaws.

The first picture that came into my mind was precisely what I describe in the first line of the poem: waking up at night and standing in the hall with my little brother, hearing the loud voices, not understanding, and feeling afraid. I remember that as I stood there trembling, I thought to myself, "I'm trembling like a leaf," and I realized that I was experiencing the reality behind the cliché. As a small child I was afraid of violent weather, especially floods, probably because I associated them with family discord. In the poem these images came involuntarily to me—the rain had claws; I heard thunder as the skies clapped over me. Also, as I listened, I felt my smallness, my helplessness, and this feeling of being a helpless victim of their anger found its image in picturing my head as a "pingpong ball / between the paddles of their anger" and my feeling of being "shaken / like a mouse / between their jaws."

A more cheerful poem about the smallness of childhood, the feeling of being small in a world of giants, is Anne Sexton's "The Fury of Overshoes." In the poem, she speaks in a child's voice, saying, "Remember, big fish, / when you couldn't swim / and simply slipped under / like a stone frog?" and reflects on how "the world wasn't / yours. / It belonged to / the big people." Sexton continues, nostalgically recalling, "Oh overshoes, / don't you / remember me, / pushing you up and down / in the winter snow?" and yearning, "where are the big people, / when will I get there, / taking giant steps / all day, / each day." Through this voice, she plunges directly into the details of those feelings as though she were experiencing them in the present. The reference to "giant steps" slyly nods to the game "May I?" that children play, evoking the authentic sense of being small and surrounded by giants.

The South American poet Cesar Vallejo, in his poem "To My Brother Miguel: In Memoriam," uses a childhood game of hide-and-seek to evoke themes of loss and memory. Vallejo recalls playing at a specific hour when their mother would calm them with "There now, boys . . ." This game becomes a poignant metaphor for death as the speaker remembers how his brother, Miguel, once hid "one night in August, nearly at daybreak" and was never found again. The only direct reference to death is in the phrase "dead afternoons," but the sorrow culminates in the final plea, "Listen, brother, don't be too late / coming out. All right? Mama might worry." The plaintive last two lines, spoken in a child's voice, make you as the reader feel the pang of his sorrow.

Philip Levine's poem "Child Trapped in a Barber Shop" transforms a child's experience into a poem about the universal fear of being trapped. The speaker's image of a "six-year-old red face / calling for mama" conveys the child's distress, while the line "because your case / is closed forever, hopeless. . . ." hints at a deeper existential fear. The poem shifts to a collective voice with, "We've all been here before," emphasizing the shared experience of vulnerability and resilience. The imagery of enduring the "electric storm / of the vibrator" and the "true blade mowing / back and forth" symbolizes the trials of growing up, ending with the sobering realization: "You think your life is over? It's just begun."

> **EXERCISE 5.** *What event or impression sticks in your mind from childhood? Were you ever frightened by adults quarreling, as I was; did you feel very small in a world of giants, as Anne Sexton did? Do you remember playing games with a brother or sister like Vallejo? Were you ever trapped inside a store or room like Philip Levine? Do you remember your first day at school? Think back to your earliest memory and put it down in your notebook in any form that comes to your hand: prose paragraphs, brief jottings, whatever preserves the moment for you. Then, taking the language you've used in your description, write a poem, keeping to the simplest and most specific language you can. The very process of verbalizing your memory may release other memories, perhaps a flood of memories. The more you think about your childhood, the more you will remember.*

It is through memory that you understand your relation to your family, your personal and public history, and eventually, your relationship to the rest of the world. Memory about human relationships is charged with emotion: you may feel extremes of love and hate. Literature is filled, for instance, with poems about fathers. Dylan Thomas has written a beautiful poem about his father, the famous villanelle on his father's death, "Do Not Go Gentle into That Good Night." Theodore Roethke's "My Papa's Waltz" captures a tender and complex moment between a father and son as they waltz around the kitchen. The poem's structure, with its abab rhyme scheme and three-beat rhythm, imitates the 3/4 time of a waltz, evoking the steady, swaying cadence of the dance. For example, in the lines, "The whiskey on your breath / Could make a small boy dizzy; / But I hung on like death: / Such waltzing was not easy," the alternating rhyme and consistent rhythm enhance the playful yet tense nature of the scene.

All the details—the whiskey on his father's breath, the pans rattling on the shelf, the father's hand caked with dirt and battered on a knuckle, the boy's head that comes as high as his father's waist and keeps getting scraped on the father's belt buckle—all these create a picture that is vivid and complex in its reality, both funny and sad.

Robert Francis's poem "That Dark Other Mountain" reflects on the speaker's memories of his father, who could descend a mountain faster than the speaker, even though the speaker was "the first one up." The poem uses vivid, concrete details of their hikes, such as the father's confident movement—"legs braced or with quick steps he slid / the gravel slopes"—while the speaker picks "cautious footholds." Francis lists actual New England mountains, including "Black, Iron, Eagle, Doublehead," to root the poem in a tangible setting. The surprise comes in the last two lines, hinted at in the title, when the poem shifts from describing their mountain descents to a final metaphor that elevates the poem to a poignant reflection on mortality and loss: his father beat him down "that last other mountain, / And that dark other mountain"—the mountain of death.

EXERCISE 6. *Think about your father, his life, his character, his relationship to you. Did he ever comfort or protect you? Did you become friends? Was he away during your childhood? Is he alive? Describe any incident or fact about him that comes into your mind. If you find it hard to write about your mother or father—and sometimes not enough time in your life has elapsed for you to get perspective on that relationship—write about your grandmother or grandfather or any other relative who was important to you. Relationships with* *grandparents are often poignant, precious relationships that provide you with imagery you can reach out to more easily. I have a picture of my grandfather hanging in my study. One day, when I was looking at it, I found myself writing this poem about him:*

I BECOME MY GRANDFATHER

Grandpa, I
want to tell you
simply:
that picture of you,
the handsome one with
curly gray hair,
amorous eyes,
arms folded in satisfaction—

I have looked
at you since I was
a little girl:
my grandfather.

Today I thought:
he's like some friend of mine,
a man I could love,
a sweetheart.
And reckoned
I'm now older
than your picture
by one year.

The ancient Greeks in their wisdom made Memory the mother of the Muses. The children of Memory were Calliope, the muse of music, Clio of history, Euterpe of flute playing, Terpsichore of dance, Erato of lyric and love poetry, Melpomene of tragedy, Thalia of comedy, Polyhymnia of sacred poetry, and Urania of astronomy (considered an art in ancient times). It is clear that every creative act is born of some kind of memory.

We have dealt in this chapter chiefly with memories of childhood and family relationships because it is these memories that give you access to your basic and most profound sources of poetry. The longer you live, the more material you store in your memory—the experience of love, marriage, work, having children, growing up, growing old—all the events and relationships that surround the history of your life, and these recollections, in one form or another, can become the material for poems. But as you grow older, your early experiences, your childhood and family, seem to become more and more vivid, and it is these memories that the creative act takes as its focal point. By practicing, by exercising your memory, by putting into words every event that has remained meaningful to you, you will begin to learn how to transform memory into language, and ultimately into poems.

Some students have said to me, "I find it difficult to tell the true details of this event. Do I have to tell the truth?" This is a decision that every writer has to make—whether to use the material of life directly or to disguise and transform it in some way. Every writer at some point overcomes the initial reluctance to reveal personal secrets because of the realization that there is no human experience that is unique or alien to other human beings. Human experience is universal. Only the telling of it can be new.

When memory comes to the surface, catch it and write it down. Don't worry about its significance. Everything human is significant. That is what poetry demonstrates.

IV. BRINGING DREAMS TO THE SURFACE

> What joy is there in taking the poet at his word, in dreaming with him, in believing what he says. . . .
>
> —Gaston Bachelard, *The Poetics of Reverie*

Memory is a primary source for the poet not only in waking life, but also in the life of dreams. For thousands of years dreams were thought of as magic and prophetic. But the truth is that dreams tell you only what you have been and what is. They tell you how you feel about your life.

Dreams draw their material from memory—the memory of childhood events and of places long ago, as well as the memory of places and events that happened yesterday. Nothing that you have once experienced can be entirely lost, whether it is a major event or a trivial one. And these experiences—the meaningful, private experiences of your life—rise up in your dreams, whether you are aware of it or not.

How do you get in touch with that material for your poems? You can bring your dreams to the surface by thinking about them, by watching for them, and, above all, by keeping a journal of your dreams. Dreams are potential poems.

Everyone dreams, even those who believe that they never do. If you tell yourself before you go to sleep that you want to remember what you dream, chances are that a dream will stay in your mind when you wake up. The more you practice paying attention to your dreams, the more accessible your dreams will become and the more possibilities they will suggest for poems.

The best method for catching your dream is to keep your journal at your bedside and to start writing whatever you can remember as soon as you wake up. It is not necessary to be exact and literal. Whatever you write will come out of the same frame of mind that produced your dreams of last night. Free association from the starting point of a dream can lead to the revelation of rich fantasies, forgotten events, critical secret thoughts. You will find that you are producing images, ideas, thoughts, and memories that have the potential to lead you into a poem.

Dreams and poems come from the same deep recesses of the mind. The methods that the mind uses to make a dream resemble the processes it uses to make a poem. The only difference is that making a poem is a conscious act and making a dream is not.

If you examine your dreams, you will find that they tend to disregard logical connections, and instead often portray events by using disguise and distortion. Dreams tend to reduce your thoughts to the most condensed expression possible, which is why they sometimes use a kind of symbolic shorthand, similar to the images poets use in writing poems or the objects in a surrealist painting. Like poems, dreams tend to function on at least two levels, sometimes using words, sometimes visual images, that go beyond their obvious and immediate meaning.

Often in a dream contradictory and ridiculous images crowd one another. Wallace Stevens's poem "Disillusionment of Ten O'Clock" humorously critiques the dullness of reality by describing an absence of vibrant and imaginative elements. He denies the existence of colorful, whimsical scenes, such as green or purple garments with unusual patterns, which makes readers visualize these vivid images despite their supposed absence. The line "People are not going / to dream of baboons and periwinkles" emphasizes how ordinary life stifles creative dreams. Only the old sailor, asleep and drunk, breaks free from this dullness, dreaming vividly of "catching tigers / In red weather." The poem's striking, contradictory images invite readers to see it as a celebration of imaginative freedom. Readers in fact *are* seeing baboons and periwinkles. You can easily picture the poem as a painting.

Dreams are full of psychic energy, forming a bridge between primitive, colorful, verbal and pictorial forms of expression and the language with which you consciously express your waking thoughts. In this sense, dreams can be regarded as unrealized poems. If you go to sleep with the intention of remembering your dream, the dream may stay with you after you awake. E. E. Cummings's poem "Now I Lay (With Everywhere Around)" explores the transient nature of waking life, contrasting it with the permanence of night and sleep. He writes, "Sunlight is / only loaned," and then equates sleep, night, and snow with winter and death. But he also says that when you lie down to dream ("of something which nobody may keep"), you can comfort yourself by dreaming of Spring, satisfying your wish for eternal renewal.

EXERCISE 7. *Write a poem about sleeping—ways of going to sleep, how you arrange your room, how you feel about your bed, the sensation of sinking down into various levels of consciousness, what you see when you close your eyes. Try to recall memories of sleeping when you were a child. How did darkness and the night affect you?*

I have filled many notebooks with my dreams, some of which I have made into poems. In fact, by paying attention to dreaming, I have developed a facility for going back and changing the ending of a dream if I don't like the way it ends the first time I dream it. I have noticed, too, that my dreams have adopted some of the techniques of film: dollying in for close-ups, superimposing landscapes on one another, showing multiple points of view.

Here is a poem based on a dream I had, in which the details are exactly the way I saw them in the dream:

IN THE LOBBY

In the lobby while people shook hands
and flashbulbs of friendship popped like smiles,
while you said hello and hello to everyone
who didn't matter and I stood stylishly by
pretending I didn't know you
suddenly
I took my machine gun and,
dressed as I was in maroon velvet,
mowed down the popular lecturer with
his witty charm and good wife,
his friends, clingers, all parasites
and passersthrough, all those related to me
by birth, marriage and death,
until finally I could see the ceiling.

The walls were absolutely bare and solitary.
Across the tiled floor only you were left.
You smiled, took my arm, and we
began to go home together.

Clearly, this is a wish-fulfillment dream. Some time before the dream, in a crowded lobby, during the intermission of a play, I had actually seen the person I address as "you" in the poem. The phrase "flashbulbs of friendship popped like smiles" (in the dream there were flashes, as from a newspaper reporter's camera) suggests my feeling that everyone was putting on an act, and that all relationships were hypocritical except the one relationship that concerned me. In the dream, I experienced a wonderful sense of relief, blasting away everyone who was irrelevant to me, and I was conscious in the dream, as I was shooting the machine gun, that I was wearing an elegant maroon velvet dress. The conclusion—the end of the dream and the end of the poem—was the wish that we "began to go home together."

Many people have recurring dreams. Some return repeatedly to certain landscapes that exist only in their dreams. If you can remember such a dream and describe it, you will discover that the description is packed with emotional connotation for you. Dreams are naturally surreal. The irrationality of dream symbols and landscapes have had a strong influence on such painters as de Chirico, Marc Chagall, Salvador Dali, Max Ernst and René Magritte. A painting by Chagall or Magritte, which literally uses dream imagery, or surrealism, can be the ignition point for a poem. In my poetry writing classes, I find that hanging up large color reproductions of pictures by these or other surrealist painters stimulates and releases in my students the kind of imaginative and fantastic invention for their poems that is usually reserved for dreams.

EXERCISE 8. *If you have access to a book of reproductions by de Chirico, look at one of his flat, lonely landscapes, with its muted colors and its strange, isolated columns and stairways. Or find a painting by Dali or Magritte. You might be reminded of one of your own dream landscapes. Write a description of the picture, as though you were within it, or write whatever it suggests to you, even if it seems farfetched. Invent a dream landscape. Let your imagination go.*

I often dream of water images—swimming, being on a raft or ship, or in a well—sometimes pleasant, sometimes threatening. This probably accounts for my fascination with the ocean and my desire to live beside it. I feel that it is my primal element. The morning after a wedding I wrote this poem about waking up:

RACHEL WAKING

She's in a well,
the walls covered with
slippery moss between

wet stones.
Under the water asleep,
holding her breath.
The clock strikes,
shooting her to the surface.

Her nose and the top of her head break through to air.
She scatters the scum lazing on the surface, the dragonfly resting,
the flat leaf of autumn.

She climbs,
sliding up the slippery walls,
dreams clinging to her ankles.
She wants to fall back.

But up there standing in crisp grass, Jacob
waits by the well, leaning his elbow against
the day, tossing idly in his hands
her brand new morning.

When I woke up, I remembered the details in the dream: the sensation of rising from beneath the surface of the water, struggling to wake up, the feeling that I was climbing the walls of a well toward a promise waiting for me up in the morning air. One of the most effective dream poems is Louise Bogan's "The Dream." In this poem, Bogan portrays a powerful, mythic scene where a "terrible horse" embodies a part of the speaker's life that is monstrous and uncontrollable, infused with fear and long-held retribution. The speaker identifies herself as a "coward complete," lying on the ground, overcome by fear. Yet, another, stronger figure—a woman—appears to confront the beast, representing the courageous part of the speaker. This figure advises the speaker to give the horse "something of yours as a charm," symbolizing an acknowledgment of herself. When the speaker, in an act of submission and recognition, throws her glove, the once-terrifying horse is transformed and "puts down his head in love." The poem uses the imagery of the horse, the cowardly speaker, and the brave woman to illustrate the internal conflict and reconciliation within one person. By the end, the disparate parts of the speaker's soul come together, achieving a sense of peace.

Whether or not Louise Bogan actually dreamed this dream hardly matters. Her mind invented that dream, creating a mythic portrayal of her life. The terrible horse is part of herself, a monstrous part of her life that is out of control, a part of herself that she fears. She is the coward lying and weeping on the ground, and she is also the other woman, the courageous woman, who knows how to tame the beast by giving the terrible horse (the nightmare) a talisman, in other words an acknowledgment of herself, a recognition. As soon as she does this ("like a lion in a legend"), the beast is tamed, the fear is put to rest, and the monster puts down his head in love. The separation of the person into three elements is a kind of displacement, a way the mind uses to illustrate, through symbolic images, the warring elements within one person. In the end of this dream-poem, the warring parts of her soul are brought together, and she is finally at peace with herself.

Whether you remember it or not, your dream life creates a pattern of images that ultimately forms a portrait of the self who is the dreamer. Yeats says in his poem "Among School Children":

> O body swayed to music, O brightening glance,
> How can we know the dancer from the dance?

How can we know the dreamer from the dream? In essence, they are one.

If you can learn to make your dream life operative in your creative life, if you can learn to draw out of your sleep those essential, dynamic words and images, you will open up a rich and inexhaustible source of material for your poems.

V. THE LAW OF RECURRENCE

> If, as I believe, the urge to make a kind of music is as much a characteristic of biology as our other fundamental functions, there ought to be an explanation for it. . . . The rhythmic sounds might be a

> recapitulation of something else—an earliest memory, a score for the transformation of inanimate, random matter in chaos into the improbable, ordered dance of living forms.
>
> —Lewis Thomas, "The Music of This Sphere"

Poems make shape out of chaos. What we are given, living in the world, is a chaotic mass of impressions, experiences, sights, sounds, feelings, and thoughts, as complex as a mountain landscape with masses of stone, trees, waterfalls, and pastures. Painters take a piece of that landscape and put a frame around it, arranging what they see so it makes sense to the eye. That is called *composition*. Writers must also select. The way that they *arrange* their selections, the way they compose the details, is governed by certain fundamental aesthetic laws that are inherently satisfying to the human imagination.

Robert Frost called poetry "a momentary stay against confusion." He felt that the *stay* had to consist of a formal arrangement of subject matter—that is, he used traditional modes of meter and rhyme for his material, remarking that writing a poem without regular form was like playing tennis without a net. But form does not have to be rigid in order to give shape to a poem. It does, however, have to conform to a certain pattern.

Is there a primary aesthetic law that governs the human imagination? What governs the pattern of the poem?

The most important law is the law of *recurrence*. That is, the return or repetition of an element with predictable regularity. It is a reflection of the recurrence of the beat and rhythm in nature: the coming in and going out of the tides and waves, the phases of the moon, the patter of raindrops, the cycle of the seasons. The law of recurrence is found in our bodies: our breathing, our pulse, our heartbeat, the rhythm of our walking. The patterns of recurrence in art are man's natural response to the great pulse of the universe and the pulse in his own body. Human beings chop wood, row boats, rock cradles in the same recurrent rhythm as the waves beating on the shore and the pulsing of their blood. Many poets believe that the rhythm of the universe, the inherent pattern in the spiritual as well as the physical world, proves that there is an essential pattern or inscape inherent in every poem.

Children find pleasure in clapping their hands rhythmically. Infants clearly enjoy the repetition of sound—rhyming words, repeating patterns of vowels and consonants. There is only a short leap from walking to dancing; only a short distance between talking and singing, namely, an intensification of recurrence.

The two basic kinds of recurrence that govern poetry are *rhythm* and *sound*, or, to put it more technically, *meter* and *rhyme*. The simplest examples of these recurrences can be found in children's nursery rhymes:

Ride a cock horse
to Banbury Cross
to see a fine lady
upon a white horse.

If you say the poem out loud, you will find there are two stresses or downbeats on each line, on ride, horse, Ban-, cross, see, lad-, -pon and horse. Note that stresses occur on the accented syllable, not on the whole word. The unaccented syllables together with the accented or stressed syllables give the effect of a galloping horse—which is another example of rhythm in nature. Notice that the rhyme here—cross and horse—is really a half rhyme, that is, only the "o" and "s" of cross and horse are the recurrent sounds.

An example of a much more mysterious nursery rhyme that uses regular meter and full rhyme is "There Was a Man of Double Deed":

There was a man of double deed
Sowed his garden full of seed.
When the seed began to grow,
'Twas like a garden full of snow;
When the snow began to melt,
'Twas like a ship without a belt;
When the ship began to sail,
'Twas like a bird without a tail;
When the bird began to fly,
'Twas like an eagle in the sky;
When the sky began to roar,
'Twas like a lion at the door;
When the door began to crack
'Twas like a stick across my back;

When my back began to smart,
'Twas like a penknife in my heart;
When my heart began to bleed,
'Twas death and death and death indeed.

If you read this poem out loud, you will find that there is recurrence in the rhythm—there are four beats or stresses in every line—and in the rhyme, where every two lines rhyme in couplets. This ancient device of recurrence—rhythm and rhyme—has always been central to poetry, used in countless variations.

In Muriel Rukeyser's poem "Rune," the repetitive structure features rhymes and three stresses per line, creating an incantatory effect. Each stanza weaves a series of lines such as, "The word in the bread feeds me" and "The word in the moon leads me," emphasizing the varied and profound ways words influence life. The progression includes contrasts like "The word in the war kills me" and "The word in the body mills me," showcasing the power of words in nurturing, shaping, and destroying.

The word in the man takes me.
The word in the storm shakes me,
The word in the work makes me.
The word in the woman rakes me,
The word in the word wakes me.

The brilliant rhymes, four in each stanza, and the three stresses in each line, give an effect of incantation.

Whether a poem is in irregular free verse or in regular or fixed form, it is essential for a poet to know how to mark the accented syllables in every line. This is one way to discover what kind of a recurrent pattern the poem contains. For the moment we will look at the recurrence of rhythm in regular forms.

EXERCISE 9. *Type or write the poem "Rune," leaving plenty of space between the lines. Then mark each accented syllable with an accent mark ('). The accent falls where the normal speaking voice stresses the syllables in a sentence. If you listen carefully as you say the line out loud, you will find where the accent falls. Write* *the number of syllables accented at the end of each line, and you will see the pattern of rhythmical recurrence. Then follow the same procedure for any poem quoted in my book that you particularly like, and finally, for a poem of your own.*

In language, rhythm is created by the pattern of accented and unaccented syllables, as in the word *never*. Here are the basic units of rhythm:

trochee—néver
iamb—agáin
dactyl—phýsical
anapest—interrúpt
spondee—néwbórn

When one of these units is repeated throughout a line, then the line is metrically regular. When the number of stressed syllables is the same in every line, it is also considered regular. The poet is free to make endless variations and combinations of these units.

The rhythm of speech and singing—instinctive to all human beings—came long before the names for the units were invented. The language of poetry encompasses the following kinds of recurrence:

1. Letters — The same letter at the beginning of two or more words within a line, called alliteration ("Let me not to the marriage of true minds . . .").

   The same vowel and consonant at the end of a word, in two or more adjacent lines, called rhyme ("seed" and "need").

   The same vowels in words within or at the end of the line, called assonance ("pain" and "mail").

   The same consonants within or at the end of the line, called consonance ("horse" and "cross").

2. Syllables — An equal number of syllables in every line, or a parallel arrangement of syllables in every stanza, called syllabic poem, haiku, cinquain.

3. Words — The recurrence of the same word or group of words, either within the line or at the end of the line, as in the sestina.

4. Lines — The recurrence of whole lines, in various forms of refrain, as in the ballad, triolet, villanelle, and pantoum.

Assonance and consonance are often used in slant rhyme, sometimes called half-rhyme, in which only part of the end words rhyme, as in "cross" and "horse." Emily Dickinson is the first American poet to use this kind of half-rhyme extensively, a daring innovation for her time, when most poetry rhymed fully. Here is one of her poems in which she uses slant rhyme:

465

I heard a Fly buzz—when I died—
The Stillness in the Room
Was like the Stillness in the Air—
Between the Heaves of Storm—

The Eyes around—had wrung them dry—
And Breaths were gathering firm
For that last Onset—when the King
Be witnessed—in the Room

I willed my Keepsakes—Signed away
What portion of me be
Assignable—and then it was
There interposed a Fly—

With Blue—uncertain stumbling Buzz—
Between the light—and me—
And then the Windows failed—and then
I could not see to see—

In the first stanza the rhymes are "Room" and "Storm" (consonance); in the second, "firm" and "Room" (consonance); in the third, "be" and "Fly" (semi-assonance because the final vowels are phonetically related); and finally, in the fourth stanza the full rhymes "me" and "see" mark the end and climax of the poem.

There is a close relation between the recurrence of words in poetry and the recurrence of sounds in music. Some poets hear the melody of the poem before they write the words. Shelley's notebooks, for instance, often show his marking for the meter of a poem before he wrote the words. Lyric poetry, since its first appearance in written form in the sixth century B.C.E. in the poems of Sappho, was meant to be sung to an instrument. The very name—lyric—shows poetry's early relation to a musical instrument, the lyre. The recurrence of tempo and the repetition of themes in music is closely parallel to the return and recurrence of meter and rhyme in poetry. The poet who has a musically sensitive ear has a great advantage. You can develop this sensitivity by reading poetry out loud, by listening to the chiming of sound and the flow of cadence, and by allowing yourself to become aware of the beauty of recurrence.

I am fascinated by parallels between poetry and music, and I often try to write in words certain forms that give me great pleasure in music: rounds, theme and variations, even a poem modeled on a trio of Schubert. Several poems of mine have been set to music by composers. Here is one, very strong in recurrence, that has been set to music by the composer Robert Stern:

ROUND

I keep my clocks a little fast
so time won't take me by surprise.

Lest crows tread harshly round my eyes
I keep my clocks a little fast.

I push ahead the hands of past
before the future tints my hair.

I race the hours through the air
so time won't take me by surprise.

Before the spider bygone dries
I cobble cobwebs on my last.

I keep my clocks a little fast
so time won't take me by surprise.

Notice the end rhymes: surprise, eyes, dries and fast, past, last. Note the repetition of the two lines "I keep my clocks a little fast" and "so time won't take me by surprise." Also note the alliteration in "time won't take me," "ahead the hands," "before the spider bygone," and "I cobble cobwebs."

The recurrence of syllables in a pattern means using the same number of syllables in every line or the same numerical variations in every stanza. The most complex example of this latter device is found in the poems of Marianne Moore, the greatest innovator of this form. Here are a few stanzas from her poem, "The Fish":

THE FISH

wade
through black jade.
    Of the crow-blue mussel shells, one keeps
    adjusting the ash heaps;
        opening and shutting itself like

an
injured fan.
    The barnacles which encrust the side
    of the wave, cannot hide
        there for the submerged shafts of the

sun,
split like spun
    glass, move themselves with spotlight swiftness
    into the crevices—
        in and out, illuminating . . .

Notice that every five-line stanza has the same pattern:

First line: one syllable
Second line: three syllables (plus rhyme with line one)
Third line: nine syllables
Fourth line: six syllables (plus rhyme with line three)
Fifth line: eight syllables (no rhyme)

It is a marvelous *tour de force* and a device worth playing and experimenting with.

Sometimes a syllabic pattern provides a perfect solution to a poem whose very subject is the imposition of form on matter. I was working on a poem about the experience of having my portrait painted, that is, of *reality* being turned into *form*. I tried the poem with various line lengths, both metrical and irregular, but the poem never seemed to have the right shape until I hit on the idea of using a syllabic pattern, with three syllables to a line. Here is the poem:

SITTING FOR A PICTURE

The painter
narrows his
eye, measures
along his
finger, looks
at her up-
sidedown then
backwards in
a mirror.

Not touched the
girl on the
couch begins
to wear his
grammar. Per-
spective flat-
tens her curves

buttock brow
she becomes
more than her
self, catch for
a palette.

She gives off
faint power
like perfume
or buddha
she sits in
his eye like
an apple.

The idea of imposing three syllables per line on the poem exactly matched the subject matter: namely, that I, a three-dimensional creature, was being transformed into two dimensions by the painter and that the laws of space and perspective were being "imposed" on my reality.

EXERCISE 10. *Write a syllabic poem of at least 8 lines. If a new poem doesn't come easily to you, take one of the poems you wrote in Exercises 1 through 8 and turn it into a syllabic poem. The trick is not to break too many words in order to have the lines come out with an even number of syllables, but rather to rearrange your words to make the poem come out right. Don't be afraid to experiment with the length of the line. Choose any length from three to nine syllables per line, but be sure every line is the same length.*

Another form of recurrence, which depends on the repetition of words themselves rather than letters or syllables, is the sestina, a form invented in the Middle Ages by Provençal poets and a favorite among contemporary poets.

The sestina is a poem of six six-line stanzas in which the final word of each line in the first stanza is repeated in the five subsequent stanzas in a prescribed order. The six words in the first stanza, which we will call a b, c, d, e, and f, are repeated in the second stanza, like this:

STANZA I	STANZA II
line 1, word a	line 1, word f
line 2, word b	line 2, word a
line 3, word c	line 3, word e
line 4, word d	line 4, word b
line 5, word e	line 5, word d
line 6, word f	line 6, word c

Each subsequent stanza then takes its pattern from the stanza immediately preceding by applying the same principle. The advantage of this method is that you don't have to remember a complicated numerical sequence, but in writing or analyzing a sestina can always apply this simple principle.

Here is how the pattern works out in the sestina below by Kinereth Gensler. The recurrent words are *vision*, *episode*, *wood*, *wolf*, *eyes*, *hidden*.

STANZA I	STANZA II	STANZA III
vision	half-hidden	would
episode	vision	hidden
wood	eyes	wolf
wolf	episodes	vision
eyes	wolf	episode
hidden	wood	eyes

STANZA IV	STANZA V	STANZA VI
eyes	wolf	episode
wood	eyes	wolf's
hidden	envision	hidden
episode	would	eyes
revision	hidden	wood
wolf	episode	vision

Notice that the last word of the last line of the preceding stanza always becomes the last word of the first line of the following stanza. Here is the poem:

SESTINA: AN OLD STORY

The child had 20–20 vision.
The clue was always there: that episode
where she picks wildflowers in the wood,
when, basket on her arm, she meets the wolf
and still won't hurry, still can't keep her eyes
from thickets where blue hyacinths lie hidden.

We see her next at the door, half-hidden
by flowers, basket, hood—a vision
from our first picture books. She is all eyes,
all innocence, a pawn in episodes
whose end is preordained: the wolf
is slain; she learns to fear the wood.

"Come in my dear!" he cries, as we knew he would.
He's tucked in bed, his whiskers hidden
by Grandmother's nightcap, but he looks like a wolf.
Could any child, with even partial vision,
be fooled by such a flimsy episode?
Some secret lay behind that snout, those eyes,
some great unfolding. With her own eyes
she'd seen those wondrous changes in the wood,
watching a stone move (cautious, its head hidden),
watching the leaf with wings, the snake's episode
of shed skin. Do people undergo revision?
Old people? Grandmother? Is she this wolf?

Now (in that queer, high-pitched voice), the wolf:
"Come closer, child!"—"But, Grandmother, what big eyes
you've got!" (What ears! What teeth!)—Could she envision

herself transformed, made meek, incurious, or would
she wait to learn the secret hidden
from children until the final episode?

The hunter dominates that episode.
He does not hear her cries, he hears the wolf's
loud snoring. And she, swallowed alive, hidden
in that dark gut, sees through corrected eyes
how wrong it is to dawdle in the wood,
how dangerous to trust her small girl's vision.

She learns: meet each new episode with downcast eyes.
Avoid: wolf, flowers, turtle, butterfly, snake, wood.
Be good. Be safe. Stay hidden. Abandon vision.

Notice that after the six stanzas there is a three-line envoy that uses all six words, two to a line. The poem is metrically regular, that is, there are five main stresses to each line. The only irregularities are that "wood" also appears as "would" and "episode" as "episodes"—a liberty that makes the poem linguistically more interesting. Robert Francis wrote this description of a sestina: "If you drape thirty-nine chains over your arms and shoulders and then do a dance, the whole point of the dance will be to seem light and effortless—If six words are to be repeated over and over . . . they should be so 'useful' the ear will keep track of all their recurrences . . . and enjoy the pattern of chiming."

In writing a sestina, it is helpful to choose words that can be used as both nouns and verbs, like *vision* and *would*. The mark of a good sestina is that the reader doesn't recognize the repetition of words immediately because they fit so well into the meaning and movement of the poem. It is only in the third or fourth stanzas, when you begin to notice that the last word of the last line of the preceding notice stanza is the same as the last word of the first line of the following stanza that you realize the poem is a sestina.

EXERCISE 11. *Take the six words from Kinereth Gensler's Little Red Riding Hood sestina—*eyes, wood, hidden, episode, vision, wolf*—and see what kind of a sestina you can make out of them.*

> *The hardest part is beginning. You will be surprised, after you write the first two stanzas, how the repetition begins to flow with a momentum of its own, and how easy a seemingly complicated form can become. This is a form that is much easier than it looks. If you prefer, invent your own six words.*

The recurrence of lines in a poem has been handled in various ways through the centuries and, like all other recurrences described here, is always subject to variation and invention by the individual poet. I consider the villanelle one of the most difficult forms of line recurrence, and also one of the most beautiful. In the villanelle, the first and third lines of the first three-line stanza are repeated alternately in the following four stanzas, and then are brought together as the final two lines in a final stanza. Each three-line stanza rhymes *aba*, except for the last stanza, which rhymes *abaa*. Theodore Roethke's villanelle "The Waking" contemplates mortality and the approach to life in anticipation of its inevitable end. It begins:

> I wake to sleep, and take my waking slow.
> I feel my fate in what I cannot fear.
> I learn by going where I have to go.
>
> We think by feeling. What is there to know?
> I hear my being dance from ear to ear.
> I wake to sleep, and take my waking slow.

The poem is about mortality and about how to live in expectation of the inevitable end of living. Notice that all the lines are end-stopped, that is, there is punctuation at the end of every line, until stanza five, the climax of the poem, where the end of the first line "to do" runs over to the next, "to you and me."

> Great nature has another thing to do
> To you and me; so take the lively air,
> And, lovely, learn by going where to go.

This is followed by the injunction "so take the lively air, /And, lovely, learn by going where to go." Notice, too, how Roethke uses short sentences within the line, especially in the last stanza, where the short statements heighten the intensity of the poem.

The cadence and sound of a poem, like rhythms and tonality in music, can have a strong emotional effect on both writer and reader. The effect can be pleasurable, soothing, or exciting, depending on the pattern of recurrence in rhythm and sound. Only by analyzing the stresses and listening to the music of the poem can you see the patterns of recurrence within it. You will find that recurrence in some form almost always strengthens the poem's beauty and power.

VI. FINDING THE ORGANIC FORM

> In poetry, technique is another name for morality: it is not a manipulation of words, but a passion and an asceticism.
>
> —Octavio Paz

Every poem has its appropriate form, and the poet must discover what it is, in somewhat the same way as Rodin said he discovered the innate or organic form inside the stone as he chipped away at it. An arbitrary shape cannot be forced on a poem. The poet changes, rewrites, and experiments until he finds the right shape and pattern for his subject.

Emerson said, "Ask the fact for the form." He meant that implicit within the subject is its inevitable shape. Are you writing a song or love poem? Probably the lines would want to be short, possibly rhymed. A sonnet might be just the right pattern. Are you writing a narrative, a dramatic monologue? You might find that longer lines, perhaps five-stress blank verse, would be most appropriate. Are you writing about uncertainty or unhappiness? You may find that lines broken in a pattern of free verse are the best way to express the subject matter. The *way* that the poem is said is inherent to *what* it is saying.

How can you know what forms to choose among? First, by reading poetry copiously and discovering how other poets have solved the problem of matching form to subject. Second, by training yourself in traditional forms, even if you don't intend to write strictly in every case. That is why it is important to own a book of forms, such as the *Book of Forms* by Lewis Turco, the *Poetry Handbook* by Babette Deutsch or *Rhyme's Reason* by John Hollander. There you will find all the patterns that poets have invented through the centuries.

It is equally important to have in front of you an example of the form you want to use. Mere description is not enough. The more examples of the form you read, the better you will understand it. Practicing different forms is for the poet what bar work is for the ballet dancer. It strengthens and stretches the muscles, including muscles you wouldn't ordinarily use, and thus gives you a technical mastery that becomes evident when the real performance—your own poem—begins.

The more patterns of rhyme and line lengths you have practiced, the more you will have to draw on when you are looking for the appropriate shape for your poem. I believe, with many other poets, that there is one inevitable shape inherent in every poem and that it is the task of the poet to be the sensitive and receptive intermediary for finding that shape. There are no absolute rules to guide you. Finding the form that is organic to your poem requires humility, energy, and the willingness to experiment and discard until you solve the problem.

How do you know when you have found the organic form? Partly by a sense of satisfaction and triumph, partly by the gradual development of experience and taste. You will find, as you work, that you are becoming more confident. Sometimes, miraculously, the poem will emerge in its inevitable organic form at the first trial. But that is rare.

One of the simplest and most pleasurable forms to begin with is the *haiku*, borrowed from the Japanese. Here are the characteristics of the classical Japanese *haiku*:

1. It is a poem of seventeen syllables, sometimes divided into 3 lines of 5-7-5 syllables, respectively.
2. It is a small poem that evokes emotion through the suggestion and juxtaposition of two precise concrete details.
3. The impact of the poem depends entirely on the association between the two ideas or pictures.
4. The first line always includes some word or expression that indicates a season, time of year, age of life, or place.
5. The conclusion, implicit in the third line, points toward a human emotion.

The following *haiku* are from the seventeenth, eighteenth, and nineteenth centuries. It was considered part of the education of every Japanese man and woman to be able to write an elegant *haiku*.

The temple bell stops—
but the sound keeps coming
out of the flowers.

—Basho, seventeenth century

Cricket, be
careful! I'm rolling
over!

—Issa, nineteenth century

blossoms on the pear
a woman in the moonlight
reads a letter there

—Buson, eighteenth century

Notice that the poem by Issa has not been translated into the traditional seventeen syllables.

EXERCISE 12. *Look out the window and observe the season, the time of day, the effect it has on the changing scene. Write a haiku, selecting one or two concrete details to begin with, images from nature or the seasons, keeping the seventeen-syllable count in the three lines, 5-7-5, and ending with a human observation, an expression of your own emotion.*

A variation of the haiku is the cinquain, invented by the American poet Adelaide Crapsey. It consists of five lines, unrhymed, with the following syllabic pattern:

first line: two syllables
second line: four syllables
third line: six syllables

fourth line: eight syllables
fifth line: two syllables

Here is an example of the cinquain, called "The Warning" by Adelaide Crapsey:

Just now,
Out of the strange
Still dusk . . . as strange, as still . . .
A white moth flew. Why am I grown
So cold?

The poem has the sensitive, slight form, suggestive of a more profound meaning, that is exactly appropriate to its subject: the sudden, mysterious apparition of a delicate moth.

It cannot be emphasized enough that the only way to find the organic form of a poem is to experiment until you are satisfied that the form visually and orally matches the subject. It is interesting to see how stanzas of two, three, or four lines can change the effect of the whole poem. If my poem "Round" were written in three-line stanzas, it would look like this:

I keep my clocks a little fast
so time won't take me by surprise.
Lest crows tread harshly round my eyes

I keep my clocks a little fast
I push ahead the hands of past
before the future tints my hair.

I race the hours through the air
so time won't take me by surprise.
Before the spider bygone dries

I cobble cobwebs on my last.
I keep my clocks a little fast
so time won't take me by surprise.

Although the lines fall easily into multiples of three, the three-line stanza form is not as inevitably appropriate to the poem as the two-line stanzas that I finally settled on. It would be possible, also, to write the poem in four-line stanzas, but that, too, lessens the effect of the poem as it progresses from refrain to refrain.

The number of lines in a stanza have traditionally ranged from one to nine. Among the poems that find their appropriate form in three-line stanzas, one of the most interesting inventions is the medieval Italian form called *terza rima*, which has continued to fascinate poets through the centuries. In Dante's handling of the form, the three-line stanzas rhyme in an interlinking way like this: *aba, bcb, cdc, ded*, and then a final rhyming couplet, *ee*.

One of Robert Frost's loveliest poems, "Acquainted with the Night," is written in *terza rima*, a form that interlocks rhymes to create a sense of movement. The speaker reflects, "I have been one acquainted with the night," setting a tone of solitude and introspection. Frost uses this pattern to express a melancholy journey through the city, as in "I have walked out in rain—and back in rain. / I have outwalked the furthest city light." The speaker's isolation deepens as he describes passing "the watchman on his beat" and averting his gaze, "unwilling to explain." The poem's rhythm and rhyme propel the narrative while reinforcing its themes of loneliness and detachment. The "luminary clock against the sky" becomes a haunting image, indicating that time is indifferent, "neither wrong nor right." Notice how the interplay of rhymes gives a sense of forward movement, portraying the poet's melancholy walking through the streets at night.

Other twentieth-century poets have introduced variations into the form. Archibald MacLeish used *terza rima* in his long documentary narrative about the conquest of Mexico, called "Conquistador," but he introduced half-rhymes (consonance and assonance) as well as full rhymes, as in this passage:

> I am an ignorant old sick man: blind with the
> Shadow of death on my face and my hands to lead me:
> And he not ignorant: not sick
>
> but I
>
> Fought in those battles! These were my deeds!

These names he writes of mouthing them out as a man would
Names in Herodotus—dead and their wars to read—

These were my friends: these dead my companions:
I: Bernal Diaz: called del Castillo:
Called in the time of my first fights El Galan:

The *me* in the second line of the first stanza rhymes assonantly with *deeds* in the first line of the second stanza, but the word *deeds* rhymes almost fully with *read* in the third line. *Companion* and *Galan* rhyme consonantly (the *n*'s) with *man*, the next to the last word in the second line of the preceding stanza—a quite unusual variation. Yet despite the variations on the form, MacLeish's treatment is considered to be strict and formal within the flexible limits that he has established.

Like the *terza rima*, the *sonnet* is an old form that originated in Provence and was used widely in Italy, England, and America up to the present. The word *sonnet* means little song and is particularly appropriate for a short observation, usually personal and subjective. The traditional sonnet is a fourteen-line rhymed poem in iambic pentameter (five stresses to a line), comprised of two parts: the first eight lines (the octave), and the last six lines (the sestet), usually following a prescribed rhyme scheme. The octave often states a single thought, idea, or problem, which is summed up or resolved in the sestet. There are several variations in the sonnet form: The Italian or Petrarchan sonnet, a favorite among poets during the Renaissance, which rhymes *abaabba cdecde*; the Spenserian sonnet, which rhymes *abab bcbc cdcd ee*, and has three rhyme-linked stanzas and a final couplet, unlike the two-stanza Italian sonnet; and the Shakespearean sonnet, which rhymes *abab cdcd efef gg*, made up of three stanzas that are not rhyme-linked, and a final couplet. Here is an example of the Shakespearean sonnet:

SONNET 116

Let me not to the marriage of true minds
Admit impediments. Love is not love
Which alters when it alteration finds,

Or bends with the remover to remove.
O, no! it is an ever-fixed mark
That looks on tempests and is never shaken;
It is the star to every wandering bark,
Whose worth's unknown, although his height be taken.
Love's not Time's fool, though rosy lips and cheeks
Within his bending sickle's compass come;
Love alters not with his brief hours and weeks,
But bears it out even to the edge of doom.
  If this be error and upon me proved,
  I never writ, nor no man ever loved.

The excellence of Shakespeare's one hundred and fifty-four sonnets in sequence has been a perennial challenge to poets. As a consequence, the sonnet has become a much-abused form, culminating in the *tour de force* of Merrill Moore, who wrote over a hundred thousand sonnets. Among contemporary poets, the sonnet has undergone some changes: unrhymed sonnets, sonnets with fewer than five stresses to the line, even fifteen-line sonnets. I believe, however, that the essence of the sonnet form is its adherence to a fourteen-line length.

EXERCISE 13. *Write a fourteen-line, rhymed sonnet, five stresses to the line. Follow, if you wish, the Shakespearean sonnet, with its climactic couplet at the end. If you don't want to start on a new subject, try fitting one of the drafts you wrote in the first eight exercises into a sonnet. Try to think in terms of statement and resolution.*

One of the most flexible and commonly used forms is blank verse, which is written in unrhymed iambic pentameter. Every line must have five recurrent stresses and a minimum of ten syllables. Blank verse is especially appropriate for dramatic and narrative poems. It offers a broader canvas than other forms because there is no limit to the number of lines that a poem may use.

Shakespeare uses blank verse, occasionally interspersed with songs and lyrics, for the dialogue in his plays. Milton uses it spectacularly in his epics, *Paradise Lost* and *Samson Agonistes*. Here are the famous first lines from *Paradise Lost*:

Of Man's first Disobedience, and the Fruit
Of that Forbidden Tree, whose mortal taste
Brought Death into the world, and all our woe,
With loss of Eden, till one greater Man
Restore us, and regain the blissful Seat,
Sing Heav'nly Muse . . .

Blank verse was also a favorite form of Edwin Arlington Robinson and Robert Frost. Here is a passage from Robinson's *Tristam*, based on the legendary love story of Tristram and Isolt:

Isolt of the white hands, in Brittany,
Could see no longer northward anywhere
A picture more alive or less familiar
Than a blank ocean and the same white birds
Flying, and always flying, and still flying,
Yet never bringing any news of him
That she remembered, who had sailed away
The spring before . . .

The cadence of five accented syllables to a line seems peculiarly suited to English poetry, either because we have read so much of it in our literature, or because the vocabulary and sentence structure of English speech falls naturally into that pattern.

EXERCISE 14. *Write at least ten lines of blank verse, telling a story or recounting dialogue. Try to think in terms of a five-beat line. Use simple conversational language. You will find that your words will fall easily into the pattern.*

Regularity of meter and rhyme, regular recurrence, may be satisfying to poet and reader, but some poets have felt that the rigidity of absolute regularity is monotonous, artificial, and inappropriate to contemporary subject matter. During the past one hundred years, many American poets have come to feel that the line is governed by an "organic" musical phrase, the duration of the speaking or singing breath. It is not as insistent or obvious as regular rhyme and meter, but it is still as natural as the human pulse. This poetry is called "free verse" because it has "freed" itself from traditional set forms. In actuality, it is still governed by an organic recurrence that is called *cadence* rather than meter. Recurrence in free verse is more subtle than in fixed forms. It uses repetition of sounds and words within the line and occasionally the recurrence of rhyme. Stresses recur in a looser but still identifiable pattern, a pattern that more nearly follows the natural cadence of conversation. Line breaks, the shape of the poem, the length of the line, all depend on the breath and pauses of the poet or speaker reading the line. In free verse, the organic structure of the poem—its meaning and the way it is said—entirely dictates the poem's form. Many of the model poems in this book are in free verse because that is a dominant form used by the majority of contemporary American poets.

One of the most important variations on form in the twentieth century is the triadic stanza invented by William Carlos Williams. His intention was to control free verse with a "variable foot" based on the normal measure of American speech, because, as he said, "Man and the poet must keep pace with this world." Here are a few triadic (three-line) stanzas from his poem, "Asphodel, That Greeny Flower":

Of asphodel, that greeny flower,
    I come, my sweet,
        to sing to you!

My heart rouses
    thinking to bring you news
        of something

that concerns you
    and concerns many men. Look at
        what passes for the new.

You will not find it there but in
    despised poems.
        It is difficult

to get the news from poems
    yet men die miserably every day
        for lack

of what is found there.

As Kenneth Rexroth described Williams's poetry, "His poetic line is organically welded to American speech like muscle to bone."

In writing free verse, how does the poet know when to break the line? In regular meter, in which each line is supposed to have the same number of stressed and unstressed syllables, the end of the line comes after the appropriate number of recurrent stresses. The metrical control of the number of the line is apparent even when the poem is written without any break at the end of the line. In the famous papyrus manuscript of poems by the Greek poet Sappho, the poems are written continuously back and forth, the way an ox ploughs a field, in a pattern called *boustrophedon* (meaning how an ox turns a plough back and forth).

If the Shakespearean sonnet quoted earlier were written in this fashion, would you be able to figure out the correct line breaks?

Let me not to the marriage of true minds admit
impediments love is not love which alters when
it alteration finds or bends with the remover
to remove o no it is an ever fixed mark that
looks on tempests and is never shaken it is

And so on. Both rhyme and meter guide you to the correct line breaks despite the dizzying arrangement above. Here they are, as written by Shakespeare:

Let me not to the marriage of true minds
admit impediments. Love is not love
which alters when it alteration finds
or bends with the remover to remove

You can see that if the poem is in a regular fixed form—if it follows exactly the same pattern of stresses in every line—the line breaks are readily apparent. It is comparable to the bars or measures in music. You can tell by listening to a piece of music, for instance, that it is in three-fourths time, and thus you know that the measures will be divided after every three whole beats. In the same way, it is clear in Shakespeare's sonnet that there must be a line break after every five stresses.

But what of the line endings in free verse? Without the same number of recurrent stresses, each line must be judged separately. Sometimes the controlling factor may be stress count in an irregular pattern, but what usually determines the line ending is the breath-phrase, the natural break in the line according to breath, phrasing, and meaning. Although the decision must be made by the poet, it is not merely intellectual or willful; it must be perceptive and intuitive in terms of the organic shape within the poem.

What shape does your poem want? Where does the line need to break? Read it out loud to find out.

Here is a short free-verse poem of mine, written without any line breaks:

> a veil fell just now between me and the white
> ocean—one of the shutters of evening is closing—
> the blind hands of tides are feeling their way
> below the cliffs and mountains beneath the forest
> of water among the weeds and eyeless fish along
> twilight canyons to the underside of light

EXERCISE 15. *Type or write out these lines on a separate piece of paper. Then read it out loud, listening to where the natural phrases or clusters of meaning occur. The end of each phrase is a place for a line break. Mark the phrases with a slant line (/), then write the lines with the line breaks that you would prefer. Compare your version of the poem with my final draft (below). Finally, write your own free-verse poem on a subject of your choice.*

The natural line breaks can be chosen from among these possibilities:

a veil / fell / just now / between me / and the white
ocean / one of the shutters / of evening / is closing /
the blind hands / of tides / are feeling their way /
below the cliffs / and mountains / beneath the forest
of water / among the weeds / and eyeless fish / along
twilight canyons / to the underside / of light

Those are the possibilities for organic line breaks. After writing the poem out several different ways, I discovered that it wanted to go like this:

a veil fell just now

between me and the white ocean

one of the shutters of evening is closing

the blind hands of tides
are feeling their way
below the cliffs and mountains
beneath the forest of water among

the weeds and eyeless fish
along twilight canyons to the

underside of light

I discovered that not only the break at the end of the line but the spaces between lines and stanzas can dramatize the movement of the poem. I wanted to choreograph the poem on the page so that its shape and meaning would coincide. I used the first line as the title and decided not to use any punctuation, but to let the placing of the words make the poem comprehensible. Notice that every line, up to "beneath the forest of water," breaks at the expected end of the phrase.

Why, then, did I leave the word "among" irrationally at the end of the line rather than as part of the whole phrase, "among the weeds and eyeless fish"? Because the regularity of phrases began to seem monotonous to me, and I wanted to arrest the reader's attention. The same explanation applies to "to the" at the end of the next to the last line. I knew my phrase, "underside of light," was the best part of the poem. If I had written "to the underside of light" on one line, it would have been perfectly correct, but the words would not have stood out nearly as much as when I wrenched them apart from "to the"—a discordance, an unsmoothing that does not destroy the essential lyric quality of the poem.

A poet can manipulate the words at the beginnings and ends of lines for emphasis and dramatic effect, using a line break where it would not be expected. But there must always be a good reason, appropriate to the meaning, for not following the natural phrasing.

The only form that does not use line endings at all, but is written in the form of a prose paragraph, is the prose poem. The prose poem first made its appearance during the nineteenth century in the work of Baudelaire, Rimbaud, and Mallarmé. It has since attracted the attention of many European and American poets, among them Francis Ponge, Zbigniew Herbert, Russell Edson, and Michael Benedikt, because it is a challenge to the ingenuity and imagination of the poet.

Although it does not have line breaks, the prose poem, which is a poem written in paragraph form, must have the compression of a lyric poem, short and compact, and must be written with economy and intensity. It often has a narrative to tell. Because it does not employ the arrangement and space that a verse poem uses, it must use other forms of recurrence: parallel sentence structure, cadence, alliteration, assonance, consonance, and even internal rhyme.

What often distinguishes the prose poem is its use of surrealistic or dreamlike imagery, creating a cumulative metaphorical effect. In David Ignatow's prose poem "The Juggler," the poet presents an unusual scene where the juggler extracts a "live rabbit, tiger cub, a rooster, a monkey, [and] a musical instrument" and tosses them into the air. The objects "squawk, growl, chatter, crow," while the instrument plays music, prompting the reader to wonder, "In protest? Who can tell? It is music and that's all." This chaotic act symbolizes the poet's role in manipulating language and ideas—alive, unpredictable, and full of sound. The juggler's laughter underscores this connection, as "nobody wonders why he uses live things," suggesting a deeper relationship between the poet's creative process and the living elements of the world.

The whole poem is actually in itself a metaphor: the juggler is the poet who manipulates live things, they make sounds, even the oboe is in this sense alive. Wit often plays an important part in the tone of the prose poem. It is playful and at the same time serious; irrational and profound.

The forms described in this chapter and the preceding chapter are just a few of the forms available to the poet searching for the right shape for his poem. The only way to be sure you have found the right shape is to develop a repertory of forms by reading, imitating, and practicing the forms of other poets. Mastery of form, whether you are training yourself in fixed forms or are dealing with the more difficult problems of free verse, does not come easily. On the one hand, it is difficult to submit to the challenge of a fixed form. In free verse, on the other hand, you must be sure there is a good reason for everything you do. There is, as Octavio Paz says at the head of this chapter, a morality to technique, a passion and an asceticism, whether you are writing in a traditional form or inventing a new one.

Finding the form for your poem means learning how to discover the organic necessity within the poem. By gathering knowledge and experience, you will ultimately find the right shape for your poem. There are few experiences more satisfying or exhilarating.

VII. THE ART OF REVISION

> In the eyes of others, a man is a poet if he has written one good poem. In his own he is only a poet at the moment when he is making his last revision to a new poem.
>
> —W. H. Auden, *The Dyer's Hand*

The French poet Paul Valéry remarked that a poem is never finished; it is only abandoned. He was saying that your original intention, the vision in your mind, is rarely realized in the final work. This is partly because your control of the material—both content and form—is often flawed.

But it is also because as soon as you contact that great source of creative energy within you, you discover there is a dynamic force outside you that can sometimes move in a direction different from your original intention. When this occurs, it is wise to yield to it. You must be sensitive to the potent energy in your work, be able to recognize it and be willing to follow it without losing your control. It is like riding a spirited horse. You guide it along the path you intend to ride, but the animal's will, direction, and speed also guide you. The two energies must fit together.

The process of accommodation between you and the poem is practical as well as metaphysical. After you have finished a draft of the poem that is more or less the way you want it; after you have brought it as far as your experience can take you, there is a great temptation to sit back and admire your creation.

You have learned to let your first words come as unself-consciously as possible. You have learned to suspend the judgmental part of your mind as you reach into the primary sources of your material. You have then learned to look for the right form for your words, the organic shape for the content. You have typed the poem in the best and clearest way you can invent. The question you must then ask yourself is not *How beautiful is this poem?* but *What's wrong with this poem?*

This doesn't mean that you let your heart sink in disappointment or that you allow yourself to be overcome with discouragement at your own work. It means using a cool, critical detachment to find the flaws in the poem and to mend them. But how do you achieve this detachment? One of the best and most useful ways to gain perspective on what you have written is to read it aloud. If you can find a willing ear, read it out loud to someone else. Read with a pencil in your hand, and mark whatever seems flawed to you. You can detect a weakness by hearing the hesitation in your voice, by stumbling over a word, by the judgment of your eye. Be sure that your text matches your voice, that is, that the line breaks occur where you really want them, judging by the natural breath phrases and clusters of meaning. Be sure that you are using space where the dramatic movement of the poem requires a pause, that the poem looks the way it sounds. The poem on the page may be viewed as the score for a spoken performance. It should be written in such a way that anyone who reads it will know exactly how you intend it to be read.

Better than reading aloud to yourself or to someone else is to record the poem. I frequently use recordings when I revise a poem, especially when I reach a point at which I have lost objectivity but feel that something is still wrong. I record the poem, and then, a while later, I play it back to myself, listening to it as though someone else had written it. Recording the text this way provides an extra dimension, an added perspective, that enables you to judge your work more quickly and accurately. Using recordings not only helps you spot the flaws in your work, but also trains the sensitivity of your ear by teaching you to listen carefully. By constantly reading aloud and playing back the recording, you will learn to read aloud clearly and expressively. This not only helps to develop your characteristic style and cadence but prepares you for poetry readings in the future.

Writing poetry and constantly reading other poets means that you are continually developing and sharpening your judgment. W. H. Auden once remarked that his ambition was eventually to have perfect judgment about his own work. I doubt this is possible, although I think it is possible to know when something is wrong, or occasionally to know that a poem has come out surprisingly well. But it would take a superhuman poet always to have perfect judgment.

It is useful, if you have access to a workshop, to read your work aloud to other writers and to get their reactions and suggestions. A group of poets working informally together can be helpful to each other. Better still, if there is an accomplished poet leading a workshop, you will be able to gain a great deal by studying with her or him and learning to criticize your own poems. Robert Lowell tried out his new poems on fellow poets to get their reactions. Ezra Pound rewrote the whole of T. S. Eliot's *The Waste Land*, suggesting passages to be eliminated, changed, and rewritten. If Eliot had not accepted Pound's help, the poem might not have received the acclaim it now enjoys.

As a young poet, I never took part in a workshop, but I knew what I wanted to do and how to go about it: namely to read everything I could lay my hands on, to imitate those poets I admired, to compare my work to theirs, and slowly to develop taste and judgment. Later I found friends among other, older poets, who were very helpful to me.

It is not enough, of course, merely to ask the question, *What's wrong with this poem?* You must look it over from head to toe, as you would a child you are about to send out into the world. Here are some of the questions you must answer:

1. Does the poem have a title? Is the title appropriate?
2. Are the line breaks in the right place?
3. Does the poem have enough space? Should it have more stanzas, or would it be better to keep the lines in one cluster?
4. Have you used too many adjectives? Adjectives tend to weaken a noun, unless they are extraordinary or precise. The more adjectives you use, the weaker the poem will be.
5. Are there too many adverbs? Remember that the strength of a poem, as with all writing, lies first in its verbs, and then its nouns. The verbs must be lively, the nouns specific.
6. Have you avoided abstract language?
7. Have you used the passive voice when the active would be much more effective?
8. Have you explained too much?
9. Does the poem continue after it is actually finished?
10. Does the poem really start after the first few lines?

Two danger spots to watch for are the beginning and the end of a poem. Young poets often begin a poem with a sort of warming-up exercise—like making a running start before a jump—and the real poem begins after the first several lines. If you recognize that you have done this, find out where the poem really begins and then eliminate those first lines. Some poems keep going on, making unnecessary explanations or repeating an already well-made conclusion after the end. In that case, you must have the courage to delete those last lines.

Are there enough clues so that a reader would know what you are talking about? If not, you need to expand.

Does the poem sing? Does it follow the natural emphasis and cadence of your speaking voice?

Here are some worksheets of a poem of mine, showing the various stages of revision through the six drafts that brought the poem to its final published form:

<u>Draft 1</u>

Directions for Building a Fire

Two logs are best.
~~If you add a third~~
~~it upsets the balance.~~

They must barely touch:
set them close enough to draw juice from the embers,
far enough apart so the ~~spark~~ ~~flame~~ fire
won't be smothered.
If one leans too much on the other
it ~~the fire~~ goes out.
You must discover
that ~~the~~ brushing distance where the ~~flame~~ spark
ignites them both ~~pours up~~ and burns them together.

In a little while
time changes the relation.
One loses in the flame
more than the other.

Let me step back
so you may move an inch forward.

This poem began when I was at the MacDowell Colony, where I tried to build a fire every morning in my cabin. As I tried to make the logs ignite and keep burning, it occurred to me that what makes a fire catch and burn is essentially the same quality that keeps a human relationship going: a skillful combination of touching and not touching. I wanted the poem to portray this, rather than say it. As is common in my writing, my first draft was longer than the final version. My initial concern was to get down everything I could think of about my experience in building a fire.

The first stanza in Draft 1 seemed rather banal to me, too flatly explanatory. I wanted the poem to begin with a more enigmatic and challenging line. I crossed out lines two and three and decided to try for a better first line.

"They must barely touch"—This line uses the word *must*, which carries out the intention of giving directions, but in Draft 2 I tried leaving it out.

"Set them close enough to draw juice from the embers"—by Draft 2, I had added the imperative "set them," to carry out the idea of giving directions but was still not sure this phrase belonged. The real inspiration

Draft 2

Directions for Building a Fire

Two logs are best.

They ~~must~~ barely touch;
~~set them~~ close enough
to draw juice from the embers,
far enough apart so ~~the fire~~ neither
will ~~won't~~ be smothered.
If one leans ~~too much~~ on the other
the fire goes out.
You must discover
that brushing distance where the sparks
ignites them both
and, Then burns them together.

In a little while
time has changed the relation.
One loses in the flame
more than the other.

Let me step back
so you may move an inch forward.

in this new line was adding the word "juice." Drawing "juice" from the embers was now superimposing a word usually applied to a living organism upon an inanimate object—namely, a fire—thus implying a condition that leads toward a human metaphor.

It is interesting to note that all the problems in this poem are confined to the first two stanzas. There are very few changes in the last two stanzas, only slight alteration in the words and their position on the page, throughout the six drafts.

Looking at my metrical patterns in Draft 2, I discovered that most of the lines were in two- or three-stress meter, and some in five-stress. This discovery gave me the idea of writing the whole poem in equal lines of five stresses each, as shown in Draft 3. But reading it over, I knew it was wrong. Filling out every line to make the five stresses had resulted in a poem that was prolix, explanatory, and dull. I decided to abandon the idea of five-stress lines. Something was wrong in my conception of the poem. I put the poem aside for several years. Yes, years! It contained a good idea, but I didn't know how to make it an immediate experience rather than a dull explanation.

When I picked the poem up again, I realized my mistake. It was that I had been trying to give directions. I was making the poem didactic, robbing it of its immediacy. I decided to call the poem simply "Laying a Fire," and was at once relieved of the dogmatic tone of the earlier versions. Now I was narrating, not explaining.

Draft 3

Directions for Building a Fire

When the real fire starts two logs are best.
Only in rare instance can you add a third
and then it usually upsets the balance.

The two logs must barely touch.
Close enough to draw juice from the embers,
far enough apart so their generative tongues
won't be smothered. If one leans on the other
the fire goes out. The two have a secret design,
a brushing distance each must discover
where the fullest flame pours up and burns them together.

In a little while time has changed the relation.
One has lost in the flame more than the other.
Let me step back so you may move an inch forward.

Draft 4

LAYING A FIRE

The fire starts when two logs meet.
They must barely touch.

Close enough to vitalize the embers,
enough apart so every tongue can move
freely. If one leans too hard on the other
the fire coughs and smokes.
A brushing distance
makes a better flame.

In a little while time changes ~~their~~ relation. The
One loses in the fire more than the other.

I'll step back. You
move an inch forward.

I wanted to preserve the idea of starting with two logs. Now, in Draft 4, my first line was, "The fire starts when two logs meet." I followed this with my original second line from Draft 1, "They must barely touch." The third line was giving me trouble: "Close enough to vitalize the embers . . ." The word "vitalize" was wrong. It was a Latinate, multisyllabic word instead of a simple one. In Draft 5 I went back to "draw up from the embers," but it wasn't until the sixth and final version that I rediscovered the word "juice" from Draft 2 and decided it was the right one. Back on Draft 4 come the lines, "enough apart so every tongue can move / freely." I liked the inspiration of using the word tongue—it was doing a double service, suggesting a tongue of flame and, I hoped, a human tongue, thus helping the double meaning (condensation) implied in "juice" to be carried a step further.

Draft 5

LAYING A FIRE

The fire starts when two logs meet.

They barely touch.

Close enough to draw up from the embers,
enough apart so every tongue moves
freely.

If one leans too hard on the other
the fire coughs and smokes; a brushing distance
makes a better flame.

In a little while time changes their relation.
One loses in the fire more than the other.

I'll step back. You
move an inch forward.

But then I was in trouble. The next four lines weren't working. They were slipping back into that explanatory, didactic tone. In Draft 5 I tried the same lines with different spacing, but they were still wrong. It wasn't until Draft 6 that I realized these lines were redundant. I had already said what was essential about being close and yet apart in lines three and four. It took courage, but I threw lines five to eight away.

The next two sentences—"In a little while time changes their relation" and "One loses in the fire more than the other"—had been carried practically intact from the third stanza of Draft 1. It seemed clear to me that since they were both five-stress lines, it would be pleasant to vary the cadence of the poem by keeping them whole, especially since they are used in anticipation of the last two lines, which change suddenly from a third-person point of view to the poet speaking. By this device I was first hiding the metaphor, then hinting at it (by "juice" and "tongue"), and finally letting it emerge.

<u>Draft 6</u>

LAYING A FIRE

The fire starts when two logs meet.

They barely touch.

Close enough to draw juice from the embers,
enough apart so every tongue moves
freely.

In a little while time changes the relation.
One loses in the fire more than the other.

I'll step back.

You
move an inch forward.

Since I was no longer giving directions but describing a dramatic event, I could change the "let me step back" to "I'll step back." But those two, short final lines in Draft 5 seemed too neat to me. I wanted to break them up, since this was a surprise ending. And so, in Draft 6, I dropped down the "You" as though "You" were really moving an inch forward.

Ten years after I first began this poem, the final draft, Draft 6, was published in the *New Republic*. Is it possible to write a poem that doesn't need revision? Yes, it is possible, but it doesn't happen frequently. When a poem comes full-blown and perfect, it is a gift. I have received a few such gifts, as have other poets, but it is not common. Usually a "given" poem is short, and you know at once that it is flawless. But you might also feel that you had nothing to do with it, that it came from a source outside yourself.

There are some poets who believe that the first draft, just as it comes from pen or keyboard, is somehow sacred because it reflects the elemental, unself-conscious mind at work. Don't let them fool you. In most cases, the work will be careless and entirely forgettable. You may find many of these first drafts in current magazines, but the models you are looking for are careful, well-made poems.

After you reach a point in your revising when you have lost your objectivity, it is useful to put the poem face down on your desk for at least three days. But sometimes, if there are knots in the poem that you cannot unravel, it may take months, even years to finish it, as with my poem, "Laying a Fire."

Never throw away a failed poem. Put it in a folder and let time pass. If you go on reading and writing and developing as a poet, you will be able at some point to pick up that failed poem and know exactly what you need to do to solve the problem. Even if you can't use the whole poem, you may discover lines or phrases in it that you can use in another poem. Don't let impatience deprive you of a great advantage—the passage of time. Time is one of the tools of the writer. Use it.

VIII. THE ULTIMATE TASK

Come, said my soul,
Such verses for my body let us write (for we are one)
That should I after death invisibly return,
Or, long, long hence, in other spheres,
There to some group of mates the chants resuming
(Tallying earth's soil, trees, winds, tumultuous waves),
Ever with pleas'd smile I may keep on,
Ever and ever yet the verses owning—as first, I here and now,
Signing for soul and body, set to them my name.

—Walt Whitman, Invocation to *Leaves of Grass*

> Which part of me is me?
>
> —Spoken by a four-year-old child

In every work of art you look for the signature of the maker. Eventually you are able to recognize the maker from the work—Rembrandt in his portraits, Emily Dickinson in her poems, Mozart in his music. The poet Stanley Kunitz once told me that what he looks for in a poem is the person behind the poem, and if there is no one there, if the poet is hidden behind a poem that is too abstract or impersonal, he is disappointed.

Whether you realize it or not, what you are doing in the course of your work is defining who you are. When you have written and accumulated enough poems, they will begin to make a portrait of you, not an external portrait, but an internal one. This does not mean that you want to concentrate on writing exclusively egocentric and confessional poetry, but it does mean that whether you write about your own experience or not, you are making a characteristic individual imprint.

Direct self-confrontation is sometimes frightening. We are afraid of monsters inside ourselves, and we are afraid of the blemishes we may find, as we saw in Louise Bogan's poem, "The Dream." Yet to follow a simple exercise of self-confrontation often helps to put aside some of those fears.

Looking in a mirror and then immediately writing about it is one of the best ways I know for filling in the lines of your internal (as well as external) portrait. Are mirrors true? In some societies mirrors are thought to be magic: They will refuse to reflect an evil person, and if you want to identify a devil or vampire, you can hold a mirror up to its face and there will be no reflection. In Orthodox Jewish households, mirrors are covered over with sheets during the period of mourning so that the mourners won't be distracted from their grief by their own faces and their everyday lives. Some pre-modern cultures believe that mirrors, like photographs, steal the living reality of the subject. Do mirrors know more than they show? Remember the famous mirror in the nursery rhyme:

> Mirror, mirror on the wall
> Who's the fairest one of all?

asked the wicked Queen, even after she believed she had murdered Snow White, and the mirror answered:

Queen, you are full fair, it's true,
But Snow White is fairer still than you.

Randall Jarrell's poem "From the Night Before the Night Before Christmas" offers a glimpse into a young woman's private reflection as she studies herself in the mirror. She questions, "Do I really look like that?" and moves between moments of self-critique and brief admiration, noting her "beautiful golden—anyway, yellow" hair and "How white her teeth are." Despite this, she ultimately wonders, "What do I really look like? / I don't know. / Not really. / *Really*." The poem is remarkable because it is written by a man who has insight into how a young woman may think of herself while she examines herself in a mirror, looking for her own reality.

Sylvia Plath's poem "Mirror" offers a unique perspective as the speaker embodies the voice of a mirror, stating, "I am silver and exact. I have no preconceptions." The mirror presents itself as a neutral observer, "unmisted by love or dislike," capturing images with an impartial, god-like quality. The poem shifts when the mirror becomes "a lake," reflecting a woman who "bends over me, / Searching my reaches for what she really is." This woman's quest for self-understanding leads to disappointment. From the mirror's point of view:

She comes and goes.
Each morning it is her face that replaces the darkness
In me she has drowned a young girl, and in me an old woman
rises towards her day after day, a terrible fish.

That image of the future face of old age as "a terrible fish" characterizes her horror at the thought of aging.

EXERCISE 16. *Look in a mirror for one minute. It may be difficult and even a little embarrassing to look deliberately at yourself, but you must persist. After the first shyness, you will begin to see. What do you see? Your physical characteristics, of course. You may also notice your resemblance to your mother or father, or to other members of your family. You may see the passage of time. You may remind yourself how you looked when you were younger or think* *about how you will look when you are older. Write your mirror poem as quickly as you can, letting your mind seize on any aspect of the mirror experience it wants to, even if it ranges away from your actual image. Try to keep the freshness of the first impact, using direct and simple language to describe how it makes you feel, what it makes you think about.*

Self-confrontation takes many forms. It can be a kind of revelation, almost like an epiphany, at that moment when you recognize the central reality of your life. In Stanley Kunitz's poem, "The Illumination," the speaker describes being in a hotel room where his "life / rolled in its socket / twisting my strings." Past mistakes rise up—"the parent I denied, / the friends I failed, / the hearts I spoiled"—culminating in the haunting realization of "a history of shame." This moment of reckoning is intensified by the sudden appearance of Dante, "laureled and gaunt, / in a cone of light," symbolizing guidance and judgment. The figure's response, "I know neither the time / nor the way / nor the number on the door . . . but this must be my room, / I was here before," underscores a shared human struggle. The final, blinding image of the key in Dante's hand represents the instant of complete revelation and self-recognition.

Adrienne Rich, in her poem "Diving into the Wreck," explores the profound process of self-confrontation, symbolized by a solitary dive into deep, unknown waters. She begins with preparation, saying, "First having read the book of myths / and loaded the camera, / and checked the edge of the knife-blade," emphasizing the deliberate readiness for exploration. She acknowledges the loneliness of her endeavor: "not like Cousteau with his / assiduous team . . . but here alone."

As she descends, Rich captures the tension and vulnerability of the experience: "I go down. / Rung after rung and still / the oxygen immerses me." The imagery of "blue light / the clear atoms / of our human air" conveys the shift from familiar to foreign territory, underscoring the sense of isolation and uncertainty as she continues, "I crawl like an insect down the ladder / and there is no one / to tell me when the ocean / will begin." This descent represents the journey into the depths of self-awareness, where confronting the hidden wreck within oneself becomes an act of courage and discovery.

She sees the changing colors of the water as she descends, the underwater life, and then the poem moves into a more intense phase, what she came for:

> the thing I came for:
> the wreck and not the story of the wreck
> the thing itself and not the myth
> the drowned face always staring
> towards the sun . . .
>
> This is the place.
> And I am here, the mermaid whose dark hair
> streams black, the merman in his armored body . . .
> we dive into the hold.
> I am she: I am he
>
> whose drowned face sleeps with open eyes . . .
> we are the half-destroyed instruments
> that once held to a course

Rich is saying that she herself is both the explorer, and the victim, together with all victims, male and female. She wants to look steadily and without flinching at the "half destroyed instruments that once held to a course." Whatever it is that has characterized her life, the shipwreck, the drowning, the survival of relics, she is willing to confront it, using all the devices that she can summon, although the event itself is so universal, so common, that her name as participant will be forgotten.

This is one of the most moving poems I know about the process of self-confrontation.

If I were to choose one poem of my own as a self-defining poem, I would choose "A Questionnaire." When I wrote it, I wasn't consciously aware that I was defining myself. What was paramount in my mind at the time was that I had been spending many days filling out real questionnaires and grant applications, and at the same time, my children were asking my help in filling out their college applications. I began to be obsessed with the basic questions. I dreamed about them. I thought, "Does one ever give the true answer in a questionnaire? One may give the factual answers, but something essential is missing." I then decided to write my own questionnaire, giving answers that were not necessarily factual, but that felt true and essential. Here is the poem:

A QUESTIONNAIRE

Describe your early education.
At six, standing on the low stone wall
beside my grandfather, I was taller than he.
Wearing my white beret, hair cut short,
with leather leggings to my knee, I put my hand
on his shoulder possessively
and sang him his lullaby, *a moloch veynt*,
an angel weeps, an angel weeps.

What is your permanent address.
A flat rock in Central Park
where an innocent policeman
found me with my first sweetheart.
Under Cambridge clocks chiming each quarter hour.
Beside the sea.
Beneath Mount Zion.
On Boston's broad Victorian bosom.
Across the pond where you are standing, laughing at me

Male or female.
Both. When I saw the Greek Hermaphrodite
I recognized myself and you, each
two in one. Now I know why
the Masai warriors grow brave
by drinking blood and milk.

Are you married.
Yes, many times.
I marry my first loves
over and over. Like coming home.

Describe a crucial event in your life.
At twenty, I died and was born again. For a while
I died every day. One day when I was dying
beside the sea, which ignored me,
when my guts ran empty and I started sinking
into that bottomless hollow
beneath the bed, I suddenly heard
(through the window, in my head)
the notes of the *Appassionata*
calling me back into the world.

List your awards and honors.
Three children.
One, a yellow tearose.
Two, a winedark peony.
Three, a young fox, heart's desire.

Give a brief statement of your plans.
To fly.
To swim across the pond.
To tell what I know.
To love you harder.

This questionnaire by no means covers all the possibilities of asking meaningful questions about your life. Other suggestions made by students are: Have you ever been in jail? What is your mother's maiden name? Where were you born?

EXERCISE 17. *Write your own questionnaire, using either these questions or any others that come to your mind. You can write an entire poem based on just one question. Whatever you write for this exercise, you will find that your answer is pointing towards an insight into yourself, your past, your life and character.*

Remember that self-definition is never final. As you live and write, and as you change with changing circumstances and relationships, your definition will change. But accept the present revelation: it is your reward for the humility and honesty you bring to your poem.

IX. COMMUNICATING THE POEM

> This is my letter to the World
> That never wrote to Me—
>
> —Emily Dickinson

Part of the basic motivation for writing a poem is to share your perceptions with someone else, to communicate your feelings, to send your poem out into the world.

But if you write a poem with publication in mind from the beginning, you will tend to distort either the form or the subject to fit what you imagine to be marketable. Your first responsibility is to come as close as possible to realizing and expressing your own vision of the poem, to revise and be willing to work towards that personal vision. Only then is it time to think about submitting your poem to a magazine.

How do you know when you are ready? The Roman poet Horace in his *The Art of Poetry* suggests that you put a poem away for six months before you can make a proper judgment about it. You may not be willing to wait that long. Poets both new and experienced are eager to see their work in print, but getting published is often a difficult and disappointing process. Not everyone has the experience of Theodore Roethke, who wrote this description of his first attempts to publish his poetry:

> My first verses, and dreadful they were, I sold for $1. About a year later when I was moping through the Harvard Yard one night, I saw a man I thought might be Robert Hillyer. I said boldly, "Pardon me, Sir, I think I have some poems you might like." A look of pain came over his face. "Come to my office at eleven," he said. . . . Ushered in by his secretary, he took the verse, started reading. Suddenly he wheeled in his chair. "Any editor who wouldn't buy these is a fool!" he said.

The three poems were subsequently published in *The New Republic* and *Commonweal*, and for the rest of Roethke's life, he had little difficulty in publishing.

For the beginning poet, however, it is important to begin modestly. Many young writers, with dreams of instant fame, send poems to the major national magazines first. These magazines receive so many thousands of poems every month that most of them never reach the eyes of the poetry editor, but are screened by first and second readers. Your chances of success are better if you submit your work to little or literary magazines first, or to newspapers or magazines that publish poetry. Look at the newspapers and magazines online or on the newsstand. There is no better way to discover the wide range of publications that use poetry, even though some of the smaller ones pay little or nothing, except perhaps in copies.

Be sure to read a recent copy of the magazine before you submit a manuscript to it. Reading the magazine helps you judge whether your work is likely to fit into it or not although acceptance is never predictable. Only a few times have I sent a poem to a magazine with complete confidence and found that it was accepted immediately. More often, editors accept poems that I had not expected them to take. The choice often seems arbitrary.

If your work is rejected, it is important not to take it as a personal evaluation, but to rethink your choice of magazine and try again. After several rejections, it may be wise to go over the poem carefully to see if it should be revised again.

There are certain rules to follow—based on custom and courtesy—when you submit a poem to a magazine. If you send it electronically, follow their instructions. If you're submitting your work by mail, follow these steps for a polished presentation. Use standard 8½ × 11 white paper and print your poem clearly, single or double-spaced, on one side only. Include your name and address in the upper corner of every page and be sure to keep a copy for yourself. You can submit one to six poems at a time. Always enclose a self-addressed stamped envelope (SASE) with enough postage for a return. Address the envelope to the poetry editor by name, if possible, and consider including a short note about your writing background or previous publications to add a personal touch.

Generally, it is not a good idea to submit the same poem to more than one magazine at a time. If a magazine keeps your poem for more than three months, it is appropriate to send a courteous inquiry, giving the date of your submission and asking for a report. If the magazine keeps your work for more than six months, you may want to let them know you are withdrawing the poem, and then feel free to send it somewhere else.

It is important to keep a record of where and when you send every poem. You may find it useful to keep one notebook listing the titles of the poems you send out, entering the date, the name of the publication you send each one to, and the date of rejection or acceptance. I keep two loose-leaf notebooks arranged in alphabetical order: one for the titles of the poems I send out, and one for the titles of the magazines to which I send them. In this way I can tell at a glance where any one poem has been sent and also what poems I have sent to a specific magazine. Other poets prefer a computer or file card system, since it is easy to arrange alphabetically and to add or remove the entries. Whatever system you use, you will find it essential to keep a record of what you send and where.

If you are fortunate enough to have published in several magazines and have thirty or forty finished poems, you may be ready to publish a chapbook or a book of poetry. Most trade publishers are reluctant to publish poetry by unknown poets, particularly since the sale of books of poetry is usually low and unprofitable.

The best market for books of poetry is the small presses and the university presses. You can find a list of these in publications like *Literary Market Place*, which gives valuable information to writers about markets, competitions, and awards.

Publication of your poetry is not the only way to share it with others. During the past twenty years, public poetry readings have grown in popularity and proliferated all over the country, from small-town schools and libraries to college and university campuses; from private living rooms to bookstores, art galleries, and community centers.

Young poets may think it daunting to read publicly to strangers the poems they have labored so long in private to perfect, but they will find it an exhilarating and rewarding experience to see an audience respond to their words. If listeners show that they are interested and moved by what they hear, it is immensely encouraging for the poet.

When you read your own lines aloud in public, you find out many things about your own poems—rhythms, choice of language and subject—that may not have been evident to you when you worked alone.

I have often changed a word or line break as the result of hearing myself at a reading.

In recent years, partly through the generosity of the National Endowment for the Arts, poetry readings have become more lucrative for poets. Grants have been given to libraries, community centers, and academic centers so that poets can receive a higher fee for readings. Fees can vary, but the amount of the fee is not what makes a poetry reading satisfying. The satisfaction lies in the sense of communication between poet and listener.

Listen to other poets as often as you can. There are many recordings of poets reading their poetry. If there are no poetry readings near you, organize your own. An audience does not have to be large in order to be stimulating.

I quoted two lines from a poem by Emily Dickinson at the head of this chapter because, despite the fact that she is one of the greatest of American poets, and despite the fact that she tried to publish her poems for many years, she never succeeded during her lifetime. She corresponded extensively with Thomas Wentworth Higginson, a prominent and influential contributor to *The Atlantic*, but because her poetry was different from most of the poetry then being printed, he did not have the foresight or courage to recommend publication of her work. But she communicated constantly. She sent poems to her friends and family, all the people she cared for. Her letters, which are full of poems, are poems in themselves. Here is the entire poem quoted at the beginning of this chapter:

> This is my letter to the World
> That never wrote to Me—
> The simple News that Nature told—
> With tender Majesty
>
> Her message is committed
> To Hands I cannot see—
> For love of Her—Sweet—countrymen
> Judge tenderly—of Me

Emily Dickinson must have known somehow, intuitively, that at some point her message would reach the world. She died in 1886. In 1890,

Mr. Higginson published some of her poems, but it was not until 1955 that a complete collection appeared.

What does this mean for you? It means you must be patient, must persevere, must believe in yourself and your poems. The process of writing is in itself the important thing, the joy and the goal. If the finished product is excellent, chances are it will not forever stay hidden from the world.

WORKS CITED

Ammons, A. R. *Collected Poems: 1951–1971*. W. W. Norton, 1972.

Bashō. "The Temple Bells." *The Sea and the Honeycomb*, ed. Robert Bly. Beacon Press, 1971.

Bogan, Louise. *The Blue Estuaries*. Farrar, Straus and Giroux, 1966.

Buson. "Blossoms on the Pear." Trans. Harold G. Henderson, in *An Introduction to Haiku*, Doubleday, 1958.

Crapsey, Adelaide. *Verse*. Alfred A. Knopf, 1922.

Cummings, E. E. *Complete Poems, 1913–1962*. Harcourt Brace Jovanovich, 1963.

Dickinson, Emily. *The Poems of Emily Dickinson*. Ed. Thomas H. Johnson. Belknap Press of Harvard University Press, 1979.

Doolittle, Hilda (H. D.). *Selected Poems of H.D.* New Directions, 1957.

Francis, Robert. *Collected Poems, 1926–1976*. University of Massachusetts Press, 1972.

Frost, Robert. *The Poetry of Robert Frost*. Ed. Edward Connery Lathem. Holt, Rinehart and Winston, 1969.

Gensler, Kinereth. *Without Roof*. Alice James Books, 1981.

Herbert, Zbigniew. *Selected Poems*. Trans. Czeslaw Milosz and Peter Dale Scott. Penguin Books, 1968.

Honig, Edwin. *The Gazabos: Forty-One Poems*. Clarke and Way, 1959.

Ignatow, David. *Tread the Dark*. Little, Brown, 1978.

Issa. "Cricket, Be Careful." In *The Sea and the Honeycomb*, ed. Robert Bly. Beacon Press, 1971.

Jarrell, Randall. *The Complete Poems*. Farrar, Straus and Giroux, 1968.

Jong, Erica. *Fruits and Vegetables*. Ecco, 1997.

Kaufman, Shirley. *Gold Country*. University of Pittsburgh Press, 1973.

Kunitz, Stanley. *The Poems of Stanley Kunitz*. Little, Brown, 1971.

Levertov, Denise. *The Jacob's Ladder*. New Directions, 1961.

Levine, Philip. *Not This Pig*. Wesleyan University Press, 1966.

Lowell, Amy. *The Complete Poetical Works of Amy Lowell*. Houghton Mifflin, 1955.

MacLeish, Archibald. *New and Collected Poems, 1917–1976*. Houghton Mifflin, 1976.

Moore, Marianne. *Collected Poems*. Macmillan, 1935.

Plath, Sylvia. *The Collected Poems of Sylvia Plath*. Ed. Ted Hughes. Harper & Row, 1963.

Rich, Adrienne. *Diving into the Wreck: Poems 1971–1972*. W. W. Norton, 1973.

Robinson, Edwin Arlington. *Collected Poems*. Macmillan, 1927.

Roethke, Theodore. *The Collected Poems of Theodore Roethke*. Doubleday, 1953.

Rukeyser, Muriel. *Collected Poems*. International Creative Management, 1978.

Sexton, Anne. *The Death Notebooks*. Houghton Mifflin, 1974.

Stevens, Wallace. *Collected Poems of Wallace Stevens*. Alfred A. Knopf, 1923.

Swenson, May. *New and Selected Things Taking Place*. Little, Brown, 1965.

Unamuno, Miguel de. *The Tragic Sense of Life*. Trans. J. E. Crawford Fitch. Dover, 1954.

Vallejo, César. *Neruda and Vallejo: Selected Poems*. Ed. Robert Bly, trans. John Knoepfle and James Wright. Beacon Press, 1971.

Whitman, Ruth. *The Marriage Wig and Other Poems*. Harcourt Brace Jovanovich, 1968.

———. *Blood & Milk Poems*. Clarke and Way, 1963.

———. *The Passion of Lizzie Borden: New and Selected Poems*. October House, 1973.

———. *Permanent Address*. Alice James Books, 1980.

Williams, William Carlos. *Collected Earlier Poems*. New Directions, 1938.

———. *Pictures from Brueghel*. New Directions, 1955.

Yeats, William Butler. *Collected Poems*. Macmillan, 1940.

About the Author

Ruth Whitman (1922–99) was a renowned poet, translator, and performer. She published fourteen volumes of poetry—original works and several translations of Yiddish poetry, including *An Anthology of Modern Yiddish Poetry* (Wayne State University Press). Whitman won numerous awards, fellowships, and grants, including a 1984–85 Senior Fulbright Writer-in-Residence Fellowship to the Hebrew University of Jerusalem and a 1974–75 National Endowment for the Arts Creative Writing Grant. During her career, Whitman taught at many universities, including Harvard, Radcliffe, and MIT.

About the Editor

David Houghton is an adjunct professor of English in New England. He coauthored *The Chinese of the Mendocino Coast* with Dorothy Bear and teaches writing, rhetoric, and literature. He is the son of Ruth Whitman.